BONATTI

ON

MUNDANE ASTROLOGY

Treatises 4, 8.1, *&* 10
of Guido Bonatti's
Book of Astronomy

Translated by Benjamin N. Dykes, Ph.D.

From the 1491 and 1550 Latin Editions

The Cazimi Press
Minneapolis, Minnesota
2010

Published and printed in the United States of America
by the Cazimi Press
621 5th Avenue SE #25, Minneapolis, MN 55414

ISBN-13: 978-1-934586-10-5

PUBLISHER'S NOTE:

This reprint of Treatises 4, 8.1, and 10 of Guido Bonatti's *Book of Astronomy* has been excerpted from the out-of-print 1st edition, published in 2007. The text reflects the original pagination for each Treatise, and has not been revised or updated to reflect new translation conventions or citations in more recent translations. The Table of Arabic Terms has been removed (a more recent version can be found at: www.bendykes.com/reviews/study.php).

Students should also consult *Works of Sahl & Māshā'allāh* (2008), which contains much mundane material, now translated into English.

Dr. Benjamin N. Dykes
The Cazimi Press
May, 2010

TABLE OF CONTENTS

Book Abbreviations:

Abu 'Ali al-Khayyat:	*The Judgments of Nativities*	*JN*
Abū Ma'shar:	*Liber Introductorii Maioris ad Scientiam Iudiciorum Astrorum (Great Introduction to the Knowledge of the Judgments of the Stars)*	*Gr. Intr.*
	On Historical Astrology: the Book of Religions and Dynasties (On the Great Conjunctions)	*OGC*
	The Abbreviation of the Introduction to Astrology	*Abbr.*
	The Flowers of Abū Ma'shar	*Flowers*
Al-Biruni:	*The Book of Instruction in the Elements of the Art of Astrology*	*Instr.*
Māshā'allāh:	*De Receptione (On Reception)*	*OR*
	De Revolutionibus Annorum Mundi (On the Revolutions of the Years of the World)	*De Rev. Ann.*
Pseudo-Ptolemy:	*Centiloquium (Centiloquy)*	*Cent.*
Ptolemy	*Tetrabiblos*	*Tet.*
Sahl ibn Bishr:	*De Electionibus (On Elections)*	*On Elect.*
	De Quaestionibus (On Questions)	*On Quest.*
	Introductorium (Introduction)	*Introduct.*
'Umar al-Tabarī:	*Three Books of Nativities*	*TBN*
Vettius Valens:	*The Anthology*	*Anth.*

Table of Figures

TREATISE 4:
CONJUNCTIONS

On the consideration of certain conjunctions, and of certain other things which the astrologer must know and consider

Chapter 1: On the exposition of certain terms used by astrologers

This Treatise is on the more powerful things which there are in a full consideration of astrology, which would seem to pertain to judgments: whence it is necessary that you turn your whole mind and your whole intention to it, in such a way that you do not become given over to other topics until you understand its purpose. Which if you were to do otherwise, you will have deceived yourself and wasted your effort and your time; and perhaps (even if unduly), you will reproach me, affirming that I have said nothing.

Indeed the beginning of this Treatise is [on] the conjunctions signifying things which come to be in this world, and these conjunctions are six,[1] of which the first and greatest of all is [1] the conjunction of Saturn and Jupiter in the first bound of Aries, or in the beginning of Aries itself. And this comes to be only once in 960 years, which signifies great events to come in the world.

[2] The second conjunction of these, comes to pass in the first bound or degree of any one [member of a] triplicity, like that of the fiery, or the earthy, or the airy, or the watery; and this comes to be only once every 240 years.

Moreover, they make other conjunctions in each triplicity; and it is sometimes possible that they make thirteen conjunctions in one triplicity, in this way: one conjunction ends in the beginning of some triplicity which begins in another triplicity, indeed near its end, [so] that they could not be completed in it; whence it is denominated from that triplicity in which it ends. And it ends in the beginning of it, because the other twelve can all begin and be ended in that same triplicity, and thus there come to be thirteen conjunctions in the same one. This

---

[1] They are: (1) the climacteric conjunctions of Saturn and Jupiter in Aries every 960 years; (2) the mutation conjunctions of Saturn and Jupiter in a new triplicity every 240 years; (3) the conjunctions of Saturn and Mars in Cancer, which takes place every 30 years; (4) the conjunctions of Saturn and Jupiter with a given triplicity every 20 years; (5) the conjunctions of the Sun with other planets; (6) the conjunctions of the Sun and Moon.

happens if one conjunction would end in the beginning of some triplicity, indeed so that it would not go beyond 54' of the first degree of that triplicity. And these thirteen conjunctions come to be in one triplicity, just as sometimes two conjunctions of the Sun and Moon come to be in one sign, and in one solar month. For example, a conjunction of the Sun and Moon was made in the first degree of Aries, and [thereafter] there was a conjunction in Saphar[2] (which is the second month), which is comprised of 29 days; and before the Sun had left Aries, another conjunction was made in the thirtieth degree of Aries (or perhaps in the twenty-ninth), and thus two conjunctions were made in Aries. Likewise a conjunction was made on the first day of August, and before the Sun had left August (indeed so that a lunar month would have been completed), another conjunction of the Sun and Moon was made on the thirtieth day of August, and so two conjunctions of the Sun and Moon were made in one month–not that both began in it, but because both were ended in it. And so it is with the conjunctions of Saturn and Jupiter when they make thirteen conjunctions in one triplicity.

Afterwards, the conjunction is changed to the triplicity which succeeds the first, so if the first conjunctions were made in the fiery triplicity, they are changed to the earthy triplicity, and from the earthy to the airy, and from the airy to the watery; and again from the watery it reverts back to the fiery, namely to the triplicity of Aries; and from the triplicity of Aries to the triplicity of Taurus; from the triplicity of Taurus to the triplicity of Gemini; and from the triplicity of Gemini to the triplicity of Cancer; again, from the triplicity of Cancer to the triplicity of Aries, and so on *ad infinitum*.

Chapter 2: In what way the supercelestial bodies are moved, according to the diverse motions of the planets

The conjunctions of the superior, perceptibly changeable bodies, come to be according to the differences of their motions (both natural and in place); and from thence come to be their effects imperceptibly in inferior individuals.[3] And these natural motions are considered according to three divisions, because the divisions are named and considered according to the order of the successive

---

[2] *Saphar* or *Safar* is the second month of the Islamic calendar. Bonatti is counting by lunar months, so that in his proposed example, the New Moon that begins the lunar year coincides with the beginning of the seasonal year, when the Sun enters Aries. Thus the second lunar month (Saphar) would begin before the first seasonal (solar) month had completed.

[3] Reading *insensibiliter* for *insensibilibus* (in order to parallel *sensibiliter* above).

circles of the seven planets in this way: of course the first division is considered according to the motions of the three superior planets (which are Saturn, Jupiter, and Mars), according to which you will find sufficiently determined below in the Treatise on nativities. The second is considered according to the planet in the middle of the other locations, which is the Sun. The third, if indeed it is considered, is according to the motions of the three inferiors, which are Venus, Mercury, and the Moon.

For the first division of the planets (namely that of the superiors), is three-fold, and in a threefold way it impresses upon individual, inferior things; and this according to three diverse motions, namely the first, second, and third. The first motion is moved about the middle. The second is moved from the middle. The third is not moved about the first, nor from the first, nor about the middle, nor from the middle, but toward the middle.

Whence the first division of the superior planets is considered, and referred to the first motion, which presides over the middle motion, because those planets approach the first motion, and are elongated from the third motion, which is toward the middle motion. And these divisions of motions are taken to be over individual particulars of which durability is expected, as are the structures of houses, and similar things which have beginnings, and whose middle does not come quickly, and whose end comes long after their beginning. And these things are attributed to Saturn, which has an affinity with the first motion more than the others. And their middle is attributed to Jupiter, because just as Jupiter is in the middle between the other superiors, and located in the middle of them, and among those motions his motion is in the middle [in terms of speed], therefore the middle of those things is attributed to him, and even their full completion is attributed to him, and considered according to the same. And because he himself is closer to Mars (to whom is attributed the end of things) than is Saturn, and closer to Saturn (to whom is attributed the beginning of things) than is Mars, therefore to him is attributed the middle, and the full completion of things according to the same consideration. Indeed, the end is attributed to Mars, because he himself is posited at the end of the first division, and because the end makes for the destruction of things; and on account of this wars and battles and contentions are attributed to him, because they make more for consumption, and diminution, and destruction, than the rest.

For the beginning indicates the being of things, indeed the middle their perfection; the end the destruction of the same. And because the multitude of diverse motions are multiplied, and diversity between humans, and discord of their wills, and accordingly wars and contentions arise, which make for the destruction of things, and make their ends. And whatever may be said by certain ignorant persons about their own Creator[4] (who disposed the universe in good order, and did nothing without reason), this was the reason why these three [significations] were attributed to the three superior planets, just as [many as there are] principles in the first signification, surpassing [or preceding] those which come after (in the second signification, which are signified by the other planets).

And thus by the testimony of the Philosopher[5] the second[6] motion is moved from the middle, and the third motion moves toward the middle. And the second, middle motion is naturally attributed to the Sun (who is the greater luminary) and to his effects; and this motion is from the middle, by means of a relationship,[7] because he himself has affinity to this motion; and he is, in the order of the circles, placed circularly in the middle of the others, and whatever is referred to him is between the first motion and the third motion. And because his motion is less slow than the superior ones, and less fast than the inferior ones, for this reason he is said to be the significator of kings and the wealthy, and of magnates, of those wanting to be in charge of and rule over others; and because he himself participates with the first division, and his signification is considered [to be] stronger in the second one than any other's; and he succeeds Mars in the order of circles.

However, the third motion, toward the middle, is attributed to the three inferior planets, on account of their remoteness from the first motion which is above the middle motion; and their effects concern things that are pleasant and which are not expected to last long; and on account of their fast motion having an affinity with pleasant things, even if in a certain way they may resemble the first motion, still they have an affinity with the third motion. And their natural motions are considered according to the three divisions of the motions of the superior planets. For to Venus is given the signification of marriage, and the arrangement of the clothing of bodies,[8] and of similar things, because of her correlation to Saturn. For just as Saturn is the first and highest of the three

---

[4] Reading *de Creatore suo* for *creatorem suum*.

[5] This philosopher could be Aristotle, but it might also be Abū Ma'shar or Māshā'allāh.

[6] Reading *secundus* for *primus*.

[7] *Per relationem.*

[8] *Indumentorum ordinantium corpora.* According to Zoller (private communication), clothing was (as it still is) a way of distinguishing social class and rank, which has a kind of stability not unlike Saturn.

superior planets, and from him are considered the principles of things of great durability and great age, so Venus is the first of the three inferior planets, and according to her are taken into account the beginnings of things of which great durability or widespread effect[9] is not expected; and she succeeds the Sun in the order of circles.

Indeed to Mercury is given signification over things signifying the perfection of things which do not have great durability, like numbers, writings, and measurements, and sculptures, and the like, of which it is granted that certain ones do last a long time, but not unless they come to be [used] for the memory of things, as they improve the forgetfulness of men, and wherefore his significa-tion is associated with the signification of Jupiter (and is correlated to him, who signifies the perfection of things which last a long time). For just as Jupiter is in the middle between the superior planets, so Mercury is in the middle between the inferior planets, and succeeds Venus in the order of circles.

Indeed to the Moon is given the signification over movable things, and things that change themselves quickly, and over pilgrimages, and over all things acknowledged to change quickly, and whose end comes quickly, and whose meanings are correlated to the significations of Mars: for just as Mars is the third and last of the three superior planets, and signifies the end of things lasting a long time, so the Moon is the third and last of the three inferior planets and is akin to the third division, to the signification by Mars; and she signifies the end of things that go on quickly to their end. And thus the Moon[10] falls in the order of circles, just as will be explained at length in the Treatise on nativities.

Nor should you believe that these significations were attributed to these three planets except by reason of the need for those things which natural necessity impels toward them, just as are the customs of men, and oppositions, and [social] conditions, and laws, and according to the particular stories of living people, all of which are perfected by number and writing; and into whose debt they plainly fall, as much as in them as to wars, contentions, and journeys, and the rest of the changes which they do not take up except through perfected motion. And these aforesaid significations were attributed to the stated three inferiors, because they are secondary through a relation to the first motion or being, and [it is] on account of it that they follow from thence. And wherefore from their (and others') significations is had the foreknowledge of their effects which generally are going to come, according to their course; and through which

---

[9] *Prolixitas.*
[10] Reading *Luna* for *Mercurius.*

[course] we arrive at their particular cognitions, the which aforesaid conjunctions we would be able to judge if we wished to understand them correctly (namely [that] of Saturn with Jupiter and Mars in the aforesaid places). But concerning those motions and what is signified by them, it will be stated at greater length (and to a finer point) in the Treatise on nativities.

Chapter 3: On the conjunction of Saturn and Mars[11]

[3] The third conjunction is the conjunction of Saturn and Mars which they make at the beginning of Cancer, or in its first degree, or at least in its first bound–and this happens once every 30 years.

But you could say, "why was only the conjunction which Saturn and Mars make at the beginning of Cancer considered, when they themselves are conjoined in the beginnings of the other signs, and likewise of the other triplicities, just as in the beginning of Cancer?" To which it can be responded thus, that their conjunction was considered more so in the beginning of Cancer than elsewhere, because it is worse than all the other conjunctions they make, even if all the others are bad; and the conjunction they make in the beginning of Capricorn is less malicious, because they are received by each other, and their malice is diminished. Capricorn is the dignity of each, namely the domicile of Saturn and the exaltation of Mars, while Cancer is the detriment of each, namely of Saturn, and of Mars, because it is their[12] greatest impediment. And however much more the malefics are impeded, by that much more they do worse things, and their malice and detriment is increased. For in the other signs, they do not have manifest detriment. And even if they harm or offend in the others, still they do not kill as much as they do in [Cancer]; because then the greatest changes in the world take place, as well as the greatest accidents, which do not happen in the other conjunctions they make elsewhere. For kingdoms are changed, and terrible battles come to be, from which follow killings, suffocations, shameful captures, the destruction of kingdoms, burning by fire, and many sheddings of blood, famines, mortalities, sterility,[13] and many pestilences.

And if they were oriental, the things signified by them will happen quickly in proportion as they were close to the Sun or removed from him. And if they

---

[11] See also Tr. 8, Part 1, Chs. 18, 52, 57, 76.

[12] Reading *eorum* for *eius*.

[13] Bonatti's inclusion of this in the agricultural/weather portion of the sentence suggests this could also refer to breeding and crops.

were occidental, the things signified by them will be prolonged and delayed. Whence you will consider the Ascendant of their conjunction, namely when they come together in [one and the same] minute; and see the number of degrees of longitude which are between them and the Sun, from which you will make the signs, namely by giving 30° to each sign. If a fixed sign were ascending, and they themselves were occidental, they will signify the years of the arrival of the things they signify, according to the number of signs in degrees of distance which you come up with between them and the Sun. And if they were oriental, instead of years put months. And if the sign were common, and they occidental, instead of years put months. And if they were oriental, instead of months put weeks. And if the sign were movable, instead of years put weeks if they were occidental. Indeed if they were oriental, instead of weeks put days. And when you give one sign per year, give a month for every 2° 30', and a week for every 37' 30", and a day for every 5' 21", because within these times the things signified by them will take place, if you have reckoned the Ascendant of their perfected conjunction well.

However, you must consider there whether the angle of the 1st house is correct or removed. Because if it were correct (namely, that it is one sign, and does not make but one house), they will take place according to that which I told you in the listed, equal times [in the preceding paragraph]. If however it were removed, it will happen in another way: because if the angle contained less than 30°, it will delay what is signified–that is, if one sign were to make two houses (just as often happens). Indeed if it contained more than 30°, that is, that one sign is included there which will not be specifically named, or [if] in another way it contains more than 30°, what is signified will come quickly, and will accelerate.

So, let it be put that the fifth degree of Leo is the 1st house, and the twenty-seventh degree of that same sign is the 2nd house. In this way that sign makes two houses, and the thing signified will be delayed by one-tenth, just as one-tenth of the sign falls in another house;[14] and if more of it were to fall into it, the thing signified would slow down more; and if one-ninth of it fell in the other house, its signification would slow by one-ninth of the time. If one-eighth fell, it would slow down by one-eighth; and so on with the other parts of the sign. But if one sign were enclosed,[15] like if the twenty-eighth degree of Pisces were the 1st house and the third degree of Taurus were the 2nd house, in this

---

[14] I.e., 27° - 29° 59' Leo.
[15] I.e., intercepted.

way Aries would be wholly enclosed in the 1st house; and the thing signified would hasten in accordance with the amount of degrees which the 1st house contains beyond 30, and which ought to have been in the 2nd house, which are two degrees of Pisces and three of Taurus: and thus the thing signified will hasten by a sixth part of its time, just as one-sixth of one sign falls in that house beyond what it should have been according to the right size of the angles. And thus may you understand in the case of any proportion of a sign. Likewise if there were few degrees [between] them and the Sun, such that an entire sign could not be made from them (this is when there are less than 30).

And if the Ascendant [of the Saturn-Mars conjunction in Cancer] were such a sign that it rises in less than two equal hours, it signifies days. And if there were between them and the Sun so many degrees that an entire sign could be made from them, namely if there were 30 [degrees] and the ascending sign was one which rises in two hours, it signifies months. And if the ascending sign were such that it rises in more than two hours, it signifies years, subject to the proportion subsisting in degrees and minutes, as I said.

One must even know that the things signified by their conjunction often fall upon those things which are signified by the sign which was ascending at the hour of the middle of their conjunction, or by its Lord, and so concerning the sign in which their conjunction is.

And if they were in the eastern part when their conjunction is completed, namely that they would come together in one [and the same] minute, or they were conjoined to oriental [eastern?] planets, the things signified will happen in the eastern part. And if they were in the south, joined to planets in the south, they will happen in the southern part. And if they were conjoined to occidental [western?] planets, or they were western, they will happen in the western part. And if they were not in any of these parts, but were northern, or were joined to northern planets, they will happen in the north.[16]

Cancer, as I said, is the detriment of Saturn and Mars, because it is opposite Capricorn (which is the domicile of Saturn and the exaltation of Mars); and every seventh sign from the domicile or exaltation of some planet, is said to be the detriment of that planet. Aries is opposite Libra (which is the exaltation of Saturn); but it is not opposite any dignity of Mars—on the contrary, [Aries] is his dignity.

---

[16] It is unclear whether south and north are meant in terrestrial terms, or in terms of ecliptical latitude.

Taurus is the opposite of Scorpio (which is the domicile of Mars), but is not the opposite of the domicile or exaltation of Saturn. Whence their conjunction in the beginnings of the other signs, or other triplicities, are less than their conjunction in the beginning of Cancer, and less malicious. Indeed, Gemini is not the opposite of the domicile or exaltation of either of them.

Chapter 4: On the fourth conjunction, of Saturn and Jupiter

[4] The fourth conjunction is of Saturn and Jupiter, which occurs once every 20 years, indeed so that [there are] 12 conjunctions in each triplicity. And that it is true that they make 12 conjunctions in any [given] triplicity, is made plain by this, if you would attend to its truth: for by the multiplication of 12 by 20 or 20 by 12 (which is the same thing), they make 240, and thus they are conjoined in 240 years twelve times in turn, by making one conjunction every 20 years. And thus they make 48 conjunctions between all the triplicities before they return to the same point in which they made their first conjunction (whence they make 12 conjunctions in 240 years): for multiplying 240 by 4 makes 960 years; and then their conjunction returns to the beginning of Aries, or to the beginning of some other triplicity. And understand this about any place in which they make some conjunction: they will always return there, once every 960 years.

Chapter 5: On the fifth conjunction, of the Sun with other planets

[5] But the fifth conjunction is that which the Sun makes with the planets in his entrance into the first minute of Aries,[17] or of another planet to him in turn. For it has its [own] significations: sometimes small, sometimes great, sometimes good, sometimes bad, sometimes middling, just as is discussed in full in the Treatise on revolutions. For it would be long and laborious, nor philosophical, if it were touched on here; nor in the proper order [of topics]. And likewise if the entrance of the Sun into Aries is considered, and its Ascendant in that hour, and its minute in each year, in which one of the aforementioned conjunctions (namely of Saturn with one of the planets discussed), is obliged to take place: because in that that year the conjunction of the Sun with the planets must show greater things to be signified than in others.

---

[17] I.e., in mundane ingresses.

Chapter 6: On the sixth conjunction

[6] Indeed the sixth conjunction is of the Sun and the Moon in the same minute, which takes place once at the beginning of each lunar month; and their opposition, which is in the middle of every lunar month. And they likewise have diverse things they signify, just as is discussed in the Treatise on rains; and even certain [significations] in revolutions, which I will tell you about when it seems expedient.

Chapter 7: On the combust and incombust hours following the conjunction of the Sun and Moon, which certain people call *Albuim* or *Albuith*[18]

Some of the ancient sages, from whom I do not wish to deviate, said that after the conjunction of the Sun and Moon, from the very minute of their conjunction, there are 12 hours which are called "combust"; and after those 12 combust hours are 72 hours which are called "incombust"; and after those 72 incombust ones are 12 combust ones; and so on up to the degree and minute of the next conjunction that follows. And they said that the 12 combust hours are divided into three equal parts, by giving to each part four of these hours. And they said that he who prepares to make war in the first four hours, or goes to war, ought to fear the death of his body. And he who prepares in the second four hours to make war, or goes to war, should fear for his capture, or being wounded, or some blow, [but] without losing his life. And he who undertakes in

---

[18] From Ar. البست (*al-bust*, see al-Qabīsī, IV.23), a term of art Burnett believes derives from Sanskrit. But note the similarity between the Ar. *bust* and the Latin *combustus* (combust). There is confusion on Bonatti's part about the various ways of dividing up the hours of the lunar month. In the *Book of Astronomy* this is discussed in several places (comprising three different divisions). First, (a) he divides the month into sections of 12 and 72 hours, of which the 12 hour sections are subdivided into four-hour periods which get less and less severe. This is one version of *al-bust* (and it is repeated in Tr. 7, Part 2, 7th House, Ch. 4, as well as in Tr. 9, Part 3, 12th House Ch. 6). Then (b) he speaks of the *duodena* of the Moon, in which the month is divided up into 12-hour sections, each section being ruled by the triplicity rulers of fire, earth, air, and water. Finally (c) in Tr. 9, Part 3, 12th House, Ch. 6, he mentions another version of (b), but calls it another form of *al-bust* instead of the *duodena* of the Moon. In this case, the month is divided up as with (b), except that instead of using the natural order of the triplicities, we begin with the Sun and move in descending Chaldean order. Thus the first 12 hours are assigned to the triplicity rulers of the Sun, Venus, Mercury, Moon, Saturn, Jupiter, and so on (presumably using the sign in which these planets are when their hours are in effect).

the last four hours to make war, or goes to war, should fear the loss of his substance and of those who were with him; and he could even lose the persons who help him. And he who undertakes to plow in the first four hours, or goes to plow, should fear the loss of the fruits of his hope from that plowing. And he who undertakes to plow in the second four hours, or who goes to plow, should fear great detriment in all things that he possesses, and even in his body, [but] without losing his life. And he who undertakes to plow in the last four hours, or goes to plow, should fear the diminution of his seeds.

On the Duodena of the Moon[19]

Moreover there is another division of these hours, which is called the 12 hours of the Sun and the Moon–namely 12 of the Moon. And this is something very important to observe, namely that you should know the hour of the conjunction of the Sun and Moon and its minute, and take 12 hours after the conjunction, and divide them into three equal parts, namely by giving to each part four hours; and to give the first division to the Sun, who is the first Lord of the first triplicity, namely the fiery one; and the second you ought to give to the second Lord of the same triplicity, namely Jupiter; and the third you should give to the third Lord of that triplicity, which is Saturn; and you ought to judge according to the condition of these Lords, just as I will explain to you in what follows.[20]

Then you ought to give the next 12, which you put under the Lords of the first triplicity, to the second one, namely to the earthy one, by giving the first four hours to Venus, who is the first Lord of the second triplicity, namely the earthy one. The second four [go to] the Moon, who is the second Lord of the same triplicity. [Give] the last four to Mars, who is the third lord of that triplicity.

Then you ought to give 12 hours to the Lords of the airy triplicity, namely to the third [triplicity] after the 12 hours you gave to the Lords of the second triplicity, by giving the first four hours to Saturn, who is the first Lord of the third triplicity. Give the second four to Mercury, who is the second Lord of the airy triplicity. Give the last four to Jupiter, who is the last Lord of the same triplicity.

---

[19] These are not the same as the *duodecimae* (Tr. 5, the 89th Consideration; Tr. 9, Part 3, 12th House, Ch. 11), which are spatial divisions of the signs.

[20] As he clarifies below, each individual *duodena* is 12 unequal hours long; therefore a given triplicity ruler will rule one-third of a *duodena*.

Then you ought to give another four hours to the Lords of the fourth triplicity, namely the watery one, by giving the first four hours to Venus, who is the first Lady of the fourth triplicity. [Give] the second four to Mars, who is the second lord of the same triplicity. The last four you ought to give to the Moon, who is the last Lady of the fourth triplicity, namely the watery one.

And so you ought to do with every Lord of every triplicity, until the disposition is reverted back to the Sun, and this is continued up to the degree and minute of the next conjunction that follows. And you will consider all of these hours according to inequality, and not equality.[21]

And therefore Ptolemy said, "observe the *duodena* of the Moon,"[22] because this is that *duodena* of the Moon which he understood. For always when the Moon is in one of the *duodenae*, her condition and disposition will be according to the condition of that planet to which is deputed that third part of the *duodena* in which the Moon then is. Whence a *duodena* of the Moon must be avoided (according to the disposition of that planet to which are attributed those four hours, who is not to be placed on behalf of him for whom you elect), if you can ever avoid it, unless it should happen from the misfortune of someone that the beginning of his war, or his journey to war, should fall in one of those prohibited combust hours: for he will have to fear the danger spoken of above.[23] And so much more strongly do those four hours of the Moon's *duodenae* have an effect[24] she were badly disposed then: because then there would be no remedy for him, even if he had a good election for war: only God could avert it.

However, the aforesaid 12 combust hours are to be avoided more, because [the *duodenae*] are subordinated to [the combust hours]. And thus 12 degrees are connected to each planet, by dividing the *duodenae* themselves equally between the planets; whence are produced 84 stages between them all. For 12 multiplied by 7 makes 84. Then the eighth *duodena* reverts back to the Sun, and the

---

[21] Bonatti repeats this claim in Tr. 9, Part 3, 12th House, Ch. 6. He seems to mean that standard planetary hours should be assigned to the period between the Full Moons, so that each day, the actual daylight and nighttime hours are divided equally, which would make the hours of a given season unequal to equinoctial hours: daytime "hours" in the summer would be longer than those in the winter, for example.

[22] I am not sure where Bonatti is getting this quotation from; he could be extrapolating from pseudo-Ptolemy's *Cent.* (e.g., Aph. 60, on critical days).

[23] This is an awkwardly constructed paragraph, and Bonatti is trying to put too much into every sentence. The point is that unless you can absolutely avoid it, you should not undertake certain actions outside of the four-hour periods during which the Moon is in a good portion of her *duodena*.

[24] *Contingent.*

divisions of the *duodenae* come to be again as was said in the preceding, until they reach the second conjunction.

Then the wise said that after the aforesaid 12 combust hours, in which it is not good or useful to do anything mentioned above, there are 72 incombust hours in which one can begin or do what one wants, unless something else impedes. And [so on] until the following conjunction is reached. Whence you ought to consider in judgments, and especially to see in those matters about which I made mention, lest the beginning of some matter you (or someone else) do or intend to begin, falls in one of those prohibited hours, be it a journey or something else, and that you avoid it as much as you can.

Chapter 8: On discovering the degree of the Ascendant of a nativity, or of some question, or of some beginning, of which some information is thought to be uncertain

Having spoken about conjunctions, and the combust and incombust hours, even if it should seem not [to be] in philosophical order, still I will make mention to you of how to find the degree of the Ascendant of any beginning for which certainty is not had, provided that some indications are possessed which seem to show a closeness [to the correct time], even if they are not very certain, but as though half-certain. Because it happens sometimes that the mother or female porter or other midwives do not know the hour of the nativity of the child well; nor even do those who are taking part in some matter [of an election]; but they have it near to the truth, not far off, perhaps to the hour, or less than an hour, or thereabouts. Whence they say "this child was born around the third hour," or the sixth, or the ninth, or perhaps they say "around the middle of the night," or "around dawn," or around the first [hour of the] night, just as sometimes laypeople are accustomed to saying, or as yet others say, "it was around such an hour as when the banners are given." Or it might be the beginning of some building, or some [affairs requiring] management, and things like that. Then certainty of the hour cannot be provided to you for those judgments; but [something] near the hour is given to you.

Whence in order that you can find the exact hour of the nativity or matter, it is necessary that you reckon the planets to the hour as closely as you can, indeed that you do not depart from what the midwives say (or the mother, or someone else) by more than one equal hour. And see what sign ascends then, and consider whether the nativity (or the beginning of whichever matter it is) is conjunctional or preventional. And look at the degree in which the conjunction or prevention was made, and consider which of the planets is stronger and more powerful in the number of dignities or strengths in that degree, and see how many degrees it has traversed in the sign in which it is, and you will make the ascending degree of the sign which seems to ascend then, similar to the degree in which that planet is, which is the *al-mubtazz* in the degree of the conjunction or prevention.[25]

For example, [suppose] it seemed to you according to the reckoning which you made for the imprecise hour, that you had initial evidence that the fourth degree of Aries was the Ascendant, by your estimation, as I said, because you were able to comprehend concerning the nativity or uncertain matter; and the conjunction or prevention was in the tenth degree of Aries; and in this way the Sun is stronger in the degree of the conjunction than any other planet by his number of dignities, just as was said elsewhere. Therefore calculate the Sun for that hour, and see in which degree of whatever sign he is in—let us put it that he is in the seventeenth degree of Aquarius. Now you must change the Ascendant which you had found first through your judgment, and make it so that the Ascendant is Aries, the seventeenth degree (which at first had seemed to be the fourth degree); and you will verify the Ascendant which you seek. And if you were to find through your judgment that the Ascendant were greater than the planet that is *al-mubtazz* in that sign, reduce it to the quantity of its degrees: like if it were the twenty-fourth, or more or less, reduce it to the seventeenth just as the Sun is in its own sign.[26] And understand this in every case, and build the other houses based on this Ascendant. But because I would make for you, with the aid of God, a special Treatise on nativities, in which I will expound all of this to you, I will explain it in detail [later on], and I will not spend any more time on it here, so that the order [of topics] may be observed more rightly.

---

[25] This method is based on Ptolemy (*Tet.* III.3). See Tr. 9 for a fuller description.

[26] This shows that this method of rectification is meant to give only an initial plausible time which must then be refined further.

TREATISE 8:
REVOLUTIONS & PARTS

[PART 1:] On the Revolutions
of the Years of the World

Preface

Since after a treatment of elections nothing would seem more appropriate than to treat subsequently of revolutions of the years of the world, we should deservedly set it apart and produce a special treatise concerning them.

But first we must look briefly at what a revolution is. A revolution of the year is the circular course of the Sun from one minute of any degree of any sign, up to his return to the same point—even though it might otherwise be defined, just as it seemed to certain people. And this is considered according to two methods, namely [first] according to the revolution of the years of a nativity or other inceptions;[1] for, [secondly,] a revolution of the *year of the world* is from the entrance of the Sun into the first minute of Aries, up until he is then revolved and transits circularly through the whole zodiac, and returns to the same point. However a revolution of the year of the nativity or of other beginnings, or of some inception, is from the minute in which the Sun was at the nativity of some native, up until he then is revolved, and circularly transits the whole zodiac, and returns to the same point—and the same must be said about all other revolutions.

Indeed a revolution is, among the rest, a very useful thing, and its significations higher than the rest, [just] as it is powerful and intricate to discover its certainty.[2] For through a revolution of the years of the world is known what is going to be concerning the good and bad in that year, namely whether the year is going to be tranquil or troublesome; and whether there are going to be battles or not in the year which you are revolving. It is said likewise concerning peace. And what the standing of kings or princes, the wealthy, or great men, is going to

---

[1] In other words, the general definition of a revolution pertains particularly to nativities and elections, since the Sun may be at any degree of the zodiac when their events take place. But a mundane revolution is something more specific.

[2] *Sicut & ad ipsius certitudinem inveniendam, fortis atque implicita.* This is an awkward sentence. I think that Bonatti is saying the difficulty of delineating a revolution, and the broad and deep information gotten from one, befits its status as a chart whose significations cover an entire nation or region.

be. And likewise that of the people, and of low-class people, the religious,[3] even every one in his own nature, of every kind universally according to the customs[4] of men.

Likewise it is known what is going to be concerning things born of the ground, whether abundance or lack should be expected from them; and what their future is going to be from them, whether they will have low or mediocre prices, just as will be said concerning the Parts in its own place.[5]

For through the revolution of nativities are known the accidents of any native in his own year.[6] Whence, if you wished to know the significations of the revolutions of years, both of the world and of nativities, you will observe this arrangement according to what I hand down to you; nor should you neglect this book, but it is necessary for you to know it and to have it in your mind before all other books, since in order to know and understand it well would be a great effort,[7] so that by distinguishing the times you may harmonize the writings, lest perhaps you believe there to be contrary things in it—because they are not, if you were to consider well the things which present themselves to you to be considered. Because even if you find a saying at some time (if such there were), that "it signifies such-and-such an event," or "it signifies the multitude of such-and-such a thing," and you should find in that same chapter, "it signifies the scarcity" of that same thing, you should not accept it as a contrary, but distinguish that you may harmonize. Because one intention will be general; the other will be particular, and the special restricts[8] the general. However, it sometimes happens that someone doing the modifying speaks according to latitude, according to orientality, or according to occidentality, or according to direct motion, or according to retrogradation, and the like. For these accidents vary the significations, nor therefore are the chapters made contrary to one another.[9]

---

[3] Bonatti probably means the secular religious.

[4] *Ritus*, "rites, customs." Revolutions therefore cover all religions, cultures, and types.

[5] See Part 2 of this Treatise, Ch. 18.

[6] The world's year goes from equinox to equinox; a native's year begins at the moment of the Sun's return to the location it had at the nativity.

[7] *Industria.*

[8] *Derogat.* In other words, the presence of individual judgments tailored to a specific case does not invalidate the general rules—we must restrict and distinguish general rules when applying them to individual cases.

[9] This paragraph emphasizes the prior point. For example, Saturn in a given sign might mean one thing for weather; but what if he is both northern and retrograde—and those delineations are contrary to each other or to the testimony given by the sign? I am not sure Bonatti really has a clear answer to the problem, but he does believe the contrariety is only apparent, not real.

If you wanted to know the revolution of the year of the world, [know] at what hour the Sun enters the first minute of the sign of Aries (namely from the first second of that minute, up to the fourth and more, up to its fifth second). And if you were to find this with an exact investigation, you will reckon the planets and the houses to that hour, and to the minute of that same hour. And you will find the Ascendant as exactly as you can, and you will construct the twelve houses by their degrees and minutes, and to the minute of that hour, jut as well and exactly as you can. Likewise you will reckon all of the planets to the same minute of that hour, and you will discover most exactly their places, by degrees and minutes, and likewise the seconds, of every one of them, lest you should fall into any error. And you will consider their condition (namely how they are disposed), and in which houses, and in which signs they are. And which of them are direct, and which retrograde, and which stationary, and which [are] quick in course, and which slow; and whether any of them are northern or some of them southern amongst themselves, or from the path of the Sun.[10] For if a planet were northern from another, he who is northern of the other is said to go above him,[11] whether he were of the superiors or of the inferiors.[12] And likewise if they were southern, he who was less southern is said to go above him who is more southern. And [consider] how one of them aspects the other, or how it is aspected by him; and how one projects his own rays upon[13] the body or rays of the other, and how they aspect the angles–because the good aspects signify good; but the bad ones the contrary. And if you were to do this, you will likewise see what sign is ascending: because then you could take the Lord of the Year, and the signification of the common people generally, from the Lord of the ascending sign (unless another impedes, which deprives the Lord of the Ascendant of the rulership of the year). Nor however should you always believe the Lord of the Ascendant of the revolution will always be the Lord of the Year absolutely (as some seem to want to say, in order to make it easier for themselves). But you will take him as I will tell you below.

---

[10] In other words, which planets are north and south relative to each other, and which are north and south of the ecliptic absolutely.

[11] *Super eum.*

[12] Omitting the repetitive phrase *dicit[ur?] ire super eum.*

[13] *Super.*

Chapter 1: How the Lord of the Year may be found

After you were certain to a fine degree concerning the time of the entrance of the Sun into Aries (as was said), and of the Ascendant of his entrance, and concerning all the other houses, and the places[14] of the planets, see which planet is the Lord of the Ascendant, and how it is disposed, and where it is. For if it were direct, and free from combustion, and were in the Ascendant[15] by 3° ahead of the line or 4° after,[16] you should not seek another, because he will be the Lord of the Year or Revolution; and he will be the significator of the condition of the common people, and nothing else will be able to deprive him of that rulership. If indeed he were retrograde, or combust, he already cannot be the Lord of the Year or Revolution, because a retrograde or combust planet cannot be the Lord of the Year: for his virtue is annihilated, except for a great reason (which can happen only most rarely). Then seek the rulership from the exalta-tion. For if the ascending sign were the exaltation of some planet, seek the ruler from him: wherefore if he were in the degree of the Ascendant, or by 3° ahead or 4° behind,[17] he will be the Lord of the Year or Revolution and will be the significator of the condition of the common people, if he were free from the aforesaid impediments. If indeed he were impeded, as I said regarding the Lord of the Ascendant, he will not be the Lord of the Year or Revolution.

If by chance it were not the exaltation of some planet, or it were and the Lord of the exaltation could not be the Lord of the Year, seek then the ruler from the Sun (if the revolution were in the day) or from the Moon (if it were in the night): because the luminary whose authority it was, will be the Lord of the Year or Revolution, if it were to have some dignity[18] in the Ascendant.

Which, if again the luminary whose authority it was, could not be the Lord of the Year, then seek the significator from the Lord of the bound; which if he

---

[14] If "places" were the same as "whole signs," then there'd be little need to be so exact about the timing–so "place" must mean "exact location" here.

[15] This could also mean, "if he were in the ascending sign," which I think is the more likely interpretation. In that case, he would have to be in the rising sign *and* conjoined to the cusp within the stated number of degrees.

[16] I believe that by "ahead of," Bonatti means "in an earlier degree than the cusp's"; by "after," he means "in a later degree than the cusp's." See my Introduction.

[17] I believe that by "ahead of," Bonatti means "in an earlier degree than the cusp's"; by "behind," he means "in a later degree than the cusp's." See my Introduction.

[18] *Any* dignity at all, or only if it is *also* in the Ascendant? The context suggests it must also be in the Ascendant, but note that below, Bonatti drops the degree requirements for the luminary.

were in the Ascendant, by 3° ahead the line or 4° behind,[19] and he were free, he will be the Lord of the Year.

And if again the Lord of the bound could not be the Lord of the Year, then seek the ruler from the Lord of the triplicity, by the aforesaid method which I have told you regarding the others.

And if it were not one of these–which I told you regarding the Lord of the domicile, or the exaltation of the Ascendant, or of the bound or the triplicity, or the luminary whose authority it was (namely the Sun's in the day and the Moon's in the night)–then seek the Ruler [Lord] of the Year or the Revolution from the Lord of the tenth. And see if the Lord of the 10th house were in the tenth, or by 3° ahead or 4° behind, nor were it retrograde or combust: it will be the Lord of the Year or Revolution, and be the significator of the common people and the rustics. If however the Lord of the 10th house were retrograde or combust, or otherwise impeded, so that it could not be the significator, then seek the ruler from the Lord of the exaltation of the 10th house, if it were the exaltation of some planet. Which if he were in the tenth, free from the aforesaid impediments, and were only by 3° ahead of the line of the 10th house, or by only 4° behind, he will be the Lord of the Year and the significator of the condition of the common people. If however it were not the exaltation of some planet, or if it were and the Lord of the exaltation could not be the Lord of the Year, then seek from the luminary whose authority it was: because if it were there, and were to have some dignity there, it will be the Lord of the Year. Again, if the luminary whose authority it was could not be the Lord of the Year, then seek the ruler from the Lord of the bound of the degree of the 10th house; which if he were in the degree of the 10th house, or by 3° ahead or 4° behind, and were free from impediments, he will be the Lord of the Year, and the significator of the condition of the common people. Which if again the Lord of the bound could not be the Lord of the Year, then seek the ruler from the Lord of the triplicity of the 10th house; which if it were on the line of the 10th house, or were by 3° ahead or 4° after, it will be the Lord of the Year, and the significator of the condition of the common people or rustics.

If however you could not have the significator from the Ascendant or from the tenth, seek him from the seventh through the same method which I have told you concerning the first and the tenth. And if you could not have him from

---

[19] I believe that by "ahead of," Bonatti means "in an earlier degree than the cusp's"; by "behind," he means "in a later degree than the cusp's." See my Introduction and the instances below.

the seventh, seek him from the fourth by the same method. And if again you could not have him from the fourth, seek him from the eleventh by the same method.[20] And if again you could not have him from the eleventh, seek him from the ninth by the same method. And if again you could not have him from the ninth, seek him from the fifth through the same method. And if again you could not have him from the fifth, seek anew from the third–always by beginning from the Lord of the domicile, then from the Lord of the exaltation, after that from the luminary whose authority it is, then from the Lord of the bound, lastly from the Lord of the triplicity. And it seemed to certain ancients that you could do the same thing with the Lord of the face.[21]

And whichever planet you were to find in any of the aforesaid places (after the failure of the aforesaid significators to have the rulership of the year),[22] if it were to have some dignity there (and if it were to have only a face there), and it were free from the impediments, as was said about the others, it will be the Lord of the Year or Revolution. And if there were more planets in one of the aforesaid places, the one which was more authoritative (or the *al-mubtazz*) by the multitude of strengths[23] in that place, will be the Lord of the Year or Revolution. And if they were equal in strength, the one which is closer to the line should be preferred. And if they were oriental, he who is closer to the Sun exceeds the other. And if both were equidistant to the Moon or the Sun, the one to be preferred will be he who is changed more quickly from the degree in which he is.[24] And if one of the aforesaid planets were to aspect one of the listed houses by a trine or sextile aspect, by 2° ahead or 3° after,[25] and were to have some dignity there, he will be the Lord of the Year, after you did not find the other aforesaid [conditions met].

And if the ascending [sign] were the domicile or exaltation of some luminary, and [the luminary] were to aspect the Ascendant by a trine or sextile aspect, by 2° ahead or 3° after, or it were in the second from the Ascendant, it will be the

---

[20] Now the numbers of the houses/signs switch to Arabic numerals, but resume their spelled-out form with the third sign; therefore I treat all of these as being whole sign houses.

[21] Bonatti agrees with this rule, as the next paragraph will show.

[22] Lit., "after the falling [away]…from the rulership of the year."

[23] I am not sure whether Bonatti or his source means an equal-point or weighted-point *al-mubtazz*.

[24] This is similar to the horary principle that certain planets can be favored if they change their sign more quickly (see Tr. 6, Part 2, 6th House, Ch. 4), but here it is important that the planet actually be in the proper sign.

[25] This suggests the use of aspects to house cusps, which is rare in Bonatti. I believe that by "ahead of," Bonatti means "in an earlier degree than the cusp's"; by "after," he means "in a later degree than the cusp's." See my Introduction.

Lord of the Year. If however it were not so, look at the Lord of the Ascendant, and the Lord of [the ascending sign's] exaltation; and see if the luminary whose authority it was, were in the domicile of one of them, and aspected him by trine or a sextile aspect, nor were it cadent from the Ascendant, and were in a strong place: because he[26] will be the Lord of the Year.

And certain people preferred the luminary whose authority it was, to the planetary *al-mubtazz*. I however do not see a reason why this should be, always putting the Ascendant before the tenth and the other houses; and the 10th before the 7th, the 7th before the 4th, the 4th before the 11th, the 11th before the 9th, the 9th before the 5th, the 5th before the 3rd, as was said.[27]

And if one of the luminaries were not in one of the aforesaid places, see if the planet in whose domicile the luminary (whose authority it is) is located, is in one of those places. Because he will be the Lord of the Year or Revolution, whether he has a dignity there or not. Which if again it were not so, look at the Lord of the hour of the revolution: which if he were in one of the aforesaid places, he will be the Lord of the Year or Revolution, and the significator of the condition of the common people or the rustics.

And may you always understand [this] concerning any significator, if it were on the line of the house in which it was, or by 3° ahead or 4° behind[28]–always preferring the Lord of the domicile to the Lord of the exaltation, and the Lord of the exaltation to the Lord of the bound, the Lord of the bound to the Lord of the triplicity. For the Lord of the domicile has five strengths, the Lord of the exaltation has four strengths, the Lord of the bound has five strengths,[29] the Lord of the triplicity has three strengths. And even though the Lord of the bound has as many strengths as the Lord of the domicile does, and more than the Lord of the exaltation does, still they are preferred on account of their excellence.

---

[26] I.e., the domicile or exalted Lord of the Ascendant, whichever one is aspected by the powerful luminary.

[27] Bonatti's point may be this: "Certain others, *instead of* going through the houses to look for *al-mubtazzes* when *all else fails*, simply revert to the sect ruler and look no further."

[28] I believe that by "ahead of," Bonatti means "in an earlier degree than the cusp's"; by "behind," he means "in a later degree than the cusp's." See my Introduction.

[29] I am not aware of any other time when the Lord of the bound is given the same numerical weight as is the Lord of the domicile: usually the Lord of the bound is given two strengths in medieval texts.

Which again if it were not so, know the places of the Lord of the signs in which the luminaries are, and the place of the Lord of the sign in which the luminary (whose authority it is) is, and count him with[30] the other significators.

Wherefore if all of the significators failed to be the Lord of the Revolution, the one of them who is more authoritative by the multitude of strengths will take charge as the Lord of the Year, at least until the Lord of the Ascendant or of the 10th goes direct (if it were retrograde), or escaped [the Sun's rays] (if it were combust). Which if again it were not one of these, the disposition then is reverted to the luminary whose authority it is. And if the revolution were in the night, and the Moon were under the rays of the Sun, then the Sun will take charge instead of her.

Abū Ma'shar (with whom it seems to me good and fitting to agree) said that the significations of the Lord of the bound and the Lord of the triplicity and the Lord of the hour are to be considered in two places only: namely in the 1st and in the 10th house. And some believed strongly that he was self-contradictory, for he says elsewhere that their significations are considered in all the aforesaid places–but it is not so [that he is self-contradictory]. Where he says that they are to be considered in the first and the 10th, he understood by their own nature. For where he says that [they are to be considered] in all other places, he understood accidentally.[31] And there are five testimonies of good or evil,[32] and thus both [of these statements] are to be followed.

Moreover,[33] if the Lord of the bound or the triplicity or hour were in the Ascendant or in the 10th, and the Lord of the Ascendant or the 10th were in the degree of its own exaltation, or in 1° in front, or 1° in back (nor could he[34] be

---

[30] *Mitte ipsum in numero.*

[31] Note below Bonatti that includes the Lords of the bounds, triplicity, and the hour in his list of considerations–so I am not sure what is gained by distinguishing their natural and accidental significance.

[32] I do not understand this statement.

[33] This is an somewhat awkward paraphrase of Māshā'allāh, *De Rev. Ann.*, Ch. 6: "If the Lord of the Ascendant were in the horoscope, namely by three degrees before or behind its cusp, not cadent nor removed from the angle of the Ascendant, it will not be necessary in this case to look at another planet. Likewise the Lord of the exaltation of the sign of the Ascendant, if it were in the degrees of its own exaltation. Indeed, if the Lord of the triplicity were in the Ascendant, it will have one-third of the strength of the Lord of the Ascendant; and the Lord of the bound has one-fifth of the strength (and this according to the quantity of their strength in the signs); and the Lord of the hour has one-seventh. And know that this happens if they were in the Ascendant or the Midheaven–if however they were in the west or in the angle of the earth, their strength would be decreased; likewise it would be decreased more if they were in the eleventh, ninth, and fifth."

[34] I believe this refers to the Lord of the Ascendant or the 10th.

the significator), and one of them[35] were to have rulership of the year, he will gain for himself from the signification of the Lord of the first: namely the Lord of the triplicity, one-third; indeed the Lord of the bound will have one-fifth; also the Lord of the hour, one-seventh–according to how strong they were. Indeed in the other places this does not happen to them, but rather they decrease their strength in them.[36]

And however much I were to name places and houses for you, from which may be known the Lord of the Year or Revolution, I want you to know that they are not of equal strength. For the Ascendant and the 10th exceed the other houses in strength; the 7th is below the 10th, the 4th is below the 7th, the 11th is below the 4th, the 9th is below the 11th, the 5th below the 9th, the 3rd below the 5th. Whence according to the house from which the Lord of the Year was taken, according to that [house] will be the stronger or weaker significations in that year, or semester, or quarter, in the regions over which the revolution was. Wherefore it will be necessary for you to consider according to the part of the clime in which you were, or whose revolution it was. For it could be a revolution which is not a year, just like when a year is revolved according to semesters or according to quarters.[37]

Therefore, what remains are the testimonies by which the significations are known in these places. They are four, of which the first is the Lord of the domicile, the second the Lord of the exaltation, the third is the luminary whose authority it is, the fourth is the planetary *al-mubtazz* in the place from which is taken the revolution by nature, and the place of the circle in the hour by which the year is revolved. After you could not operate through the Lord of the Ascendant or the Lord of its exaltation, or by the luminary whose authority it was, see if one of them were in one of the angles (after the failure of the aforesaid),[38] and were in the degrees of the cusp, or by 2° ahead or 3° after,[39] nor were it impeded: it will be the Lord of the Year. And if the planetary *al-mubtazz* were impeded, so that it could not be the significator, then take as the

---

[35] I believe this refers to the Lord of the bound or triplicity or hour.

[36] My understanding of Māshā'allāh is that *if* any of the lesser Lords is in the Ascendant or 10th, *and* either the domicile or exaltation Lord is the Lord of the Year, then that lesser Lord will participate in the rulership, albeit more weakly. But Bonatti believes the lesser Lord will be the Lord of the Year if the domicile and exaltation Lords *cannot* be Lord of the Year–and that the lesser Lord's ability will be weaker than if it had been the domicile or exaltation Lord.

[37] See below.

[38] That is, if none of them could be the Lord of the Year by the conventional method.

[39] I believe that by "ahead of," Bonatti means "in an earlier degree than the cusp's"; by "after," he means "in a later degree than the cusp's." See my Introduction.

significator the planet in whose domicile is the luminary (whose authority it is), if it were fit to receive the signification. And if it were not fit to receive the signification or the rulership of the year, then the disposition and rulership of the year reverts to the luminary whose authority it is, after the failure of all the aforesaid. And if one of the luminaries were to commit its own disposition to the Lord of the Ascendant, [the Lord of the Ascendant] will be the Lord of the Year or Revolution (nor will it be necessary for you to look to another).

After it seems that you have found the Lord of the Year, you will even see if he were in the domicile of some planet, and were joined to it from a praiseworthy aspect, wherefore he gives it his own virtue, and makes him the Lord of the Year, if it were in an optimal place from the Ascendant; and more strongly so if some luminary (or the Lord of the domicile in which the luminary is) were to aspect them (or either of them).[40]

And the Sun could even be the Lord of the Year if he were receiving and collecting the lights or strengths of the planets–like if the revolution were in the night, and the planet who ought to be the Lord of the Year were nocturnal, and were under the rays of the Sun.

And if all the aforesaid [conditions] were missing, the disposition or rulership of the year will revert to the Lord of the Ascendant, whatever his condition was, and in whatever place he was.

And because it might be difficult for you to always consider together all the things that were said, I will abbreviate for you a little rule, and will recount for you the considerations and methods by which you ought to find the significator or Lord of the Year or Revolution. And there are twelve methods and fifty-four considerations.

The first of the methods is that you look to the Lords of the domiciles, from which the Lord of the Year is sought.

---

[40] This sentence is based on Māshā'allāh, *De Rev. Ann.*, Ch. 8. Māshā'allāh says, "And if the Lord of the Year appeared to you, see if perhaps he would commit his own disposition to another–that is, like if he is in the domicile of another planet, and that planet appears in an optimal place from the Ascendant, and the Lord of the Year also is conjoined to him. Because if it were so, he is made Lord of the Year who is the Lord of his sign (in which you were to find the governor of the Ascendant)." (The instructions seems to assume a best-case scenario, in which the domicile Lord or "governor" of the Ascendant is the presumptive Lord of the Year.) In other words, if the presumptive Lord of the Year is received by another, well-situated planet, that receiver will take up his disposition and be the true Lord of the Year.

The second is that you look to the Lords of their exaltations.

The third, that you look to the luminary whose authority it is.

The fourth, that you look to the Lords of their bounds.

The fifth, that you look to the Lords of their triplicities.

The sixth, that you look to the *al-mubtazz* over the places.

The seventh, that you look to the Lord of the hour of the revolution.

The eighth, that you look to the planet in whose domicile is the luminary whose authority it is.

The ninth, that you look to see if one of the planets aspects the Ascendant.

The tenth, that you look to see whether the Ascendant of the revolution is the domicile or exaltation of one of the luminaries, and the luminary aspects it.[41]

The eleventh, that you look to see if the luminary (whose authority it is), is in the domicile of the Lord of the Ascendant or of the Lord of its exaltation.

The twelfth, that you look to the Lord of the domicile in which the planet (in whose domicile is the luminary whose authority it is) is[42]–what kind of condition it has.

In the end there could be had other certain methods, but these are primary and more principal.

---

[41] Based on Bonatti's earlier statements, the aspect must be to the actual degree of the Ascendant.

[42] In other words, look at the (a) Lord of the (b) Lord of the (c) sign of the sect ruler. For example, suppose the revolution were in the day. Let the Sun be in (c) Gemini. The Lord of Gemini is (b) Mercury. Let Mercury be in Libra. Libra's Lord is (a) Venus. In this case we would look at Venus.

Epilogue

Indeed the considerations are fifty-four, as was said:

Of which the first is the Lord of the degree of the Ascendant.

The second is the Lord of the exaltation of the degree of the Ascendant.

The third is the luminary whose authority it is.

The fourth is the Lord of the bound of the degree of the Ascendant.

The fifth is the Lord of the triplicity of the degree of the Ascendant.

The sixth is the Lord of the degree of the 10th house.

Indeed the seventh is the Lord of [the 10th's] exaltation.

The eighth is the luminary whose authority it is, of the degree of the 10th house.[43]

The ninth is the Lord of the bound of the degree of the 10th house.

The tenth is the Lord of the triplicity of the degree of the 10th house.

The eleventh is the Lord of the degree of the 7th house.

The twelfth is the Lord of [the 7th's] exaltation.

The thirteenth is the luminary whose authority it is, of the degree of the 7th house.[44]

---

[43] This awkward phrasing is based on an earlier paragraph, but stands in parallel to the third consideration above. It evidently means, "see if the luminary whose authority it is, is *in* the 10th house." This same consideration will apply to other houses below. (It is also possible that Bonatti or his source is employing a rare instance of the locative case, which again would simply mean "in.")

[44] See previous footnote.

The fourteenth is the Lord of the degree of the bound of the 7th house.

The fifteenth is the Lord of [the 7th's] triplicity.

The sixteenth is the Lord of the degree of the 4th house.

The seventeenth is the Lord of its exaltation.

The eighteenth is the luminary whose authority it was, of the 4th house.[45]

The nineteenth is the Lord of the degree of the bound of the 4th house.

The twentieth is the Lord of [the 4th's] triplicity.

The twenty-first is the [Lord of the] degree of the 11th house.

The twenty-second is the Lord of the degree of [the 11th's] exaltation.

The twenty-third is the luminary whose authority it was, of the 11th house.[46]

The twenty-fourth is the Lord of [the 11th's] bound.

The twenty-fifth is the Lord of [the 11th's] triplicity.

The twenty-sixth is the Lord of the degree of the 9th house.

The twenty-seventh is the Lord of [the 9th's] exaltation.

The twenty-eighth is the luminary whose authority it was, of the degree of the 9th house.[47]

The twenty-ninth is the Lord of the bound of the degree of the 9th house.

---

45 See previous footnote.
46 See previous footnote.
47 See previous footnote.

The thirtieth is the Lord of [the 9th's] triplicity.

The thirty-first is the Lord of the degree of the 5th house.

The thirty-second is the Lord of its exaltation.

The thirty-third is the luminary whose authority it was, [of the degree of the 5th house].[48]

The thirty-fourth is the Lord of the degree of [the 5th's] bound.

The thirty-fifth is the Lord of the degree of [the 5th's] triplicity.

The thirty-sixth is the Lord of the degree of the 3rd house.

The thirty-seventh is the Lord of [the 3rd's] exaltation.

The thirty-eighth is the luminary whose authority it is, [of the degree of the 3rd house].[49]

The thirty-ninth is the Lord of [3rd's] bound.

The fortieth is the Lord of the triplicity of [3rd's] degree.

The forty-first is the planetary *al-mubtazz* in the degree of the house from which the Lord of the Year or Revolution is taken.[50]

The forty-second is the planet which was closer to the line of the house, if the planets were equal in strength.

The forty-third is the oriental planet which is closer to the Sun.

---

[48] See previous footnote.
[49] See previous footnote.
[50] Above this meant that if there were several planets in one of the above places, we must look at the *al-mubtazz* by the multitude of strengths in that place.

The forty-fourth is the planet who is changed more quickly from the degree in which it is, if more [than one planet] were oriental.[51]

The forty-fifth is the planet who more aspects the degree of the house signifying the rulership of the year.[52]

The forty-sixth is when the Ascendant is the domicile or exaltation of a luminary, and the luminary were to aspect the Ascendant by a trine or sextile aspect, or were in the 2nd.[53]

The forty-seventh is the planet in whose domicile is the luminary whose authority it is.

The forty-eighth is if one of the luminaries were to commit its disposition to the Lord of the Ascendant.

The forty-ninth is when the Lord of the Year commits its disposition to one of the planets.

The fiftieth is the Lord of the hour of the revolution.

The fifty-first is the Lords of the signs in which the luminaries are.

The fifty-second, the Lord of the sign in which the planet is, in whose domicile the luminary is.[54]

The fifty-third, when a planet which ought to have been the significator, is under the Sun's rays.

The fifty-fourth is the planet changing figure:[55] and it is he who more quickly is changed from a sign into [another] sign in the revolution of the

---

[51] This means, "if there were more than one planet *equally close* to the Sun."

[52] Above this meant that a relevant Lord could still be the Lord of the Year if it aspected the cusp of the relevant house within a few degrees (obviously after all other options were exhausted).

[53] *Secunda.* Above the text put the luminary in the second (*secundo*). Perhaps here *secunda* means "second domicile."

[54] Per the instructions above, this is the Lord of the Lord of the sign in which the sect ruler is.

year of the world, or who is oriental and more quickly becomes occidental, or who goes to the degree in which the Moon was at that time, or to the ascending degree (apart from the Moon).

Chapter 2: On the discovery of the significator of the king

After you have found the Lord of the Year or Revolution, which is called the significator of the common people or the rustics, it remains thus far for you to find the significator of the king, because it is very advantageous to consider him in a revolution of the years of the world–which you could find in this way:

Look at the Lord of the 10th house of the figure of the revolution of the year which you are revolving, to see whether he is free from combustion, retrogradation, fall, and the other aforesaid impediments. Which if it were so, and he were on the cusp of the 10th house, or by 3° ahead or 5° after,[56] he will be the significator of the king without a doubt: operate through him and do not seek another. If however you were to find him impeded by one of the aforesaid impediments, he already will not be the significator.

Then seek the significator from the Lord of the exaltation of the sign of the 10th house (if it were the exaltation of some planet); which if he were free, as I said regarding the Lord of the domicile, and he were on the cusp of the 10th house, or by 3° ahead or 4° after, he will be the significator of the king. If however he were impeded, he will not be [the king's] significator.

Then seek the significator from the Sun: which if he were free and sound as I have said regarding the others, and were on the cusp of the 10th house, or by 3° ahead or by 5° behind, he will be the significator of the king. If however it were not so, already he will not be the significator.

Then seek him from the planet which is the *al-mubtazz* in the sign of the 10th house by having a greater multitude of dignities.[57] Which if he were on the cusp of the 10th house, or by 3° ahead or 5° after, free and sound, he will be the significator of the king. If however he were impeded, he could not be the significator.

Indeed Abū Ma'shar preferred the Sun to the Lord of the exaltation.

---

[55] In Ch. 37, Bonatti defines "changing figure" as a planet moving from the sign it is in, into the next one. See Tr. 6.

[56] Here and below I believe that by "ahead of," Bonatti means "in an earlier degree than the cusp's"; by "after," he means "in a later degree than the cusp's." See my Introduction.

[57] Again, I do not know whether this is an *al-mubtazz* by weighted or equal points.

If indeed you did not find any one of them, then seek the significator from the planet which is on the cusp of the 10th house, or by 3° ahead or 4° after, and were otherwise free, and had some dignity there: because he will be the significator of the king. If indeed he were impeded, he will not be the significator of the king.

If however he did not have dignity there, and were on the cusp, or by 2° ahead or 3° after, or were the Lord of the domicile in which the Part of the Kingdom[58] were to fall, and were free and safe from the aforesaid impediments, he will be the significator of the king.

Which if again this were not so, Abū Ma'shar said that if the Midheaven were the domicile of the Sun, and the Sun on its cusp, not removed or cadent, he himself will be the significator of the king; and likewise if he were in the Ascendant received by Mars, and Leo in the Midheaven (because then the Ascendant will be Scorpio). And he said if the Midheaven were Aries, and the Sun on its cusp according to what I said, and Mars were cadent from him, [the Sun] will be the significator of the king. And if he were to aspect Mars, [Mars] will be a participator in the signification.

And [Abū Ma'shar] said if Mars were in his own place, strong, and his condition were good, and the Sun were joined to him, Mars will be the significator of the king; and more worthy than that if he were in Capricorn and the Sun were joined to him from out of the Midheaven. And he said that if his placement were to happen in the Midheaven,[59] or in an angle from the Ascendant, and the Sun were to project his rays to him, he will be more worthy in signification. And likewise if the Sun were in the angle of the Midheaven, or in other places aspecting the Midheaven (by aspects of friendship, understand), and he were the Lord of the Midheaven, [the Sun] will be more worthy in signification.

When the Lord of the Year is made the significator of the king

Which if you did not find it just as I have told you, see if the 10th were[60] the domicile or exaltation of the Lord of the Year, and he were to aspect it from any

---

58 This probably refers to the second Part of the 10th House (Ch. 13 of Part 2, below). It is extracted by taking the distance from Mars to the Moon by day, or the Moon to Mars by night, and projecting from the degree of the Ascendant.

59 The Latin reads: *si evenerit casus eius in medio coeli*. This could be read as: "If his *fall* [Cancer] were to be on the Midheaven, but that does not make sense, because Mars would not operate well as a significator of the king and the 10th house if Cancer were there. So *casus* must simply refer to his location.

60 Omitting *dominus*.

aspect except from the opposition: the Lord of the Year or significator of the common people will be the significator of the king.

Which again if it were not so, look to see if the Lord of the Year is joined with the Lord of the 10th house, or with the Lord of its exaltation, from such a place that the Lord of the 10th receives him—wherefore he commits his disposition to him, and the Lord of the Year will be made the significator of the king. Even if the Lord of the 10th house were in the domicile or in the exaltation of the Lord of the Year, and the Lord of the 10th house were received by him, he commits his disposition to the Lord of the Year; for the Lord of the Year will not become the significator of the king unless the Lord of the 10th were to commit his own disposition to him.

Which again if it were not so, see if the Sun were the Lord of the Year, and whether he has some dignity in the 10th, or if the Lord of the 10th were under the rays of the Sun (whether he had escaped from combustion or not, provided that he is not appearing from under the rays):[61] the Sun will be the significator of the king, and especially in the region in which this is.

And Abū Ma'shar said[62] if the Sun were to commit disposition to the Lord of the Ascendant, and he had some testimony in the Midheaven, the Lord of the Ascendant will be the significator of the king.

And he said that if the Midheaven were one of the domiciles of Saturn, or the sign of his exaltation, and he were on its cusp, free from combustion, Saturn will be the significator of the king.

And he said if the Sun had no testimony in the Midheaven, look at the Lord of the Midheaven and the Lord of its exaltation, to see which of them were stronger, and with more testimony, and of better condition, and collected and received more lights from the planets, and were of a better placement from the Midheaven:[63] because he will be the significator of the king.

And if the Lord of the Midheaven, and the Lord of its exaltation, and the Sun, were cadent from aspects [to the 10th],[64] and were of bad condition, nor did you find one of the aforesaid [situations], see if one of the planets aspects one of the aforesaid significators not aspecting the 10th, and [if] he himself

---

[61] I believe Bonatti means that the planet must be either combust or firmly under the beams; but if it were separating from the Sun between approximately 12° and 15°, then it would be appearing from under the rays, and the rule would not apply.

[62] Here and throughout Tr. 8, I often do not know the source of these statements by Abū Ma'shar.

[63] See previous note about Mars's "placement" (lit. "fall").

[64] *Si ceciderint…ab aspectibus.* As we will see later in the sentence, this means that they do not aspect the 10th—probably by whole sign.

aspects the 10th, so that he lifts up[65] the light of one to another: because this will strengthen him regarding the disposition of the king, and will make him whose light were so carried to the 10th, the significator of the king of that revolution.[66]

If however you found none of these, then revert to the Lord of the Year, and to the Lord of the 10th, and to the Sun: and the one of them you find stronger, or less weak, or better disposed, or less bad, or in a better place from the 10th, or one less bad, make this the significator of the king.

And Abū Ma'shar said if the Sun were the Lord of the Ascendant, the Midheaven will be Taurus. And if Venus were under his rays, the Sun will be the significator of the king, because the Lord of the Midheaven is under the rays. If however Venus had gone out from under the rays in her own light,[67] she will be more dignified in signification, for she will be in the Ascendant or in the domicile from which she aspects the 10th; and better than that is if she were in her own domicile or exaltation. And he said if Venus were at the end of an angle, and were to push her own strength[68] to the Sun (which could not take place unless she were joined to him corporally), then if Venus were the Lady of the Midheaven, she has already pushed her strength to the Sun, and the Sun will be the significator of the king. And he said the angles of the planets are the aggregate of their equation, truth, or certainty; and this is taken by the diameters of their short circles.[69]

Chapter 3: When the Lord of the Ascendant is the Lord of the Year, whence is known the condition of the king, and of his allies, and the common people, and certain men both religious and secular

However, the significator of the year or revolution having been found, and the significator of the king, it remains to discover the significator of the other diverse persons, and even whence the significators of the king are aspected– which you could know, as Abū Ma'shar says,[70] from Saturn, and from the Sun,

---

[65] Again, a reference to Māshā'allāh. See Tr. 6. Bonatti is trying to say that this planet should be transferring the light between two of the other significators.

[66] This is a fancy way of saying that if another planet transfers the light of one of the significators to the Midheaven, that significator will be the significator of the king.

[67] This is version (b) of being in one's "own light," from al-Qabīsī III.10.

[68] This seems to be Abū Ma'shar's "pushing power" (daf' al-quwwah), when a planet is in one of its own dignities and applies to another planet. See Tr. 3, Part II, Ch. 13.

[69] This is evidently an astronomical comment, but I do not see its relevance or what exactly Abū Ma'shar means by the "aggregate" (universalitas) or what role the concept of truth plays.

[70] In this Treatise, most of the citations of Abū Ma'shar seem to come from BN lat. 16204, which I have not yet been able to examine in great detail.

and from the 10th, and from [the king's] significator. Whence if you were to see these four well disposed, announce the good condition of the king, wholly and everywhere. If however you were to find them impeded, announce wholly the contrary. Which if you were to find one free and another impeded, judge according to what you saw regarding the impediment or liberation. But what is signified by Saturn is greater than any one of the them, both for good and for evil, except for the significator of the king; and the things signified by the Sun are below the things signified by Saturn, and the things signified by the Lord of the 10th are below the things signified by of the Sun in this case.[71]

How it is looked at for the soldiers of the king

And he said that you ought to look to the soldiers of the king from the 11th and its Lord: whence if you were see the 11th fit, and its Lord well disposed, and Mars [well disposed], announce even the condition of the king's soldiers to be good. If however you were to see it unfit, and its Lord impeded, and Mars likewise [impeded], announce the contrary of what I said. If however [either] the Lord of the 11th or Mars were impeded, and the other one were free, announce their condition to be middling.

How it is looked at for wealthy and great men who are below the king

However, you would take the condition of wealthy and great men who are below the king from Jupiter, and make him a participator with the Lord in whose domicile he was: which if you were to find him strong, and well disposed, announce their condition to be good. If however you were to find him badly disposed, announce the contrary.

How it is looked at for bishops and other secular clerics

Indeed you would look for bishops and other secular clerics (and the Pope and cardinals, and even for legal officials[72] and canonists, and counselors) from Jupiter and the Lord of his domicile, and from the ninth and its Lord: which if you were to find them free and well disposed, announce their good condition. If however you were to find one strong and another weak, you will announce a

---

[71] So the order of priority is: significator of the king, Saturn, Sun, Lord of the 10th. This seems to pertain both to the order of their effectiveness, and the quality and quantity of the very things signified.

[72] *Legistis.*

middling result according to the weakness or according to the strength which you found.

How it is looked at for soldiers of the king and his allies, and bearers of arms

For soldiers and allies of the king, and bearers of arms (for the sake of making money from the war),[73] you will take[74] [it] from Mars; which if you were to find him well disposed, announce their good condition. If however you were to find him badly disposed, announce the contrary.

How it is looked at for the religious who live under a Rule[75]

Indeed, for the regular religious serving God, and who have been placed for this purpose that they may serve God (nor should you trust every caped religious person, but those who have dedicated themselves to their God, among which [you should] count monks, and especially those wearing black vestments); and for old men and the decrepit, and low-class people doing heavy works,[76] like ditchdiggers, and the like, you will look from Saturn: which if you were to find him free, namely made fortunate and strong, announce the good condition of the aforesaid; if however you were to find him to the contrary, announce the contrary.

How it is looked at for women

However you will take the condition of women from Venus and her place: which if you were to find her well disposed, announce the good condition of women, and especially young women; if however you were to find her poorly disposed, announce the contrary.

How it is looked at for merchants and tradesmen[77]

Indeed the condition of merchants and tradesmen, and painters, and scribes, and judges, and the wise, and instructors, and especially those educated in the

---

[73] I believe this refers to those we now call "war profiteers" or those with munitions contracts.

[74] Reading *accipies* for *aspicies*.

[75] Sometimes called in English the "regular religious" (*religiosi regulares*), i.e. those who live in monasteries and convents.

[76] Reading the old people, the decrepit, and low-class people in the nominative, not the ablative/dative.

[77] *Merzarioribus*.

quadrivium, and boys, and adolescents and the like, you will take from Mercury: which if you were to find him free and well disposed, announce their good condition; if however you were to find him impeded, judge the contrary. However the condition of merchants varies from the condition of the others, wherefore it is looked for [merchants] from the Lord of the Year, and from the Ascendant and its Lord, and from the Moon, and from Jupiter just like Mercury; but Mercury and Jupiter prevail over the others in the signification of merchants.

How it is looked at for low-class and common people

You will look for the low-class and commoners, and sailors on smaller ships, from the Moon; which if you were to find her free and well disposed, announce their condition to be good. If however she were impeded, announce the contrary.

And in all the aforesaid matters, make the Lord of the Year a participator, and the Lord of the domicile in which you were to find the significator whose signification you seek. And mingle them together, and see how they fare, and how they are conjoined. For if they were all free, namely fortunate and strong (that is, the planet naturally signifying the matter and the planet in whose domicile it was, and the Lord of the Year), judge everywhere good concerning the signification which you seek. If however all were sound and one impeded, judge more good than evil. If indeed two were impeded, and one sound, judge more evil than good. And according to their liberation or their impediment, more or less, and according to the Ascendant which there was then–according to that you will judge the increase or decrease of the good or evil. For if[78] the Ascendant or the 10th were one of the domiciles of a planet naturally signifying the signification sought, like if something signified by Saturn were sought and the Ascendant or 10th is Capricorn or Aquarius; and if something signified by Jupiter were sought, and the Ascendant or the 10th is Sagittarius or Pisces. And if something signified by Mercury were sought, and the Ascendant or the 10th is Gemini or Virgo.

---

[78] In this paragraph and the next, Bonatti's "if" suggests he will later say "then," followed by instructions–which he does not provide. But his point seems to be that we ought to see if (a) a domicile belonging to the superiors or Mercury is on the Ascendant or the 10th. If so, then the things signified by that planet will be prominent. Or if (b) a domicile belonging to Venus, the Moon, or Mars is on the 7th or 4th, what they signify will be prominent.

However for Venus and the Moon it is otherwise: for if something signified by Venus were sought, neither the Ascendant nor the 10th is considered, but the 7th and the 4th. For if Taurus or Libra were the 7th or 4th, it will harm or profit like the Ascendant or the 10th harms or profits for Saturn and Jupiter and Mercury. And if the 7th or 4th were Cancer, on account of the femininity of [the houses] and [the planets'] places.[79] Indeed for Mars the Ascendant and the 10th are considered on account of their masculinity; the 7th and the 4th, on account of their nocturnality.[80]

Chapter 4: What the Lord of the Year or Revolution would signify in the places in which it fell at the hour of the revolution

And when you have discovered the Lord of the Year or Revolution and the significator of the king, and of [those] others whose significators are considered in revolutions, in this chapter we must consider those things which seem to be able to take place in the revolution.[81] But first concerning the general accidents of the year, apart from the situation of things born of the earth,[82] and the like, about which will be spoken of elsewhere in its own place and time.

Therefore, see in what place the Lord of the Year or Revolution were to fall in the hour at which the year is revolved, in the figure which you are erecting. Because if it were to fall in the Ascendant or in a place of friendship to the Ascendant, it signifies good, and joy, and tranquility for persons of that clime,[83] and of that region[84] according to the nature of the house in which it were to fall, as is said elsewhere. If indeed it were to fall into a place of enmity to the Ascendant, it will signify impediment, anger and contrariety, and all the more strongly so if the Lord of the Year were the Lord of the Ascendant. For if it were to fall in the 6th (which is one of the houses inimical to the Ascendant), infirmities will happen to men of that region in their bodies, and harm in small animals which are not ridden; and the more strongly so if the house were a sign

---

[79] In this paragraph Bonatti means that the eastern hemisphere is masculine, so one looks for the signification of the masculine planets from it (*viz.*, the Ascendant and the MC); the western hemisphere is feminine, so one looks for the signification of the feminine planets from it (*viz.*, the 4th and 7th).

[80] Mars is a masculine, nocturnal planet.

[81] *Devenire*, which has more of a connotation of coming down into reality.

[82] I.e., agriculture.

[83] The climes were areas of terrestrial latitude (see below).

[84] The regions seem to be construed more in terms of terrestrial longitude, and are related to measurements in right ascension.

signifying such a subject.[85] If however it were to fall in the 7th, contrarieties and whisperings and wars will happen to them. If indeed it were to fall in the 12th, enmity and treachery will happen to them. And all of these will happen according to the nature and substance of the sign in which the significator is. And this does not only have a role for the [domicile] Lord of the Ascendant, but it also has a role for the Lord of the exaltation, and of the bound, and the triplicity, and all the other significators of the revolution. But the things signified by the other [rulers of the sign] are below what is signified by the [domicile] Lord of the Ascendant, according to the being [or condition] of each of them, whether the things they signify are good or evil.

And their significations will be more strongly evil if it happened that the Lord of the Year or the Revolution were retrograde, even though this happens most rarely: however, the disposition of the planets could be so bad that of necessity the Lord of the Year would have to be retrograde, and then it would need the support of another planet who would lift him up and render his light to the Ascendant, or be rendered from planet to planet until it then were found by the planet who would render its light to the Ascendant[86] (or to the 10th, if it were the significator of the king).[87]

Chapter 5: On the knowledge of the accidents which are going to come in the year, and in which parts they ought to happen

And even though it can be most difficult to see in what directions, and in which regions, and in which climes, the accidents which are going to happen in the revolution (or the year which you revolve) ought to take place, still, to me it seems fitting to know, and not to omit, what can be known of it. And I will tell you certain things through which you could know something, by God's will. For I could not tell you everything fully on account of the great confusion of cities

---

[85] Presumably he means a sign like Aries or Capricorn (rams and goats), and not Pisces (fish).
[86] Remember that, according to the rules, candidates for the Lord of the Year must be rejected if retrograde. Bonatti is saying that if all of the candidates are in such bad shape that the best candidate is retrograde, then one will need its light to be transferred back to the Ascendant (through either one or several other planets) in order for the signification to be good. This last point about allowing multiple planets to transfer light comes from Māshā'allāh and is confirmed by Bonatti in several places (as we have already seen in Tr. 6).
[87] In other words, when judging the condition of the king separately (through the significator of the king), the light of a retrograde significator of the king must ultimately be transferred to the 10th.

and regions which there are given to understand.[88] For since the coming of the Lord there are 18,345 ancient cities or villas and castles, and other identical city habitations in the climes, without [those] having been newly put together, just as I have found stated by certain ancient sages.

Of which Messala the Indian[89] said that there are twelve exceeding the others in magnitude, of which in the first clime there are two deputed to Saturn. In the second are two deputed to Jupiter. In the third are two deputed to Mars. In the fourth are two deputed to the Sun. In the fifth is one deputed to Venus. In the sixth are two deputed to Mercury. In the seventh is one deputed to the Moon.

Whence, if you wished to know the accidents which are going to come in the region in which you are, from the revolution or year which you are revolving, you will note the Ascendant according to the ascensions of the city or the region in which you are, and see up to how much to the west: because the thing signified will be extended only that much, provided the Ascendant does not yield to alteration (indeed that it passes away by crossing 5°) by giving 53 *miliaria* to each degree (and a certain [measurement] approximating a *miliarium* by which the ancient sages measured, which is 4,000 cubits, according to equal cubits).[90] And what is signified will be extended only how much as there is of the nature of the Ascendant. Like if the Ascendant were the fifth degree of some sign, what is signified by that Ascendant will last toward the east up until five degrees after those five which had already gone across the line [of the Ascendant]; and toward the west up to three degrees from those five which are already beyond the line of the Ascendant. And thus what is signified will be extended from the place in which you are, toward the east by 265 *miliaria* and toward the west by 159 *miliaria*; and thus there are 424 *miliaria* in all. And what is signified will be extended that far, even if perhaps sometimes this is discerned in terms of more or less [i.e., approximately], in proportion as the planets aspect a place or Part, or the planet signifying the matter.

You, however, from your own industry, consider this, and according to longitude and according to latitude. Because it could sometimes be that what is signified would be extended 90° in front and 90° in back; and by that much to the right, and that much to the left. However, you must work it out lest the

---

[88] *Dare intellegere.*

[89] *Messala Indus.* This does not appear to be Māshā'allāh himself, since he does not make a statement like this in *De Rev. Ann.*

[90] It is unclear whether this approximation by cubits is meant to be a *miliarium*, or a measurement on top of a *miliarium*; I note that this measurement is never named or mentioned again, so it must be roughly equivalent to a *miliarium*.

region be so disposed that this impedes the going out into[91] of some direction, either by good or evil. Because if the particular site of the region were good, it will increase the good and decrease the evil, just like mountains, valleys, lakes, swamps, and similar places altering a region. You will observe this same thing in all climes, lands and regions, according to their Ascendants and according to their divisions, and according to their horizons.

Chapter 6: How the earth is divided into two primary divisions

For the earth is divided into two primary divisions, of which one is from the eastern quarter and from the southern quarter,[92] because their heat in which they agree, unites them, and makes one, resemble the nature of the other. The second is from the western quarter and from the northern quarter,[93] because their coldness in which they agree, unites them and makes one resemble the nature of the other.

Chapter 7: How it is divided according to three other following divisions

Moreover, the earth is subdivided into three other following divisions, namely into the superior, the middle, and the inferior. And these three divisions are fitted to the three superior planets, namely Saturn and Jupiter and Mars; and therefore for them it is stronger than for others. Because from them descend greater significations than from others. For even though the others participate with them, still the virtue of [the superiors] is much greater and stronger than the virtue of the inferiors.[94]

For the first division, namely the superior one, which is northern, which is the seventh clime, and whatever is inhabited from the earth outside the climes

---

[91] *Exitus* can mean "going out/forth" or "end, conclusion" or "event, result." I believe Bonatti is saying we ought to be aware not just of the distances involved, but of the actual geography of a land, so that we do not make predictions about regions which cannot support the relevant activity.

[92] In other words, the area above the horizon, from the Ascendant to the Midheaven to the 7th.

[93] In other words, the area below the horizon, from the 7th to the *Imum Coeli* to the Ascendant.

[94] This paragraph recalls the statements in Tr. 4 on the planetary regions, namely that the regions are divided into the superiors, the middle (the Sun) and the inferiors, and that the inferiors are lesser versions of the superiors, with lesser powers and shorter effects.

determined by the ancients, toward the arctic pole, is attributed to Saturn, whose participant is the Moon; which is clear through these things: because on account of the slowness of Saturn, and his darkness, and the thickness of those parts of the air, the smokiness of the land of those earthly and thick regions,[95] the mass of those inhabiting those regions are of little knowledge, and little intellect, and are forgetful but nevertheless lustful; nor does piety reign in them. But nevertheless if at some time it came upon one of them to adhere to the sciences, often he would exceed others, just like our most reverend predecessor Abū Ma'shar Tricas, who, even though he studied in Athens, was still a Latin, just as he himself confessed in the Treatise *Agiget*.[96] And even certain others, even though they are rarely found, like Michael Scot in my own time; and a certain other younger man, namely Albert the Teuton of the Order of Preachers.[97]

That the Moon would participate with Saturn is clear on account of their obstacles and stealth which happens to them on account of the obstacle of the Moon and her instability and sudden change and alteration; and because of their saffron and white and often red colors,[98] and on account of the opposition of [Saturn's and the Moon's] domiciles.

The second division, namely the middle part, which is the sixth, fifth, and fourth clime, is attributed to Jupiter, whose participant is Mercury–the domiciles of whom are opposed. And even the Sun participates with him in the fifth and in the fourth clime, and in the southern part of the sixth, and this appears through these [facts]: because those living in these regions are more often wiser and more compliant than the others, and especially those living in Italy (if they are not very intent on earning money). For the citizens of those climes are good, and of a more certain intellect and a deeper and sharper form of thinking; and piety thrives in them, and truth in certain ones of them, and religion more so than in some others, and a prophetical manner. And this happens more in the

---

[95] *Ipsarum terrestrium et grossarum.*

[96] The entire last half of this sentence is bizarre. Again we see Bonatti believes Abū Ma'shar was a Latin European who studied in Athens. Also, I do not know the significance of the title "Tricas" (cf. the name Abū Ma'shar Trax in Tr. 10), but Bonatti's point may be that just as people in the Arctic might act against type by pursuing the sciences, that Abū Ma'shar (allegedly a Latin) also acted against type. The name of the Treatise *Agiget* is another form of the book called *Axiget* in *Gr. Intr.* I.5.1671, which is described by Abū Ma'shar (or John of Seville) as a "book of courses," and which the Latins call the Canons–it is the Latinized form of *Zij*.

[97] I.e., Albert the Great. See Introduction.

[98] Bonatti is referring to the skin color variation of the inhabitants–which is presumably related to the colors attributed to the planets.

northern part of the fourth clime, and in all of the fifth, and in the southern part of the sixth–but in Italy more so than in the other regions, even though ibn Sina[99] seems to want to say something else. For he put the greater temperature under the circle of equality [rather] than elsewhere.[100] However, he did not speak as an astrologer, but as a doctor: and therefore he was deceived in his opinion.[101]

That Mercury is a participant with [Jupiter] is clear on account of the sharpness of their way of thinking, which is fit to learn and work with every mystery, and to learn and comprehend every [form of] wisdom, and knowledge, both mathematical and natural, and theological; and even for learning all mechanical arts, even though certain ones of those living in the seventh clime are fit for certain mechanical masteries. And it is even clear on account of the diversity of commixtures of [the inhabitants'] colors, of white, red, black, and the like; and because their domiciles are commingled and composed; and on account of the temperate heat and appropriate thinness of the air of their climes, and the moderate smokiness of the land.

And that the Sun would participate with him in the aforesaid climes, is clear through this: because they know above all others how to rule by means of guidance; they even knew rhetoric and ethics and politics above other men. And this is the division excelling over all other divisions, and it is better and more dignified than the rest.

Indeed the third division, namely the inferior one, which is south from the others, which is the third, and the second, and the first clime, is attributed to Mars, whose participant is Venus, the domiciles of whom are opposed. And these appear through these [facts]: because those living in these climes are predators and cutters of roads, and thieves. For they employ a filthy, venereal form of worship; they [sexually] abuse men and brute animals; they are drinkers and gamblers, following an unfit way of drinking and gambling, and often are bestial in all of their actions, immoral men, of a shameful life, and in all of their actions they are foul and tasteless, and impudent men, and have an irregular and reprehensible way of life.[102]

---

[99] *Avicenna.* See Introduction.

[100] I am unclear what this sentence refers to, although is probably described in the *Canon* (see next footnote).

[101] This must refer to ibn Sina's *Canon*, one of the most influential medical textbooks of the medieval period.

[102] If the lands ruled by the Persians and Arabs fall in this division, I think we can see why Bonatti is forced to conclude Abū Ma'shar had to be a Latin and not a Persian.

That Venus participates with him, is clear on account of their lust, the worship of Venus and of drinking and games; but Mars reduces all these to shamelessness and ineptitude. Also, their colors are often burnt and horrible, and often are black and swarthy on account of the deep heat and dryness in their skin, even though this happens more in one region than in another; which happens on account of the excessive heat of the Sun's rays, heating and destroying the disposition of their places, and on account of the intense heat of the air, and its excessively destructive thinness–even though al-Farghānī seems to want to say that winter there is of an even complexion. However, this is true with respect to our winter and our summer; for the Sun is exactly as far from the equator when it is in Cancer, as when it is in Capricorn.

Chapter 8: How the earth is divided into seven other divisions

Again, these two and three divisions are subdivided into another seven divisions according to the number of the seven planets–which are called climes, which are fitted to the seven planets.

For the first clime is fitted to Saturn, who is higher and superior and slower than the rest of the planets.

Indeed the second clime is fitted to Jupiter, who immediately follows after Saturn in slowness, and succeeds [him] in the order of circles.

The third is fitted to Mars, who immediately follows after Jupiter and succeeds [him] both in slowness and in the order of circles.

The fourth is fitted to the Sun, who follows after Mars in the order of circles.

The fifth is fitted to Venus, who follows after the Sun in the order of circles.

The sixth is fitted to Mercury, who follows after Venus in the order of circles.

Indeed the seventh and last one is fitted to the Moon, who follows after Mercury in the order of circles, because she is inferior to the rest of the planets and faster than the rest.

Whence every planet disposes more over the clime deputed to it than the others, even though each of them has something to do over every clime—sometimes according to more, sometimes according to less. Likewise the signs rule over regions, and imprint in them whatever is according to their nature. Wherefore the fiery ones imprint more over hot regions, the earthy ones over dry ones, airy ones over moist ones, watery ones over cold ones.[103] Because the signs do not signify over the parts of the world by places or through their position, but through their [elemental] nature. Whence, if there were a hot region over which a fiery sign rules, what is signified [by the sign] will happen more strongly than [it would] in a cold [region]. For it tempers the coldness in the cold one; and because [a wet sign] moistens in a wet [region], it tempers the dryness in a dry region, and *vice versa*.

Just as Aries, Leo and Sagittarius (which are the first triplicity), heat in the eastern parts, in the northern parts they temper the coldness, because they are fiery, and are eastern signs. Whence if the Ascendant were one of those signs, it will strengthen what is signified, and increase it; and the eastern wind is hot and dry.

And just as Taurus, Virgo and Capricorn (which are the second triplicity) dry out in the parts of the south, in the parts of the west they temper moisture because they are earthy, and are southern signs. Whence if the angle of the 10th were of those signs, it will strengthen what is signified, and will increase it; and the southern wind is hot and moist.

And just as Gemini, Libra, and Aquarius (which are the third triplicity) moisten in the parts of the west, they temper dryness in the parts of the south because they are airy, and are western signs. Whence if the angle of the 7th house were of those signs, it will strengthen what is signified, and will increase it; and the western wind is cold and moist.

---

[103] The attributions here are not the standard Stoic or Aristotelian ones—they derive from a combination of wind and elemental considerations (see below).

And just as Cancer, Scorpio and Pisces (which are the fourth triplicity) make cold in the northern parts, in the eastern ones they temper heat, because they are watery, and are northern signs. Whence if the angle of the 4th house were of those signs, it will strengthen what is signified, and will increase it; and the northern wind is cold and dry.

And even the planets help this: for if what is signified were in the north, and Saturn ruled over what is signified, he will help it, and will make it appear to a greater degree; and more strongly so if Mercury were to help him, and what was signified were of coldness. And if it were in the west, and Jupiter were to rule over it, what is signified will be increased, and more strongly so if the Moon were to help him, and what is signified were of moisture, and [Jupiter] will make it appear to a greater degree. And if it were in the southern parts, and Mars were to rule over it, it will be increased if it were something signified of dryness, and he will make it appear to a greater degree. And if it were in the eastern parts, and the Sun were to rule over it, and it were something signified of heat, the Sun will help it, and will make it appear to a greater degree. If however Venus were a participant, she will temper some of the heat.[104]

Another division of the earth

And after these two, and these three, and these seven divisions, again the earth is divided into another twelve divisions following the number of the twelve signs, and following the degrees transited from the east to the west.[105]

For Aries is adapted to the first clime; whence Mars, who is the Lord[106] of Aries, rules over the things signified by that clime from the east to the west; but the Lords of the bounds participate with him, and the virtue of the Lord of the bound prevails over the virtue of the Lord of the domicile in the particular significations of revolutions. For Jupiter, who has the first bound of Aries, disposes over the significations of the revolution of the first clime, from the beginning of the inhabitable earth from the direction of the east toward the west for 318 *miliaria*.[107] And after him, Venus for 424 *miliaria*. And after him, Mercury

---

[104] Bonatti considers Venus to be primarily cold and moist, but with a certain "hidden heat" (Tr. 7, Part 1, Ch. 11).
[105] Bonatti follows his own (erroneous) version of Ptolemy's bounds, which I will leave standing as they are.
[106] Reading *dominus* for *domus*.
[107] Bonatti is multiplying the number of degrees in each planet's bound by 53 *miliaria* (see above).

for 371 *miliaria*. And after him, Mars for 265 *miliaria*. And his signification is stronger then because he has the virtue of the bound and the virtue of the domicile [Aries]; and so it goes with the others. And after him, Saturn for 212 *miliaria*. Then the disposition reverts to Jupiter and to the rest of the others until it reaches to the end of the inhabitable region toward the west.[108]

Taurus is adapted to the southern half of the second clime, and Venus (who is the Lady of Taurus) rules over its signification from the east to the west. And Venus, who has the first bound of Taurus, rules its significations and disposes over them from the beginning of the inhabitable earth from the east toward the west for 424 *miliaria*. And its significations will then be without the participation of anyone, because she is the Lady of the domicile and the Lady of the bound, and therefore they appear to a greater degree. And after her, Mercury for 371 *miliaria*. After him, Jupiter for 371 *miliaria*. And after him, Saturn for 106 *miliaria*. And after him, Mars for 318 *miliaria*. After him, the disposition reverts to Venus, and she rules the significations for 424 *miliaria*, and so on for the rest of the Lords of the bounds.

Indeed Gemini is adapted to the northern half of the second clime. And Mercury, who is its Lord, rules over the significations of its half from the east to the west, but [the Lords of the bounds] participate with him in the bounds.[109] For Mercury himself rules the first bound, and his signification will appear strong then (because he is the Lord of the domicile and the Lord of the bound) for 371 *miliaria*. And after him, Jupiter for 318 *miliaria*. And after him, Venus for 371 *miliaria*. And after her, Mars for 318 *miliaria*. After him, Saturn for 212 *miliaria*. Then the disposition reverts to Mercury and so one for the rest, up until the end of the inhabitable earth to the west.

Cancer is adapted to the southern half of the third clime, from the east to the west. And its Lady the Moon rules the significations of the clime from the east to the west, and the Lords of the bounds participate with her. For Mars, who has the first bound of Cancer, rules the significations of the revolution which ought to be from the beginning of the inhabitable earth from the direction of the east to the west for 318 *miliaria*. And after him, Jupiter for 371 *miliaria*. And

---

[108] Bonatti seems to be imagining that along each strip of latitude defining the clime, sections of longitude will be ruled by each bound ruler in succession. But he clearly thinks that there are well-defined boundaries to where the inhabitable parts of the clime begin and end (i.e., due to ocean boundaries). Since the discovery of the Americas, where might these boundaries begin and end?

[109] Reading *terminis* for *termino* (although the sentence is more truncated than its parallel ones in other paragraphs, and may have been garbled in transcription).

after him, Mercury for 371 *miliaria*. [And after him, Venus for 371 *miliaria*.][110] And after her, Saturn for 159 *miliaria*. Then the disposition reverts to Mars, and to the rest of the other planets, until it reaches the end of the inhabitable earth toward the west.

Leo is adapted to the northern half of the third clime from the east to the west. And the Sun, who is its Lord, rules over the significations of that half generally, but the Lord of the bounds [do so] with him particularly.[111] For Saturn, who is the Lord of the first bound of Leo, rules the significations of the revolution from the beginning of the inhabitable earth from the direction of the east toward the west, for 318 *miliaria*. And after him, Mercury for 372 *miliaria*. After him, Mars for 265 *miliaria*. After him, Venus for 318 *miliaria*. After her, Jupiter for 318 *miliaria*. Then the disposition reverts to Saturn and to the rest of the planets in succession, until the end of the inhabitable [earth] is reached.

Virgo is adapted to the southern half of the fourth clime, from the east to the west. And Mercury, who is the Lord [of Virgo], rules the significations of that half from the east to the west generally, but the Lord of the bounds participate with him; and he himself, who is the Lord of the first bound of Virgo, rules over the significations of the revolution which ought to be from the beginning of the inhabitable earth toward the west, for 371 *miliaria*. And after him, Venus for 318 *miliaria*. And after her, Jupiter for 265 *miliaria*. After him, Saturn for 318 *miliaria*. After him, Mars for 318 *miliaria*. Then the disposition reverts to Mercury, *etc.*, as was said for the others.

Libra is adapted to the northern half of the fourth clime from the east to the west. And Venus, who is its Lady, rules over the significations of that half generally from the east to the west, but the Lords of the bounds participate with her. For Saturn, who is the Lord of the first bound of Libra, rules the significations of the revolution which ought to be from the beginning of the inhabitable earth, from the direction of the east toward the west, for 318 *miliaria*. And after him, Venus for 265 *miliaria*. And after her, Mercury for 265 *miliaria*. After him, Jupiter for 424 *miliaria*. And after him, Mars for 318 *miliaria*. Then the disposition reverts to Saturn, *etc.*, as was said for the others.

Scorpio is adapted to the southern half of the fifth clime. And Mars, who is its Lord, rules over the significations of that half generally, from the east to the west, but the Lords of the bounds participate with him. For Mars himself, who is the Lord of the first bound of Scorpio, rules over the significations of the

---

[110] The text omits Venus, who fits here.
[111] Remember, the luminaries do not rule any bounds.

revolution which ought to be from the beginning of the inhabitable earth from the direction of the east toward the west, for 318 *miliaria*. And after him, Venus for 371 *miliaria*. After her, Jupiter for 424 *miliaria*. And after him, Mercury for 318 *miliaria*. After him, Saturn for 159 *miliaria*. Then the disposition reverts to Mars, *etc.*, as was said of the others.

Sagittarius is adapted to the northern half of the fifth clime, from the east to the west. And Jupiter, who is its Lord, rules over the significations generally from the east to the west, but the Lords of the bounds participate with him. For Jupiter,[112] who is the Lord of the first bound of Sagittarius, rules over the significations of the revolution which ought to be from the beginning of the inhabitable earth, from the beginning of the east toward the west, for 424 *miliaria*. And after him, Venus for 318 *miliaria*. After her, Mercury for 165 *miliaria*. After him, Saturn for 318 *miliaria*. After him, Mars for 265 *miliaria*. Then the disposition reverts to Jupiter, *etc.*, as was said for the others.

Capricorn is adapted to the southern half of the sixth clime, from the east to the west. And Saturn, who is its Lord, rules over the significations of that half generally, from the east to the west, but the Lords of the bounds participate with him. For Venus, who is the Lady of the first bound of Capricorn, rules the significations of the revolution which ought to be from the beginning of the inhabitable earth, from the direction of the east towards the west, for 318 *miliaria*. And after her, Mercury for 318 *miliaria*. After him, Jupiter for 371 *miliaria*. After him, Saturn for 318 *miliaria*. After him, Mars for 265 *miliaria*. Then the disposition reverts to Venus, as was said for the others.

Aquarius is adapted to the northern half of the sixth clime, from the east to the west. And Saturn, who is its Lord, rules over the significations of that half universally, from the east to the west, but the Lords of the bounds participate with him. For this same Saturn, who is the Lord of the first bound of Aquarius, rules over the significations of the revolution which ought to be from the beginning of the inhabitable earth, from the direction of the east towards the west, for 318 *miliaria*. And after him, Mercury for 318 *miliaria*. And after him, Venus for 424 *miliaria*. And after her, Jupiter for 265 *miliaria*. After him, Mars for 265 *miliaria*. Then the disposition reverts to Saturn, as was said for the others.

Pisces is adapted to the seventh clime, from the east to the west. And Jupiter, who is the Lord, rules the significations of that clime universally, from the east to the west, but the Lords of the bounds participate with him. For Venus, who

---

112 Reading *Juppiter* for *Saturnus*.

is the Lady of the first bound of Pisces, rules over the significations of the revolution which ought to be from the beginning of the inhabitable earth, from the east toward the west, for 424 *miliaria*. And after her, Jupiter for 318 *miliaria*. After him, Mercury for 318 *miliaria*. After him, Mars for 265 *miliaria*. After him, Saturn for 265 *miliaria*. Then the disposition reverts to Venus, as was said for the others.

If however the clime were not of such a length [or longitude] that the things signified by the planets could be extended so much that the number of the *miliaria* could be completed, as was said, it does not refer [to anything]. For with land missing, the signification of the bound of the planet expires.

Whence, you ought to look back at the disposition, and at the condition of the planets in the revolutions of the years, both in nativities and questions, and of the world, and see if the condition of the Lord of the sign were good, because it signifies the good condition of the clime generally, according to the part which it rules. And likewise look at the condition of the planets ruling over the bounds. For if they were to agree in one being [or nature or condition], it will signify that what is signified by the revolution will appear to a greater degree, both for good and for evil. Like if the condition of the Lord of the sign and the condition of the Lord of the bound were good, it signifies complete good in the region over which the Lord of the bound rules. If however the condition of each were bad, it signifies that complete evil will appear in the region over which the Lord of the bound rules. If however they were to disagree, what is signified by them will appear less, but what is signified by the Lord of the sign will appear less than what is signified by the Lord of the bound, both for good and for evil.

Chapter 9: How the condition of the Sun is to be viewed in a revolution of the year, if it were diurnal

Also, look at the condition of the Sun and his disposition in a revolution of the year of the world (if the revolution were diurnal), and see whether he is going to be eclipsed in that year or not.

Likewise, look at the aspects of the planets to him, namely [those of] the benefics and the malefics: because the benefics signify good, the malefics on the contrary signify evil. For if the Sun were made fortunate and strong, it signifies the exaltation and eventuating of a great thing, in a diurnal revolution.

Look even at the condition of the Lord of the Ascendant, and see whether it is free from the impediments already stated, or not. Because if he were free, it signifies goodness and the tranquility of the land over which the sign that is then ascending, rules; and of the citizens of that region, and of the people[113] who are signified by that planet. If however he were impeded, it signifies impediment and detriment and evil which will come to the inhabitants of that region, and [the people] who are signified by the planet who is the Lord of the Ascendant of the revolution; and their condition will be disposed according to the substance of the sign ruling over that region that is signified by that sign. Like if Libra were ascending, and Venus (its Lady) were cadent from the Ascendant, or from the angles, impeded (either retrograde or combust or besieged by the two malefics), or made unfortunate in another way, it signifies that destruction and infirmities and sorrows will happen in Arabia, and to the inhabitants of it, and to all who are signified by Libra or by Venus. And if Leo were ascending, and the Sun were impeded, it signifies that the aforesaid impediments will happen to those of Babylonia, and to all who are signified by Leo and the Sun. If however Cancer were ascending, and the Moon were impeded by the aforesaid impediments, it signifies that the aforesaid impediments will happen to the Romans, and to all who are signified by Cancer and the Moon. And may you understand this with every sign, and with every planet, according to the things signified by each.[114]

Chapter 10: How one must look at the condition of the Moon if the revolution were nocturnal

If however the revolution were nocturnal, then look at the Moon, just as you are looking at the Sun in a diurnal revolution. Which if she were the Lady of the Revolution or disposition, and were in Cancer, you will look only at her. If indeed she were outside Cancer, then look on to the Lord of the domicile in which she is: which if you were to find him strong and made fortunate by [being

---

[113] *Gentis.* Bonatti means this both ethnically (like Arabs for Venus) and in terms of character or profession (like women for Venus). See below.

[114] There are two problems with this doctrine. (a) Suppose the chart of the revolution were cast for Italy, but the rising sign were Libra (which he says rules Arabia). Why should the rising sign, which ought to pertain to Italy, say anything about Arabia? Moreover, (b) charts for nations close to one another might have the same rising sign, but the ruler in a different condition. For instance, Libra might be rising in the charts of two nations; but she might be cadent in one and angular in the other. This would give contradictory reports about the affairs of nations ruled by Libra.

in] some strong place, or by aspect of the benefics to him, it signifies good for the citizens of that region. If however you were to find him weak, made unfortunate from the aforesaid causes, it signifies the bad condition and bad disposition of the citizens or the inhabitants of that region, and their detriment.

[Further general delineation of the revolution][115]

You may say likewise concerning the Lord of the Ascendant of the revolution;[116] wherefore if it were of good condition, it signifies the good of the aforesaid citizens. If however it were of a bad condition, it signifies their detriment.

And know that the Moon in a revolution of the night, if she were made fortunate and strong, increased in light and number, signifies the exaltation and influence[117] of a great matter and for the good.

Likewise look to see if the luminary whose authority it was (and especially the nocturnal [luminary]), is joined to Saturn by body, or by aspect. Because if [the luminary] were joined to him by body, or from some aspect, without perfect reception, the malice will be increased for it; and all the more strongly if the Moon were joined to him in the going down [or waning] of her own light. If indeed she were being separated from him then, and especially in the increase of her own light, the malice will be decreased, and it will not bring in so much detriment.

You will even see where the impeding malefic is, and of which house it is the Lord; because harm will come out from the matter which is signified by that house. Like if it were in the 2nd, it will occur because of substance, or because of something of those things which are signified by the 2nd house. If indeed it were in the 3rd, it will occur because of brothers, or because of short journeys, or because of those things which are signified by the 3rd house. If however it were in the 4th, it will occur because of parents, or inheritances, or because of those things which are signified by the 4th house. If indeed it were in the 5th, it will

---

[115] Now Bonatti switches to guidelines for delineating the rulers of all of the houses in the revolutionary figure. Section heading mine.

[116] I do not know if Bonatti means this universally, or only as part of delineating a nocturnal revolution.

[117] *Pulsationem*. Usually Bonatti (or his sources) only use this term when speaking of planets "pushing" their nature or power onto one another, but "influence" seems better her. Of course, it could mean that because of the Moon's good condition, the nature or power she does "push" will be something powerful indeed.

occur because of children, or women (who are not wives or girlfriends),[118] or because of those things which are signified by the 5th house. And if it were in the 6th, it will happen because of infirmities, or male or female slaves, or because of those things which are signified by the 6th house. If however it were in the 7th, it will occur because of wives, or partners, or enemies, or one of those reasons which are signified by the 7th house. If it were in the 8th, it will occur because of death, or because of those things which are inherited from the dead, or because of those things which are signified by the 8th house. And if it were in the 9th, it will occur because of religion, or religious men, or a long journey, or because of the search for those things which pertain to the future eternal life, or one of those things which are signified by the 9th house. If however it were in the 10th, it will occur because of a king or a kingdom, or a magistrate, or one of those things which are signified by the 10th house. If indeed it were in the 11th, it will occur because of hope, or friends, or because of those things which are signified by the 11th house. But if it were in the 12th, it will occur because of hidden enemies, or large animals, or one of those things which are signified by the 12th house.

After you have looked at the Lord of the Ascendant, and you have judged concerning his condition, then look at the Lord of the second, and judge concerning him as you have you have judged concerning the Lord of the Ascendant. Like if he were free from impediments, and were made fortunate and strong, judge the goodness and increase of substance, and likewise the profit of the citizens and inhabitants (of the region that is signified by the Ascendant and its Lord), and of those [things] which are signified by the 2nd house, in that region. If however you were to find him impeded, [judge] to the contrary.

Then look at the Lord of the third, which if you were to find him free and made fortunate, and strong, say their short journeys [will be] fortunate, and useful, and lucrative; and that brothers of that region will behave well toward each other; and the rest of the things which are signified by the 3rd house will be well disposed. If however you were to find him impeded, say the contrary.

Then look at the Lord of the fourth, which if you were to find him made fortunate and strong, it signifies that the fathers of that region will behave well toward their children, and that their fields will bring forth the produce well, and

---

[118] Wives and girlfriends are attributed to the 7th house, but what other women could he mean? One is tempted to say "prostitutes," or women as givers of sexual pleasure, but why not simply say it? Perhaps it means women generally, since Venus (who is a general significator of women) has a joy in the 5th.

the rest of the things which are signified by the 4th house will be well disposed. If however you were to find him impeded, say the contrary.

Then look at the Lord of the fifth, which if you were to find him made fortunate and strong, it signifies that the children of that region will behave themselves well toward their parents, and that there will be games and joyful things in that region, and that all the things which are signified by the 5th house will be well disposed. If however you were to find him impeded, say the contrary.

Then look at the Lord of the sixth, which if you were to find him made fortunate and strong, it signifies the health of the bodies of the citizens of that region, and that their male and female slaves, and male and female servants, will behave well toward them; and likewise that their smaller animals, and the things signified by the 6th house, will be well disposed. If however he were badly disposed, say the contrary.

Then look at the Lord of the seventh, which if you were to find him strong, it signifies that their wives will more often behave well toward their husbands, and that partners will cooperate well with partners, and there will be few enmities (unless perhaps the Lord of the seventh and the Lord of the Ascendant aspect each other at the same time, from enmity), and all the things which are signified by the 7th house will be well disposed. If however it were badly disposed, say the contrary.

Then look at the Lord of the eighth,[119] which if you were to find him made fortunate and strong, it signifies that there will be little mortality in that region, and that, except for a few, they will not die a bad death. But they will depart [this world] from in their own beds (unless perhaps the malefics impede the Lord of the Ascendant or the Moon with a great impediment), and that the rest of the things which are signified by the 8th house will be well disposed. If however you were to find him impeded, say the contrary.

Then you would look at the Lord of the ninth, which if you were to find him made fortunate and strong, it signifies their long journeys will be useful and praiseworthy, and that their religious men will be increased, and the rest of the things which are signified by the 9th house will be well disposed in that region. If however you were to find the contrary, you will judge the contrary.

Then you would look at the Lord of the tenth, which if you were to find him made fortunate and strong, it signifies that the king or the defender[120] of that

---

[119] Reading *octavi* for Bonatti's *octavae*, to match the use of places/signs in the rest of the list.
[120] *Praeses.*

region will be well disposed, and that they will behave themselves well toward their subjects, and that the rest of the things which are signified by the 10th house will be well disposed. If however you were to find him impeded, say the contrary.

Then you would look at the Lord of the eleventh, which if you were to find him made fortunate and strong, it signifies that the hopes of the citizens of that region, and their trust, will come to a good end; and that their fortune will be increased in the good, and there will not be enmities between them (except for a few), and all the things which are signified by the 11th house will be well disposed. If however you were to find him impeded, say the contrary.

Then you would look at the Lord of the twelfth, which if you were to find him made fortunate and strong, it signifies that the greater animals of the citizens of that region will be well disposed and will be increased in the good; and there will be few reproaches [or blasphemies] and few slanders between them, and that the rest of the things which are signified by the 12th house will be well disposed. If however you were to find him impeded, say the contrary.

Whence if you were to look well at all of the significators of all twelve houses, you could see how the accidents of that region will be disposed in the revolution. For according to how you were to find the Lords of the houses disposed, the accidents of the significators of each house will occur according to that—namely, according to the strength or weakness of each of them, and according to the place of the Lord of the sign from that sign itself. And the adaptation of the Lord of each house will be according to the aspect of one to another, and according to how the malefics aspect the planetary Lord (namely of that house).

Even look at the angles and their Lords more diligently and minutely than the others: because their virtue exceeds the virtues of the others.

Chapter 11: What every one of the seven planets would signify in the Ascendant, in a revolution of the year

On Saturn in the Ascendant at the hour of the revolution

You will even look at the Ascendant of the hour of the revolution, to see which of the planets is in it. Because if Saturn were there, nor were he the Lord of the Ascendant, it signifies the detriment of that region which falls under that revolution, in accordance with what is said elsewhere; and pestilences, like infirmities, death, famine, many harmful winds (if he were direct, and especially in airy signs). If indeed he were retrograde, it speaks against winds, nor will he permit them to grow strong; however the ones which there are, will be harmful. If however he were the Lord of the Ascendant, it will mitigate the aforesaid things, nor will they be so harmful.

On Jupiter in the Ascendant at the hour of the revolution: what he would signify

If however Jupiter were in the Ascendant at the hour of the revolution, it signifies the general goodness of the disposition of the year or revolution, and there will be peace and security, and good will between men of that region, more so than usual; and it will be good for its wealthy and great men; and goods will be increased and bring profit, and their business matters will be improved. And if the Lord of the Ascendant ([or][121] the Lord of its exaltation) were joined to him, or he to it (from whatever aspect, and especially from the trine or sextile, or by corporal conjunction), and it were of good condition, there will be love between the king of that region and his subjects; and the rustics will encounter good from him, and that he will please them.

On Mars in the Ascendant: what he would signify

If indeed Mars were in the Ascendant at the hour of the revolution, free (namely made fortunate and strong), it signifies there is going to be an earthquake in that region. And if he were in an eastern sign, it signifies it is going to be in the first quarter of the revolution. If indeed he were in a southern sign, it signifies it is going to be in the second quarter of the revolution. If by chance he were in a western sign, it signifies it is going to be in the third quarter of the revolution. And if he were in a northern sign, it signifies it is going to be in the last quarter of the revolution. It even signifies a scarcity of rains, and a scarcity of battles. If indeed he were impeded and of bad condition, say the contrary, namely instead of good say bad, and instead of bad say worse, except for rains (because he does not extinguish their powers so much in it).

If however he were on the line of the 10th house, or beyond it by 15' or less, or after it by 1° or less, it signifies that the king or the chief of that region will capture or imprison more of his subjects. And if he were beyond it by 15' up to 30', or after from 1° up to 3°, he will capture a lesser quantity of them. And if it were beyond it from 30' up to the end of 1°, or after from 3° up to 5°, he will

---

[121] Reading *aut* for *et*.

capture fewer. And if he were[122] beyond it from 1° up to the end of 2°, or after it from 5° up to the end of 10°, he will capture far fewer again. If however he were beyond it from 2° up to 5°, or after it from 10° up to the end of 25°, and the house was not removed, he will imprison practically none (even if some). And even though he will have imprisoned [some], still he will not kill them, nor will he mutilate them (except for few), although he will torture them.[123]

If however Mars at the revolution were on the line of the 4th house, or in the other degrees or places opposite the aforesaid, he will kill (of those whom he will capture) according to the quantity and proportion and mean by which he will capture them if Mars were in the 10th, and according to the places and degrees opposite them.[124]

Indeed if he were in the first or the 7th, in similar places and degrees, he will mutilate some of them, according to the aforementioned quantity and proportion.

On the Sun in the Ascendant: what he would signify

If however the Sun were in the Ascendant at the hour of the revolution, free from the malefics and the other impediments, and the Lord of the Year or Revolution were with[125] him, it signifies the good condition of the wealthy and great or noble men, and their joy, and the increase of the good, and the progress [or success] of things. And if he were received, it signifies the taking away of evil. If however he were not in the Ascendant at the hour of the revolution, but were outside it[126] in a good place from it, free from impediments, it signifies the same, but less so. If indeed he were impeded, it signifies their detriment, and the contrary of the things which I told you.

---

[122] Reading *fuerit* for *fuerint*.

[123] In this passage, "beyond" means "in an earlier degree than the cusp's," i.e., so that it has already passed beyond the cusp by primary motion; "after" means "in a later degree than the cusp's," i.e., so that it has not yet passed beyond the cusp by primary motion.

[124] I am not sure what Bonatti means by this sense of proportion.

[125] Bonatti probably means "in the Ascendant but not combust, or in aspect." See following sentences.

[126] *Extra illud.* This use of the neuter is another reason why the quadrant/whole sign distinction is often unclear in Bonatti. Here Bonatti seems to mean "outside the ascending sign."

On Venus in the Ascendant: what she would signify

Indeed if Venus were in the Ascendant at the hour of the revolution, namely free and made fortunate and strong, it signifies joy and gladness, and dancing, and the breaking up of battles, and especially of young women and men employing venereal practices; and the good disposition of the Arabs and their goods; and all the more so if she were with the Lord of the domicile or exaltation of the sign in which she is. And if she were impeded, it signifies the contrary of the aforesaid.

On Mercury in the Ascendant: what he would signify

If for example Mercury were in the Ascendant at the hour of the revolution, in the aspect of the benefics, and he were free from impediments (namely made fortunate and strong), and he himself were the Lord of the Year, it signifies the good condition and good disposition and the usefulness of the wise (namely of judges and medical doctors), and merchants, also writers and boys; and all the more so if he were joined with the Lord of the domicile or exaltation of the sign in which he himself is. If however he were impeded, it signifies the contrary of those things which I have told you.

On the Moon in the Ascendant: what she would signify

Which if the Moon were in the Ascendant at the hour of the revolution, or she were in the house [domicile?] of the Lord of the Year or Revolution, joined to him by body or by aspect (except for the opposition), and were otherwise free from impediments, it signifies an abundance of waters or rains, and the increase of rivers and streams, and their flooding; the increase of cold; and the goodness of the disposition of men, and that they will rejoice in the good. If however she were impeded, the aforesaid will be decreased, or perhaps annihilated.

Chapter 12: On Saturn and Mars, if they were impeded in a revolution when they are above the earth

Likewise you will look in the hour of the revolution to see if Mars and Saturn are above the earth [and] impeded, because this signifies the severity of the year or revolution. And more strongly so, if Mars were to receive Saturn, and

committed disposition to him, because it will signify severe and lasting accidents, and that the significations or detriments will appear and manifest: for
they will signify the detriment and weakness of the king or the chief, and of the
wealthy and nobles or great men (namely, those who are fit for a kingdom), and
that faith and religion will be decreased (or rather it will be annihilated), and
their religious men will suffer detriment; and there will be many robbers and
cutters of roads, or pillagers; and battles and contentions will be multiplied; and
there will be more quarrels between men than usual; and even between the
religious men themselves; and they will envy each other, and especially those to
whom pride and vainglory is fitting; and more seriously so if Saturn were in the
10th.

And by how much more the malefics were elevated above the earth, by that
much more will the accidents be more serious. And it will be thus far worse[127] if
the Moon were below the earth, and she were to commit her own disposition to
Saturn while he is located above the earth, or [if] she were joined to him by the
opposition or square aspect: because then it signifies severe detriments, and
great tribulations, and horrible and fearful things, like the death of the king and
great men and the wealthy, or nobles, or a regime change[128] for the worse; and
the more strongly so if the malefics were retrograde, or occidental, or otherwise
impeded. If however they were direct, or oriental, nor impeded, the significations will be more remitted [or abated].

And if Mars did not commit his own disposition to Saturn, the significations
of Saturn will not be so intense,[129] and the significations of Mars will be
stronger, and especially in contentions and battles. And if Saturn were to
commit his own disposition to Mars, the significations of Mars will be more
intense, and the significations of Saturn will be decreased.

And if the benefics were above the earth, namely direct, made fortunate and
strong, they signify the taking away of evil, and the increase of the good; and the
more strongly so, if Jupiter were so disposed in one of his own dignities, and
were oriental. And Venus is stronger when she is occidental, so long as she is
otherwise made fortunate. Whence if a planet goes out from under the rays of

---

[127] *Adhuc deterius.* I believe Bonatti means that this situation by itself will make things worse,
regardless of how it may be worsened by other bad conditions.

[128] *Mutatio regni,* lit. "a change/mutation of the kingdom."

[129] This word (*intensa*) forms one half of a pair with *remissiora* ("more remitted") in the
previous paragraph. They come from Hellenistic astrology, which standardly speaks of the
"intensification and remission" of planetary effects especially over time. But Bonatti does not
seem to give them any special technical role here. It is possible that his textual sources use
these terms.

the Sun, it is like a man who has grown ill and is freed, and begins to resume his own powers, and is increased little by little until he is returned to his own original strength, provided that the malefics do not aspect [that planet]–because then it is like a sick man over whom a crisis has come and he seems to have escaped; afterwards he would relapse. And when it enters under the rays, it is like a man who had been healthy and begins to grow ill; or who was a young man, and begins to grow old, until his natural heat is gone.

Chapter 13: On the planets when they enter into the degrees of their exaltation

Again, look to see if Saturn is entering into Libra, or is in it, and especially in its twenty-first degree. Because his virtue will be increased that much, and his significations will be made greater; and more strongly so if he were to receive the disposition of other planets, and especially of the malefics. For then it will signify changes, and great and wondrous and stupendous things, which was touched on [in Treatise 4] in the recounting of the conjunction that Mars and Saturn make in the beginning of Cancer.

You will even look to see whether Jupiter is entering into Cancer, or is in it, especially in its fifteenth degree: because then his virtue will be increased, and his significations made greater; and more strongly so if he were to receive the disposition of one of the benefics: for it will signify great things, and wondrous and famous and durable changes, however to the good.

Likewise you will look to see if Mars is entering into Capricorn, or is in it, and especially in its twenty-eighth degree: because then his significations will be increased and made greater; and more strongly so if he were to receive the disposition of the other planets, and particularly of some malefic. For it will signify great and terrible things of those things which seem to pertain to Mars.

And thus all the other planets: if they were found to be entering into their exaltations at the hour of the revolution, they will increase their significations and make [them] greater (namely the benefics for the good, indeed the malefics for the contrary of the good). But the significations of the superiors are considered more, because they are more powerful, and stronger, and higher, and more notable.

And Māshā'allāh said,[130] when the year is revolved, look at the benefics and malefics to see if they were to aspect from a fixed sign: what they signified will

130 De Rev. Ann., Ch. 39.

be prolonged, for good or evil. And if they were to aspect from a movable sign, this will be middling. If indeed they were to aspect from a common sign, it will be half this.

[Eclipses][131]

After this, if you knew an eclipse was going to come in that same year, or in that same revolution, look at the Lord of the sign in which you saw it was going to be: what his condition [or nature] is, and how he behaves with the Lord of the ascending sign of the eclipse to come,[132] and whether they aspect each other or not. Likewise, how he[133] behaves with the Lord of the Year or Revolution, if they were to aspect each other or not, and whether the benefics or malefics aspect him or not. Because if the benefics and the Lord of the Ascendant of the eclipse (or the Lord of the Revolution, or other benefic planets) were to aspect him, it signifies good. If however the malefics were to aspect him–unless perhaps they receive him by a trine or sextile aspect (because reception takes away from their malice, even if it does not abolish it completely)–and the aforesaid planets (or one of them) do not aspect him from a praiseworthy aspect, it signifies evil. If indeed they were to aspect him together with the malefics, nor were they impeded, they signify neither this nor that. If however they were impeded, they signify evil, slightly remitted. If indeed they were to aspect without the benefics, or the benefics without them, it signifies good, slightly remitted.

Likewise, look at the significator of the king to see whether the aforesaid planets (namely the Lord of the sign in which the eclipse ought to be, and the Lord of the Ascendant of the eclipse) aspect him or not; and whether the benefics or malefics aspect him. Because the benefics signify the good condition of the king; indeed the malefics, to the contrary, signify his bad condition. And the significations which the aforesaid planets signified, will be greatly burdened if they were impeded by the aspects of the malefics. And the condition of the king will be more strongly burdened if his significator were the Lord of the sign in which the eclipse is going to come. Because if it were, it signifies his ruin–and this will be when the Sun reaches the degree which is the 10th house at the hour

---

131 Heading mine.

132 In other words, we must cast a chart for the time of the eclipse itself. If the eclipse will be in Taurus, we must look at Venus (the Lady of Taurus) and her relationship–in the revolution–to the planet that will be the Lord of the Ascendant at the time of the eclipse.

133 The Lord of the sign in which the eclipse will occur.

of the eclipse. And if the Lord of the sign in which the eclipse is going to be, were the same as the Lord of the Year ([i.e.,] of the common people), it signifies detriment is going to come over them. And the time of this effect will be when the Sun reaches the degree which is the Ascendant at the hour of the eclipse to come. And these will either be in the persons or the affairs of the king and the populace.

For if the Ascendant of the eclipse were Gemini, or Virgo, or Libra, or the first half of Sagittarius, or Aquarius, the detriments will happen in their persons. But in Gemini, Libra, and Aquarius, they will likewise happen in birds. And these will happen more strongly if Saturn were in one of these signs, whether he were direct or retrograde (but if he were retrograde it will be worse).

If however the Ascendant were Aries or Capricorn, it will happen in sheep or goats, or other small animals, according to the substance of the sign.

If indeed the Ascendant were Taurus, or the last half of Sagittarius, they will happen in cows and other greater animals according to the substance of the sign; but in cows [it will be] more serious than in the others.

If however the Ascendant were Cancer or Pisces, they will happen in fish and other animals of the kinds [that are] in waters, which are useful to men. Indeed if it were Scorpio, they will happen in poisonous animals, and those striking with their tails or rear; and more strongly to those living in waters.

And always understand the increase of detriment when Saturn is in the sign deputed over the matter.

In order to know the time of the lastingness of the detriments from the hour of the eclipse, you will consider how many hours and how many minutes of the hour the eclipse lasted. Because if it were a solar [eclipse], it will last one year for each hour, and one month for every five minutes. And if it were a lunar [month], it will last one month for every hour, and one day for every two minutes.

And look to see where the impeding malefics are: because if they were in the tenth or eleventh, or ninth, the significations will happen in the seventh clime, and in that [area] of the earth which is inhabited outside the clime toward the arctic circle. And if they were in the first or the second or twelfth, they will happen in the sixth and fifth and fourth climes. If however [they were] in the seventh or eighth or sixth, they will happen in the third and second and first climes. But if they were in the fourth or fifth or third, they will happen in the northern parts of the region in which they happen. Nevertheless if the impeding malefics were received, they will impede somewhat less.

[Further rules][134]

And he whom God willed to be a Master[135] said if the Sun were the Lord of the Ascendant in the revolution, and Venus were under the rays, [then] because she is the Lady of the Midheaven,[136] the Sun will be the significator of the king. Then you will look to see how the king's condition is going to be in that year or revolution–which you could know by the place of [the king's] significator [i.e., the Sun] in the figure of the revolution. Therefore see where he is, and how he is aspected by the planets, namely whether benefics or malefics are aspecting; and whether he is in an angle, or in a succeedent, or in a cadent (even though this rarely happens); and whether the Lord of the domicile or exaltation of the sign in which he is, aspects him or not. Because the benefics signify good, the malefics on the contrary signify evil, just as was said to you elsewhere.

You will even look at the significators of all the houses, and the one of them you find fortunate and strong, judge the goodness of the signification of that house whose Lord he is; and the one of them you find unfortunate and weak (namely retrograde or combust, or cadent from the angles or from the Ascendant or from his own domicile), judge the badness of that house whose Lord he is. And if you were to look at all houses, see in which of them the benefics are found, because they increase the significations of those houses according to how they were made fortunate and strong, because they will increase more strongly. If however they were weak, they will increase what they increased, more weakly.

---

[134] Heading mine.
[135] Māshā'allāh, *De Rev. Ann.*, Ch. 41.
[136] I.e., of Taurus, which would be the tenth sign and in most cases on the cusp of the Midheaven.

You will even look at the Part of Fortune, which if you were to find it alone in whatever house it was, it will signify the greater fortune of its signification. If however some good planet were to aspect it, it will signify greater fortune. And if [the good planet] were to receive it, it will signify greater fortune again. If however the malefics were to aspect it from a trine or sextile aspect with reception, it will be as if it were not aspected by anyone; if indeed without reception, they will subtract one-fourth of the goodness from it. Indeed if one of the malefics were joined to it from a square aspect or opposition, or corporally, they will take all the goodness from it, and it will profit nothing.

You will even look at the house in which the Head of the Dragon is, because it signifies the increase of the significations of the house in which it is, both for good and evil. For in the 6th, it signifies the increase of infirmities, and of the other significations of that house; in the 8th, it signifies the increase of its mortality and of the other significations. And understand [this] in the rest of the houses, according to the significations of each of them.

Likewise you will look at the Tail. Because it signifies the decrease of the significations of the house in which it is, both for good and evil. For in the 6th it signifies the decrease of infirmities, and in the 8th the decrease of mortality, and of the other significations which are signified by those houses. And understand [this] for the rest of the houses.

And if the Lord[137] of a sign in which there were a benefic promising good, were free and namely made fortunate and strong, the good will be multiplied. And if it were impeded, [the good] will be decreased according to the quantity of the impediment. And if the Lord of the domicile[138] in which there was a malefic (by which evil threatens),[139] were impeded, the evil will be increased according to the quantity of the impediment; and more strongly so, if [the malefic] were northern or committed its own disposition to another malefic who is northern. And if [the Lord] were free, the evil will be decreased according to the quantity of [the Lord's] own strength.

And if the malefic who is in the domicile of the impeded planet, were to commit his own disposition to some malefic located in the sixth, it signifies a multitude of infirmities; and more strongly so, if the commission [of disposition] were from the opposition or the square aspect. If however it were from the trine or sextile aspect, it will be somewhat less than this. If indeed it were to

---

[137] Reading *dominus* for *domus*, as with the third sentence.
[138] Reading "domicile" instead of "house," to go along with "sign" in the first sentence.
[139] Reading *minatur* for *minuitur*.

commit it to a benefic, it will decrease what is signified somewhat less again. And if it were to commit it to a malefic located in the eighth, it signifies mortality; and if it were to commit [it] from the opposition or square aspect, it will be more serious. If however from the trine or sextile, it will be somewhat less than this. If indeed it were to commit it to a benefic, it will be decreased in it more again. And if it were to commit it to a planet in the ninth, long journeys of the citizens of that region will be impeded. And if it were to commit it to a planet in the tenth, it signifies the impediment of the officials and the governors of that region. If however it were to commit it to a planet in the eleventh, it signifies the impediment of men's trust and of their hope. If indeed it were to commit it to a planet in the twelfth, it signifies the impediment and difficulties of greater animals, and enmities, and contentions, and battles and captures. And understand thusly for the rest of the houses, for each one according to their significations, just as I have touched on for you elsewhere.

Which[140] if Venus were not under the rays of the Sun, nor otherwise impeded by a strong impediment, she cannot avoid being the significatrix of the king, and especially if she were in Taurus (or Libra).[141]

Chapter 14: How the condition of the king and the nobles and the populace should be considered–of what sort their condition is going to be

After you have understood the condition of the aforesaid persons (namely [that] of the king and the nobles, and great men, and the common people or the rustics), you will consider what will be concerning their condition in the revolution, and concerning their accidents, and what will be between them, namely how the king may be treated by his subjects, and will follow [for] them from him, and how the citizens of that region will follow and obey their authorities and administrators or those set over them.

And you will look at the condition of each of the aforesaid following the condition of the king, which you could look at in this way. For indeed you will

---

[140] Māshā'allāh, *ibid.* Māshā'allāh also puts this after a (short) digression, as opposed to directly after the statement above about Venus and the Sun. It is unclear to me why Māshā'allāh does this, since the material in the digression is perfectly general, and does not seem to pertain only to cases where Taurus is on the Midheaven.

[141] Māshā'allāh simply says "if she were in the Midheaven," which obviously includes Taurus if the prior scenario regarding her and the Sun is meant. Bonatti seems to add Libra in order to generalize Māshā'allāh's meaning.

see in which house his significator is, because his accidents will take their root or power from the house [domicile?] in which he is, according to its fortune or misfortune, and you will see his impediments, or his escape, or his liberation from them, according to this. And if you were to see that contrarieties are supposed to happen to him, like battles and legal controversies the like, you could see what ought to happen to him from thence, which you could know through his significator and the strength or weakness of his enemies. Likewise, you will see whether journeys (long or short) ought to happen for him in the revolution, which you could know through the Lord of the ninth and through the Lord of the third. For through the Lord of the ninth you will perceive pilgrimages or long journeys; through the Lord of the third, short or nearby journeys. Whence you will see the Lord of the house of the journey at the hour of the revolution, and his place: which if he were well disposed, and in a fortunate and strong place, and were received from the house in which he is, it signifies that [the king] will journey or go on a pilgrimage of his own devices, for the purpose of finding tranquility or wandering or getting some space. And if [the significator] were in its first station, or near it by 5° or less, it signifies slowness and laziness in his pilgrimage or in journeying. And if it were retrograde or stationary in its own first station, and it were received, it signifies that he will journey, but will return shortly. If however it were like this without reception, it signifies that he will not complete his journey, but rather will suffer detriment in it, and anger or distress.

Then look at the Lord of the house [domicile?] of the journey, and see if the Lord of the domicile in which he was, is retrograde, and were to aspect its own domicile by a trine or sextile aspect: because this will signify that [the king] is going to go in order to organize and dispose his business concerns, and for the sake of his subjects. If however [the Lord of the Lord of the ninth] were to aspect [its own domicile] from a square aspect, or from the opposition, it signifies that he is going to go out in order to do battle with his rebels and enemies.

Then look at the significator of the king, to see if it were free from impediments, and even if one of the planets which is naturally inimical to it were free,[142] and that the Lord of the journey or the pilgrimage is not in the house of infirmity [the 6th] or in the house of death [the 8th]. Because this signifies the guarding and deliverance of his person in the pilgrimage or journey, in accor-

---

142 I do not understand why this latter condition is so important as to merit notice, especially since nothing more is done with it in the paragraph.

dance as his significator were sound and free from impediments. And even if the significator of the king is found free of those things which were said, if the Lord of the house of the journey or pilgrimage were impeded, it signifies impediment and sorrow according to what is signified by the house in which it is, both of the house of infirmity and the house of death, and all the others. And if the Lord of the house of the journey or pilgrimage were free from impediments, and the significator of the king were impeded, impediments which will be suspected, and which he feared, will happen to [the king] according to the significations of the house in which [the significator] was impeded, unless perhaps Jupiter were to aspect and receive him, and he himself were sound and free—because then all the malice of whatever one there was, or whatever kind, is then broken.

Chapter 15: Why the king will go on a pilgrimage, if he were going to go on a pilgrimage

However, in order to know the reasons why he will go on a pilgrimage (if he were supposed to go on a pilgrimage), you will look at the Lord of the house of the pilgrimage or journey, and you will see in which house it itself was. Because one of the things signified by that house will be the reason for the journey or pilgrimage.

For if it or the significator of the king were in the first, or were joined to the Lord of the first, his departure will be because of the salvation[143] of his own person; and it will seem more likely that he will not be on a pilgrimage, but will be in peace and quiet. But if there were another planet between him and the degree of the Ascendant, whether lighter or heavier than he, see of what nature it is: because if it were of those inimical to the significator to the king, someone will come upon him who seeks to deprive him of his kingdom or his dignity, and who will contend with him in order to take his kingdom or dignity away from him. If indeed [this] were of the things happening to him, the one who comes will be such a person that the king or commander will hand the kingdom or dignity over to him voluntarily, and will prefer him to himself. And see of which house he is the Lord: because from him will be known who it will be who is going to come to do this. Like if it were the Lord of the second, he will be of those who are signified by the 2nd house. If indeed it were the Lord of the third, he will be of those who are signified by the 3rd house. And understand thusly

---

[143] This connotes physical health, not religious salvation.

concerning the rest of the houses' significations; and perhaps that he will build in the land to which he goes.

If indeed the Lord of the ninth were in the second, or joined to its Lord, it signifies that his journey is because of a quest, namely to acquire money.

If however it were in the third–since it will be in the house of his own enemies (namely of the ninth)–it signifies that his departure will be because of making war or engaging in battles. And he will desire to journey and ride; and he will multiply the journeys–even if he does not desire with a great desire–if it were a pilgrimage.[144]

And if it were in the fourth, or joined to its Lord, it signifies that his journey will be horrible and fearful, if it were a pilgrimage. And because it will be in the eighth from its own house (namely from the 9th), it is feared concerning his death. And if one of the malefics were to aspect him then from the square aspect or from the opposition, or were joined to him corporally, or were to commit its disposition to him, he will hardly or never evade the dangers. However, he will not desire much to ride or journey, but rather he will desire to be in quiet and tranquility.

And if it were in the fifth or joined to the Lord of the fifth, it signifies his condition to be praiseworthy; and he will be in joy and dancing and delight; and he will desire to have a child, and will have one according to the sex of the sign in which Mars is, [and] the [majority] portion of the significators (which are Lord of the first and the Lord of the fifth, and the Moon, and the Lord of the domicile in which she is, and Jupiter). And it even signifies that he will build in the land to which he is going to set out, and he will think to spend time there, but he will hardly or never spend time there.

And if it were in the sixth or joined to its Lord (namely so that it commits its own disposition to it), it signifies he is going to become ill in that revolution.

And if it were in the seventh or joined to its[145] Lord, it signifies some strength of his enemies who are inimical to him, not because of the kingdom or a dignity, but for some other reason; [and] he will be intent on venereal activity more so than he ought to be.

And if it were in the eighth or joined to its Lord, from any aspect without reception, death will be feared for him in that revolution. And if the Lord of the eighth were to receive him ([and] not he the Lord of the eighth), it will be feared more so again. And if he were to receive the Lord of the eighth, nor were the

---

[144] The punctuation of this sentence is unclear.
[145] Reading *eius* for *eorum*.

Lord of the eighth to receive him, it will be feared more so again, so that it will hardly or never happen but that he will die. If however each were to receive the other, only God could make it so that he might not die; because otherwise he would not be able to escape death.

And if it were in the ninth, or were joined to the Lord of the ninth, or to some planet in it, he will be on journeys and pilgrimages both long and short. But if the Lord of the ninth were then cadent or combust, death or the greatest discomfort will be feared for him on his pilgrimage or journey. If however it were not so impeded, it signifies the journey will be good and prosperous, and that he will apply himself in affairs pertaining to religion and pity, provided that one of the malefics does not aspect him by an aspect of enmity (because that would signify that grief and sorrow will come upon him from the direction of his own household members). And if it were the first square aspect,[146] it will happen from the direction of his enemies. If however it were the second square aspect, it will happen from the direction of slaves or an opportunity [or pretext] of theirs, or that of low-class persons. And it is necessary for you to look at the sign in which the second aspect of the Lord of the house of pilgrimages is,[147] [to see] if one of the malefics were there; and to see of what substance that sign is; because if it were in the image of men, the misfortune of beasts will be feared concerning him. If however it were in the image of other animals, a blow or a bite or a poisonous puncturing will be feared, according to the substance of that sign.

And if it were in the tenth or joined to the Lord of the tenth, it signifies goodness and his strengthening in his kingdom, and that his journey will be prolonged, and that he will want to make the matters of the kingdom fit.

And if it were in the eleventh or joined to the Lord of the eleventh, it signifies the fitness of his own person, and of those following him, whether of the soldiers or of those of his own household [or of his intimates], just like a king or chief. And it even signifies the goodness of his mind; and that he will eagerly wound his subjects badly, or rather he will put down some unpunished people;[148] and that he will pay out substance in the affairs of the kingdom, and even for other reasons, in a good way, and sometimes it will disperse.

---

[146] The "first" (leading) aspect is the sinister aspect cast forward in the order of signs; the "second" ("following") aspect is the dexter aspect cast backward against the order of signs.
[147] This would be the fourth sign from the location of the Lord of the 9th, i.e., the outcome of the journey–hence the interest in seeing if malefics occupy it.
[148] Literally, "he will put down some unpunished sources," which must refer to unpunished troublemakers.

And if it were in the twelfth or joined to its Lord, he will apply himself to inquiring and investigating enemies, both his own and of the kingdom, and concerning which you [will] fear his enemies were not believed, and he will be occupied with this. And if it were to aspect the Lord of the twelfth without reception, he will get them and wound them. If indeed it were to aspect from a trine or sextile aspect without reception, he will wound them less; if indeed with reception, he will wound them little or not at all.

And he whom God willed to be a Master[149] said that whenever you were to find the significator of the king joined to the Lord of some house, it signifies that same thing [the significator of the king] would have signified if he were found in the house, provided that he commits disposition to the Lord of that house.

And Abū Ma'shar said that you ought to look in marriage celebrations just as you have looked for a journey. Because perhaps there will be a marriage on account of seeking substance. And he said, look then at the Lord of the eighth, and the Lord of the second, to see if the Lord of the eighth were to commit disposition to the Lord of the second: he will find substance from it. If however the Lord of the second were to commit disposition to the Lord of the eighth, he will [not?][150] find substance from it. And he said, [if] the Lord of the house of marriage were in the eleventh, he will marry her on account of love and delight; and more strongly so if the significator of the king and the Lord of the seventh were[151] aspecting each other. And if it were in the tenth, his kingdom will be increased from this. And if it were in the fifth, he will seek a son from it.

And Ptolemy said,[152] look at the significator of the king and the Lord of the seventh, and judge according to what I told you in the chapter on journeys. And look at the aspect of the benefics and the malefics in their own places. And he said, also look in addition in the nativities of children, and [see] how their condition toward each other will be.

---

149 Māshā'allāh, *De Rev. Ann.*, Ch. 42.
150 I believe there should be a "not" (*non*) here.
151 Reading *fuerunt...aspicientes* for *fuerit...aspicientes*.
152 I am not sure where Bonatti has gotten this quote. It does not seem to be a misread for Māshā'allāh.

Chapter 16: Why it will be feared for the person of the king, if his significator were under the rays

And[153] if the significator of the king were under the rays of the Sun, death will be feared for him in that revolution; and if it were not under the rays, but were near them by 12° in front of them (if it were of the superiors) or after[154] (if it were of the inferiors), it will be feared for him when it begins to enter the rays, according to the conjunction of the one of [these] two to which he will be joined: namely the Lord of the house of infirmity, and the Lord of the house of death. Which if it were not either of them then, death will be feared for him in the hour in which he is joined with the Sun by body (or degree by degree). Also you will look to see, if the 10th house were Leo, whether Mars aspects the Sun then, or they were joined corporally, because the killing of the king will be feared in that revolution.

However, in order that you might see whence it will come to him, look to see in whose house Mars were then: because from what is signified by that house, the reason of this wicked deed will be born. And if Saturn were to aspect him, it will happen to the king through a similar signification of difficulty; and it will be feared that the king will be poisoned in that revolution or year.

And he whom God willed to be a Master[155] said that if the Lord of the Year were combust in the Midheaven, it will be feared for the king in the same ways: and these will happen to him in the region in which it then was. And if the combustion were in the angle of the earth [the 4th] or [in] the seventh [angle], they will happen to him from someone who will come [from] outside the land. And he said that the opposition of the malefics, and their square aspect, is more serious in this case than the corporal conjunction. And he said, if the Sun were the significator of the king and he were to aspect Jupiter from the opposition, the king will be inimical to the members of his household, and will be suspi-

---

[153] This paragraph is a combination of statements largely based on *De Rev. Ann.*, Chs. 42 and 44–although the statement below about Leo being the 10th house seems to be Bonatti's own clarification or refinement. Māshā'allāh simply speaks of the Sun as the general significator of kings, but Bonatti seems to want to restrict this to cases where the Sun is actually the significator of the king according to the rules he has laid out (or, more likely, he thinks this is Māshā'allāh's own meaning, and he is simply clarifying it).

[154] By "in front," Bonatti means "in a later zodiacal degree"; by "after" he means "in an earlier zodiacal degree."

[155] Māshā'allāh, *De Rev. Ann.*, Ch. 44. Māshā'allāh does not say the "Lord of the Year," but rather the "Lord of the Ascendant of the year." Perhaps Bonatti reads Māshā'allāh as *meaning* the Lord of the Year, since in an idealized case the Lord of the Ascendant of the year would also be the Lord of the Year.

cious of them, and will be oppressed by them. And likewise, if he were opposite the Lord of the Ascendant, he will be inimical to the rustics, and will be suspicious of them and will impede them.

On the mutual reception of the planets

After this you will know which of the planets receive each other, and to what place[156] of the figure they are projecting their own rays. Wherefore in the [earthly] regions subject to the signs to which the rays are projected, the significations of those planets will have greater efficacy, and imprint more in them than in other places.[157]

Which planets are friends of the Lord of the Ascendant in the revolution

You will even know which planets are friends of the Lord of the Ascendant of the revolution, or which are enemies, and which of them aspect more, or to whom he commits disposition; and which aspect the Ascendant with a praiseworthy aspect or one of enmity. Wherefore, according to how the benefics or malefics were to aspect him or the Ascendant, you will judge concerning the significations of theirs that are going to come in that revolution.

He whom God willed to be a Master, said,[158] know that both malefics (namely Saturn and Mars), if one of them were in an angle in the revolution of the year, and were in earthy signs, direct, it signifies the destruction of trees, and the death of animals. And if Mars were to aspect the significator of the king, and he (namely Mars) were commingled with the light of Saturn, it signifies contention and the shedding of blood. And Māshā'allāh said[159] if [Mars] were in an airy[160] sign, it signifies injustices and enmities. If indeed [Mars] were [not][161] in an angle and were to aspect the Ascendant, it signifies infirmities and blood, and more severely in every land in whose sign his light was[162] (or the opposition or square aspect). And he said that if [Mars] were retrograde, it signifies pestilence. And if [Mars] were in a sign which does not[163] aspect the Ascendant, and he

---

[156] *Loca*, here meaning "signs," instead of the usual *locos*. See the next sentence.
[157] *Locis*, again meaning "signs" and the earthly regions subject to them.
[158] Māshā'allāh, *De Rev. Ann.*, Ch. 44.
[159] Māshā'allāh, *ibid.*
[160] Reading *aerio* (with Māshā'allāh) for Bonatti's *igneo* ("fiery").
[161] Adding *non* with Māshā'allāh.
[162] I.e., including the sign he is in.
[163] Adding *non* with Māshā'allāh.

were direct, it signifies infirmity and the detriment of seeds. If indeed [Mars] were retrograde, it will signify death and infirmity and blood.

Chapter 17: On those things which ought to come to the king in a revolution of the year

After[164] you were to see that the king is going to go on a pilgrimage in that year, see how the condition of the Lord of the house of the pilgrimage is, namely whether it is direct or free or impeded; and whether it is in its own domicile or a stranger's; and is going from the sign in which it is to another one of its domiciles, and is joined to the Lord of the domicile or exaltation in which it is. And see in what hour it is going to enter into its own domicile, or in which [hour] it is going to come to the place in which the Lord of the domicile or exaltation (in which it was when it was joined to him) was.[165] And see if the Lord of the ninth is retrograde: because if it were so and it were received, it signifies that he will have much space[166] in his journey or his pilgrimage, and that he will return quickly [compared to] his usual regard to a journey.[167] If however it were retrograde, nor were it received, it signifies that his journey will be difficult and irksome; and that impediments will happen to him because of his journey or pilgrimage. If however it were slower in course than in its own first slowness,[168] it signifies a long delay on his journey or pilgrimage; and that for various reasons he will be detained in it in the regions to which he goes or had gone on pilgrimage; and it will be feared for him on the pilgrimage.

And Abū Ma'shar said if it were in its own second slowness[169] he will return when the planet is direct, and his pilgrimage will not be perfected. If however it were retrograde, and the Lord of its own house were to aspect it from a square aspect, or from the opposition, it signifies that his departure will be to war, clearly with enemies turning against him, and it seems that he ought to be outside his own region. If however [the Lord of its own house] were to aspect it from a trine or sextile aspect, it seems that he is going to go against some of his

---

[164] This is based on *De Rev. Ann.*, Ch. 42.

[165] I.e., if the Lord were in Sagittarius at the hour of the revolution, and were joined by aspect to Jupiter. Then see when the Lord will come by its own motion to the degree Jupiter had been in.

[166] Earlier, this term suggested the king was able to have "space" to relax; but here it seems to mean he will travel far and wide.

[167] A more awkward paraphrase of Māshā'allāh, *ibid.*

[168] This probably means "in its own first station."

[169] I.e., in its own second station.

own subjects who are becoming (or have been made) rebels against him. If however they were joined corporally, it seems that he will arrive at the place of the contention. And when you had investigated this, look at the significator of the king: which if you were to find him free from the impediments of the malefics, nor were he joined to one of the planets who is naturally inimical to him, and the Lord of the pilgrimage [the 9th] were free, in an optimal place from the Ascendant, nor were it in a place of enmity to the Ascendant, nor were it found in the 6th or the 8th, it signifies the safety and deliverance of his body. If however his significator were free from the aforesaid impediments, or it were the Lord of the sign in which the Lord of the house (in which the Lord of the pilgrimage were) were found,[170] and the Lord of the pilgrimage were impeded, it signifies that impediment will happen to him, and his own destruction in the pilgrimage, and perhaps that some illness will happen to him which will not be of his usual types of illnesses, according to the sign in which the Lord of the house of pilgrimage is. If indeed his significator were impeded, and the Lord of the house of pilgrimage were free, what he feared in terms of an illness which he is used to having,[171] will happen to him on the pilgrimage.

You will even see whether the significator of the king is aspected by one of the planets, and whether the one that were to aspect him is a benefic or a malefic. For if it were a malefic, it signifies enmity which will happen to the king in that year or revolution. Then you will see whether the malefic has any dignity in the sign in which[172] he aspected the significator of the king. Because if he had some dignity there, the enemy will be from the land of the king according to the person which is signified by that dignity. Wherefore if it were the domicile, he will be of the greater inhabitants of his own land, and of his own household members. If however it were the exaltation, he will be of the more noble people in his kingdom, or of those who came from somewhere else and were in charge over some dignities in that kingdom, or perhaps they acquired a fortune there (signified by the aspect),[173] and great riches, and they are not of the powerful

---

[170] In other words, if he were the Lord of the Lord of the 9th. So if the Lord of the 9th were in Aries, and Mars (the Lord of Aries) were in Gemini (ruled by Mercury), Bonatti is asking whether the significator of the king is Mercury.

[171] *Accidet ei quod timebat…ex aegritudine de qua consuevit infirmari.* Māshā'allāh does not specify whether the king is accustomed or unaccustomed to having the illness.

[172] I believe Bonatti is talking about the malefic having dignity in the sign which the significator of the king is, *into which* the malefic casts his ray. Otherwise, there would be no reason to say that he has a dignity in the *king's* land (sign)–he would only have a dignity in his *own* land (sign). See Bonatti's examples.

[173] See below for hints about judging their station by aspect.

people (namely those who are fit for a kingdom and royal dignities); and they will be of more noble birth if the aspect were the second square.[174] Indeed the corporal conjunction signifies a marriage alliance on the part of women. If indeed it did not have a dignity there, he will be from the king's own particular blood-relatives. And if it were the triplicity or bound, he will be of the great citizens who are subject to the king. If the aspect were the first square,[175] it signifies the enemy[176] to be a son born not from legitimate intercourse. But if the aspect were from the opposition, the enemy will be openly adversarial to the king. If by chance the aspect were a sextile or a trine, it signifies that he will be one close to or from those close to, the king.

Chapter 18: On the conjunction of the two malefics (namely of Saturn and Mars) with a planet in the degree of its own exaltation: what would be signified from that[177]

Abū Ma'shar said, look in a revolution of the year [for] a conjunction of the malefics (namely of Saturn and Mars), to see whether they are joined with some planet which is in the degree of its own exaltation, by aspect (and it is worse if by the square or by opposition).[178] For if it were Saturn, it signifies evil and destruction in the region deputed to that planet. And if the aspect of Saturn were from a fixed sign, what is signified will be prolonged according to the quantity of degrees which there were between their bodies—for years, or months, or weeks or days. For if what was signified is supposed to be perfected within the year which you are revolving, it will signify months according to the number of degrees. If however it were going past the year or revolution, it will be prolonged for years. If however it were from a movable sign, it will signify days according to the number of degrees. And if it were not perfected in so many days, it will signify weeks. And if it were from a common sign, they will be weeks. And if it were not completed in so many weeks, it signifies months. If however Saturn did not aspect him, but some planet were to transfer their light between them, it signifies the coming of things liable to be scattered over the

---

174 The dexter square, cast backwards against the order of signs.

175 The sinister square, cast forwards in the order of signs.

176 Reading *inimicum* for *initium*.

177 See also Ch. 52 on the same topic. For more on the conjoinings of the malefics, see Chs. 57, 76; and Tr. 4, Ch. 3.

178 As the rest of the chapter shows, Bonatti is not asking whether *both* Saturn and Mars are joined to a planet *at the same time*, but whether either of them individually is so joined.

men of the region of that planet, or destruction and detriment will come over them in peoples who will not be from that region.[179] If however some planet did not transfer the light between them, and the rays of Saturn were to touch the rays of the planet located in its own exaltation (or [those] of a planet which was fit to transfer their light between them), sadness and grief will enter upon the men of that region, which they need not fear; for the fear will be dissolved and will not reach actuality, by the will of God.

On the aspect of Mars to a planet in its own exaltation

If however it were from the aspect of Mars, just as I said concerning the aspect of Saturn (and worse is if it were the square or opposition), the aforesaid will happen just as I said concerning Saturn, in a like way and for like reasons. And more so because Mars will perfect accidents which would be signified by iron and fire and the shedding of blood.

You will even look at the Lord of the ninth: if you were to find [it] in the third, it signifies the king is going to go on a pilgrimage for religious reasons, and because of the pilgrimage of eternal life, and the future age from the Creator, because this place[180] in this [matter] signifies the same that the 9th does, even though it is its nadir.

And Abū Ma'shar said if you were to see [him] in one of the houses (of the twelve houses), you should not dismiss his aspect from the places. And stronger will be the significators of the opposites: as is his signification and the signification of the sign that is the nadir of one planet; or [if] it were his domicile or exaltation, because then it signifies what I said.[181]

Chapter 19: When the Sun and Moon are joined to one of the planets or are being separated from them: what they would signify

You will consider the Sun and the Moon, and you will see how they are disposed, namely whether they are joined to one of the planets, or are being

---

[179] I am unsure what peoples are involved. Bonatti's Abū Ma'shar is definitely saying that the destruction will come over the people ruled by the transferring planet, but I do not know what exactly is denoted by the "in peoples" (*in gentibus*) clause.

[180] *Locus.*

[181] Like many of Bonatti's quotations from (or paraphrases of) Abū Ma'shar, this is unclear. I think Bonatti's Abū Ma'shar is saying that we should look to the signs Mars aspects by opposition, because (a) the domicile and exalted Lords, and (b) the planet whose descension or fall is in that sign, will be especially affected.

separated from one of them: because what is signified will be according to how
you were to see them conjoined with the planets, or separated from them, both
by body and by aspect. And Abū Ma'shar said, because the square aspect is
strong, and the sextile weak, the conjunction harsh.

Again on the accidents of the king

Again, you would look–so that you might know the accidents of the king–at
what kinds of things are going to come in the revolution which you are seeking,
to see whether the Moon is found in the 7th house or not: because if she were in
it, and were in increased light, and fast in course, and joined to the Lord of the
7th, or to the Lord of the exaltation of that domicile, or to one having two other
dignities in it, or to a benefic planet, it signifies that the rustics will adore their
king and obey him, and they will willingly listen to him and revere him, and
none of them will be contrary to him, nor will there arise an army from
someone over him, nor against him, nor will something contrary to him be
pondered, but rather he will see things which please them, and which he loves
and about which he rejoices. But if the Moon were then impeded, and were in
little light and course, nor received, it signifies the contrary of that which I have
told you. Because battles and contentions and wars will happen to him, nor will
his own subjects comply with him, nor simply will they happen to him only
when she is impeded in the seventh; but yet it will even be feared that they will
happen to him if she were impeded in other places by terrible impediments, or
were she cadent.

Again on the good or bad condition of the king

You would even look, in a revolution of the year, by means of the condition
of the Lord of the Midheaven, concerning the condition of the king (to see how
it is going to come to him in that revolution), which you could weigh carefully
through the condition of Saturn, and that of the Lord of the Year; even through
certain others of the planets just as I will expound to you. If the Lord of the 10th
house were the significator of the king in the revolution of the year, and Saturn
were combust (and more strongly so if he were in front of[182] the Sun) or were
the significator of the king, joined to the Lord of the Year, and were to commit
disposition to him; and the Lord of the Year were joined to a planet appearing
in the 8th from the Ascendant of the revolution (which is the house signifying

---

[182] I.e., in a later zodiacal degree than the Sun's.

death generally) or to a planet located in the 5th from the Ascendant of the revolution,[183] from the opposition or a square aspect, it signifies the death of the king in that year or revolution. Or [if] the significator of the king were joined to this same Lord of the Year, and the Lord of the Year were joined corporally to the Lord of the 5th or 8th in one of the other houses (or from the opposition or a square aspect), it signifies his death. And more certainly so if the Lord of the domicile in which the conjunction is, were a malefic. Likewise if the significator of the king were entering combustion, it signifies the death of the king; and he would hardly or never be able to avoid this. If however Saturn were oriental, going out from under the rays of the Sun, he will not impede the king, but his condition will be improved.

If indeed this conjunction were with a planet in the 3rd or 6th or elsewhere with the Lord of the third or sixth,[184] it signifies an infirmity is going to come to him in that revolution. And according to the significations, and through the significations of the house in which the conjunction is, and on their occasion, the contrary things which are going to come to him, will happen to him.

If however the significator of the king did not commit disposition to the Lord of the Year or Revolution, not so much danger hangs over him: for that much fear hangs over him. And this is to be understood concerning any king or one similar to a king, according to his clime and according to his region. But if he were already crossing over combustion, by as many degrees as there are degrees of his orb, up until he touches the tenth minute of the last degree of his combustion, it signifies that anger and sorrow and contention, and likewise fear, will come to the king in that revolution; and more strongly so if a malefic were to aspect him. Because if it were to aspect him, it will introduce fear over the king, and it will be feared concerning him and about him, according to the substance and signification of the house and sign in which the malefic is. Like if it were in the second, it will be because of substance. And if it were in the third, it will be because of brothers or journeys. And if it were in the fourth, it will be because of parents or inheritances. And if it were in the fifth, it will be because of children. And if it were in the sixth, it will be because of infirmity. And if it were in the seventh,[185] it will be because of his wife. And if it were in the eighth, it will be because of death. And if it were in the ninth, it will be because of long journeys. And if it were in the tenth, it will be because of the kingdom. And if it

---

[183] The 5th is the 8th from the 10th: the king's death.
[184] The 6th signifies illness generally; the 3rd is the 6th from the 10th, therefore the king's illness.
[185] The rest of the numbers are given as Roman numerals, but I have treated them as though they continue to refer to signs or places.

were in the eleventh, it will be because of allies. And if it were in the twelfth, it will be because of hidden enemies. If however a benefic were to aspect him, all of this will turn about, and turn away from him.

And in order that you might know when these things ought to happen, see when the significator of the king will be joined with that malefic. Because then will be the time of the arrival of those signified things (whether the malefic who impeded him were joined to him by body, or by opposition, or by a square aspect). You will judge according to the one of them who first arrives, or when the impeding malefic comes to the 10th of the Ascendant of the revolution, or at least to its Ascendant, unless a benefic then aspects the significator of the king or the malefic itself, so that it breaks his malice. If however this conjunction were in an angle, the time of the accidents will be when the significator is combust, or when the malefic reaches the place in which the significator of the king then is.[186]

Chapter 20: On the condition of the king with those placed under him

Indeed you could know the condition of the king with his subjects, and the condition of his subjects with him, by the conjoining of their significators to each other, or by their aspect with reception. Because he (of the significators) who receives the other, commits his own disposition to him. Whence if the significator of the king were to commit his own disposition to the significator of his subjects, the king will be of good will and peaceful to his rustics, more so than they to him. If the significator of the common people were to commit its own disposition to the significator of the king, they will be obedient, and more of good will to the king than he to them. If indeed each of the significators were to receive the other, the king will commit his own disposition to his subjects, and they to him. And one of them will want what the other wants, and each will be peaceful to the other.

Chapter 21: On the peculiar and particular condition of the king

However, you could know the peculiar and particular condition of the king, according to the daily accidents which are supposed to happen to him in the

---

[186] This must mean, "to the degree that was occupied by the significator of the king at the hour of the revolution," but "place" might also mean its *sign*.

revolution, through his significator–namely [according to] how you were to see him daily disposed to the good or to its contrary. Because according to what happens to him from day to day, up to the end of the revolution, just as he is joined to the benefics or malefics, or as he arrives at places in which the malefics were at the hour of the revolution, or to other places which were then impeded–for according to that, good things and bad things (or his liberation from them) will happen to him.

Chapter 22: What the significator of the king would signify in the angle of a house

Abū Ma'shar said when the significator of the king is in the angle of the Midheaven, it signifies the battle of the king; indeed when he is in the Ascendant, the condition of men will be diminished. If indeed he were in the western one, or in the angle of the earth, his rustics will be destroyed. And he said if the Lord of the Year or the significator of the king were going away toward a malefic planet, or to the light of a slow and malefic planet in an angle, destruction or death will be feared concerning him whose significator it was.

Chapter 23: If the significator of the king, or any other planet, were to have escaped from impediment, and were to go to its own exaltation

If the significator of the king were to stand impeded before his own exaltation, and had already escaped from that impediment, and were then joined to some benefic (and better than that, if the benefic were to receive him), and when he were separated from it, before he arrives at the degree in which he is exalted, if he were to go to it immediately, nor were he then impeded by one of the malefics, there will then be a greater strength and a stronger testimony than there ever could be.

See where the Part of the Kingdom[187] were to fall then: because if it were to fall into a place in which it is[188] impeded, it signifies contrarieties and impediments are going to come to the king in his own kingdom in that revolution. If however it were to fall into the place of [the significator's] own exaltation (toward which he is then going), it signifies the increase and goodness of his

---

[187] This is probably from al-Qabīsī below (Part 2, Ch. 19).
[188] Reading *fuerit* for *fuerat*.

kingdom, without the contrary, and without any impediment. Indeed for those wishing to resist [the king], look from the opposite places (nor however should you include among them the natural enemies of the king). Because if [the places] were impeded, [the enemies] will be impeded, and it will go badly for them. If indeed they were [not] impeded,[189] still they will not at all be weakened in these things which they want against the king.

And if the significator of the king were the significator of one of the things signified[190] and were *al-mubtazz* over it,[191] or the Part of the Kingdom were to fall on him, and the Sun were to commit his own disposition to the significator of the king, the king will rule in that revolution over all those things which are signified by Saturn, Jupiter, and the Sun, and Mercury (if he were masculine). And indeed if the Moon were to commit her disposition to him, the king will rule over all those things which are signified by Mars, Venus, the Moon and Mercury (if he were feminine).[192] It will add to his subjects in his kingdom, according to how you were to see the Lord of the domicile in which its significator was, and the Lord of the Year, and the Lord of the domicile in which the Lord of the Year is.

Chapter 24: To know when the revolution lasts through the whole year, and when through half the year, and when through a quarter of the year

It was spoken above of the revolution of years, and of the Lord of the Year. And often I have named the Lord of the Revolution to you when I made mention of the Lord of the Year, and not in vain. Because every Lord of the Year is called the Lord of the Revolution, but it does not work the other way around.[193] For the Lord of the Year is when, in the year which you are revolving, it is not sought except in one revolution. And this is when a fixed sign is ascending at the entrance of the Sun into Aries: for that revolution contains in

---

[189] Adding *non.*

[190] *Significatorum.* This could mean "of the things signified" or "of the significators." Either way there is a difficulty: if it means (a) "things signified," what are the things signified? If it means (b) of the significators, then which significators?

[191] This could refer to the *al-mubtazz* of the Part, but its gender (*eo*) is wrong.

[192] In these statements about Mercury we see a conflation of planetary gender with planetary sect which tends to occur in medieval astrology: being nocturnal is not the same as being feminine.

[193] Bonatti actually uses a traditional Latin term from Aristotelian logic, saying that it is not "converted." A judgment is convertible if we can reverse the terms, e.g., "Some cats are grey" and "Some grey things are cats."

itself all quarters of that year. And so the one that is then the Lord of the Year, will be the Lord of the whole year, and of the whole revolution. But if a common sign were ascending, the revolution will not last but through one half of the year, namely up until the entrance of the Sun into Libra: then it will be necessary for you to repeat the revolution, and the one that rules then will be the Lord of the Revolution up until the end of the second half of the year. Indeed if a movable sign were ascending, that revolution will not last but up until the entrance of the Sun into Cancer, and then it will be necessary for you to do the same for the other quarters of the year. And the Lord of the first quarter will be he whose rulership it was in the entrance of the Sun into Aries. And he who is in charge of the rulership in his entrance into Cancer, will be the Lord of the Revolution of the second quarter. And he who is in charge in the entrance of the Sun into Libra, will be the Lord of the [Revolution of the] third quarter. And he who is in charge in his entrance into Capricorn, will be the Lord of the [Revolution of the] last quarter.

And always, in every one of the aforesaid entrances, you will renew your judgment, just as you have done in the entrance of the Sun into Aries. And always make the Lord of the first revolution a participator with the Lord of the second; and the Lord of the second with the Lord of the third; and the Lord of the third, with the Lord of the fourth, until you would finish all of them. Because [such a Lord] will have one-fourth of the rulership, just as the Philosopher said.[194] And thus he who is the Lord of the whole year, will be the Lord of a Revolution; he who is the Lord of one-half will be the Lord of a Revolution; he who is the Lord of a quarter will be the Lord of a Revolution. However, with the Lord of the Year it is not so, even though he is familiarly called the Lord of the Year.[195]

What the Lord of the hour and the Part of Fortune would signify in a revolution

After you have carried out all of the aforesaid in the order by which it was described, and you have looked at all the things which were to have been looked at, as I have told you, you will then consider the Lord of the hour and the Part of Fortune, and the Lord of the domicile in which [the Part] were to fall: which if they were well disposed, they will aid the Lord of the Year and the significator of the king; which if you were to find them well disposed, they will increase

---

[194] Perhaps Māshā'allāh or Abū Ma'shar?
[195] In conclusion, only if a fixed sign is ascending will the Lord of the [sole] Revolution be a Lord of the Year.

their good. If however you were to find them impeded, they will decrease their impediment. If however they were impeded, and you were to find them impeded, they will increase their good. If however you were to find them well disposed, you will take away from their goodness.[196]

And Abū Ma'shar said, know the conjunction of the planets with the Lord of the Year, and with the significator of the king, and their conjunction with the planets, and their separation and arrival [application] with respect to one another, in the houses [domiciles?] and the aspects, and attach the broader, lesser things of their essences[197] (understand [by this] their works through the situations[198] of others), and commingle the essences[199] of the signs with these, and [know] that it may conquer over reception by nature; and learn the condition of the significators, and know their situation to one another, by difference [diversity] and binding,[200] and with reception and rendering [or returning].[201]

---

[196] These last three sentences (identical in 1491 and 1550) do not make sense, and it is suspicious that there are needless repetitions of "you were to find them impeded" and "you were to find them well disposed." My hypothesis is that the typesetter for the 1491 edition (or an earlier edition) made an error. The sentences should read: "If however you were to find them impeded, they will *increase* their impediment [and] *decrease* their good. If however you were to find them well disposed, you will *add to* their goodness."

[197] *Fige rariora minora substantiorum eorum.*

[198] *Casus.*

[199] *Substantias.*

[200] Separation and application?

[201] This paragraph is very puzzling, apart from its odd combination of concepts. First, most of Bonatti's quotations or paraphrases of Abū Ma'shar are much more straightforward. Second, it must be a quotation (rather than a paraphrase) because it does not match Bonatti's style at all. Third, it seems to be filled with strained or odd metaphors and terms, which sound much like early, pre-technical Latin translations of Arab astrologers' works. The term *casus* usually denotes the weakness called "fall," and can also refer to sudden occurrences or misfortunes, but it seems to be used here in a quasi-technical sense I cannot make exact sense of (hence my translation of it as "situation"). Likewise, an astrologer like Bonatti would not refer to the returning or rendering of light without adding "of light." It is possible that Bonatti is quoting an early Latin translation of Abū Ma'shar, and either Abū Ma'shar himself uses these kinds of terms (which in turn may derive from Greek equivalents), or the Latin translator used them as equivalents of Abū Ma'shar's words. The source may be the manuscript recently identified by me in the National Library at Paris (see Introduction), but unless we can discover the sources of this and Bonatti's other attributions to Abū Ma'shar, it will remain unclear. The paragraph reads: *Et dixit Albumasar, scito coniunctionem Planetarum cum domino anni, atque cum significatore regis, & separationem atque adventum eorum adinvicem, in domibus & aspectibus, & fige rariora minora substantiarum eorum (intellegite opera eorum per casus aliorum) & commisse his substantias signorum, & quod vincat super receptione ex natura, & cognosce esse significatorum: & scito casum eorum abinvicem, per diversitatem et alligationem, & cum receptione & redditione.* Note that the command to "understand their works" (*intellegite opera eorum*) is a plural command, not a singular command like elsewhere in the paragraph.

Chapter 25: On the knowledge of the accidents which are going to come in the climes, at the hour of the revolution

The climes are divided by the planets, just as was said elsewhere. Whence it is necessary for you to consider, in the revolution of the year, which clime each planet rules, and to know its nature [or condition], if you want to know the accidents which are going to come in the clime which the planet rules. Because the general accidents of the clime will be according to what the condition was of the planet which rules it; and the Lord of the Year (and the Lord of the Ascendant of the revolution, and the Lord of its hour) will participate. Whence, each of them will be at hand to do help or harm to the Lord of the clime, according to what its condition was, both in good and in evil. But in your memory let there always be those things which I have told you above in a chapter: what the Lord of the Year would signify in the places in which it falls, [and] how far the signification of every significator will be extended.

And you will consider the Ascendant of the revolution according to the diversity of the ascensions of any region. And if it sometimes were to happen that one planet has a signification over two climes, or rules one and participates in another, always put its signification over every region which it rules; and thus you could know the accidents which are going to come in those regions, both the general and the particular ones, both for the king and the common people. Because if the significator of the king and of the region whose year you are revolving, were stronger in the 10th house than any of the planets, [and] in its own domicile, and it were otherwise sound and free, it signifies that the king will rule over all great men of that region, and will be their master. And if there were no king in that region, these things will happen to him who is greater in it. And may you not err in the consideration of the significators of the king, because you ought to consider it according to the regions and according to the climes over which their significations are extended.

Chapter 26: What the Lord of the Year and the significator of the king would signify when they were well disposed in the revolution

In the revolution of the year which you are revolving, look at the Lord of the Year and the significator of the king to see how they are disposed, and what kind of condition they have: which if you were to find them well disposed and of good condition, and free from impediments, and they were in places of friendship to the Ascendant and the 10th, and they were in the noted aspect of the planets, received by them,[202] and they themselves were to receive them; and [if] the Sun (if the revolution were in the day) or the Moon (if the revolution were in the night) or one of the luminaries were one of the aforesaid significators (namely, that of the king or of the Year), and the luminaries (or either of them) were to aspect the Ascendant or its Lord, and the luminary were free and in a good place from the Ascendant, it signifies that those who will live in that clime or in that region (just as the signification of the Lord of the Year will be extended), will be of good condition, and that prosperity and good and accomplishment and strength will happen to them.

And Abū Ma'shar said: and better than this is if the luminary (whose authority it was), were to commit disposition to the Lord of the Ascendant: the nobles or great men and the wealthy, both those who are fit for a kingdom and others, will be subjected to the king of that same clime or of that same region, and the citizens or inhabitants of the region will be in tranquility and quiet, and good will be rendered to them.

And if some of the planets were to commit disposition to the Lord of the Year from the conjunction or some good aspect, and he were to receive them, likewise happiness and joy on all sides will happen to them, according to the natures [or substances] of the signs in which the planets are, in whose domiciles the luminaries are—especially if they were to aspect [the luminaries] (or at least one of them) from a strong and good place. Because then it signifies that in that clime or region there will be security and rest, and health in all of them, both in their things and in their persons, and they will turn their wills away from doing evil, and they will be eager to do well and to observe justice and faith, without detriment or destruction.

Again on the disposition of the Lord of the Year, according to the place in which he is, in the revolution of the year

Even look in the revolution at the Lord of the Year and the sign in which he is: which if he were of good condition, and likewise [if] the sign in which he is were well disposed, and he were made fortunate in strong in the bound of a benefic, received by one of the benefics, and he were to receive one of them, it signifies that the king or lord of that same clime or region, will be of good condition and of much attainment, more so than the other kings or great men

---

[202] My punctuation makes it seem that Bonatti is speaking of mutual reception, but it is not exactly clear whether he means mutual or only one-way reception.

of that clime or region, and likewise the Lord of the region deputed to the sign in which the Lord of the Year is, and all those inhabiting it; and prosperity and good will happen to them.

Again on the same topic

And if you were to find the Lord of some city to be free (namely made fortunate and strong), and of good condition, received by a benefic, and you knew to what sign that city or region belongs, announce joy and happiness for the citizens, and the fitness of their matters and persons. Therefore may you know what sign and what planet the city or region belongs to.[203] If however you were to find the contrary, you will judge the contrary.

What the Lord of the Year and the other planets would signify if they were impeded in the revolution

Just as you have looked at the Lord of the Year or Revolution, so it is necessary for you to look at him, and even at others, in the significations contrary to these. Therefore look in the revolution of the year at the virtue and power of the Lord of the Year and of the other planets: because the effecting of their works will be according to the places in which they were found at the hour of the revolution.

For if the Lord were impeded, and were in the Ascendant, men will be impeded in their own persons. If however he were[204] elsewhere outside the Ascendant, he will be impeded according to the substance of the sign and the house in which he were impeded: like if he were in the 2nd, substance will be impeded, and so with the rest of the houses [domiciles?] according to [their] natures [or substances], and you will judge according to what is signified by each of the houses. If however another of the planets were impeded besides the Lord of the Year, what is signified by the sign will be impeded, and [likewise] the domicile whose Lord the impeded planet is, namely following the domicile whose Lord he is after the Ascendant [in order]: like if the Ascendant were Aries, Taurus would be impeded before Libra.[205] And if the Ascendant were Taurus, Gemini will be impeded first before Virgo, and so on with the others. And the condition of the citizens or inhabitants of the region or clime deputed

---

[203] Bonatti also discusses this in the Treatise on elections (Tr. 7, Part 1, Ch. 7).

[204] Reading *fuerit* for *fuerint*.

[205] That is, if Venus were the impeded planet. She rules both domiciles, but Taurus is closer to the rising sign.

to that planet will be weakened; and they will say they are impeded, and will be openly aware of their impediments, and will say they are being put down and suppressed and deprived of their standing. And more strongly so if the Lord of the Year or Revolution were in one of the angles (and especially in the 4th) and Mars or Saturn were to aspect him; and if he were in the bounds of the malefics (and more severely so if he were at the end of a sign), unless it were the bound of the malefic who aspects him (because then it decreases something of the impediment, even if only a middling amount). And the impediment will be stronger again if he were besieged by the two malefics, because then the evil and the impediment of their citizens is doubled; and more strongly so if the besiegement were by corporal conjunction, because this will take away from them what is sought, and will bring harm to them. And if it were by opposition, the detriment will be less by one-fourth. If however it were by a square aspect, it will be less by one-third.

And Abū Ma'shar said if it were a corporal conjunction and Saturn were to impede in front and Mars behind (or one or the other malefic, you understand), [many] of the citizens will be taken captive, but few will be killed. If however Mars were to impede the significator in front and Saturn behind, many of the captives will be killed.[206] And if the planetary significator were combust, it signifies the destruction of the things and persons of the citizens of that region which it rules, and [it signifies] exiling[207] from the region on account of the unbearable impediment which will happen to them.

Again on the same topic

In a revolution of the year, know even what sign and which planet might rule in the revolution of the year over some city: because if the sign were badly disposed and the planet impeded, it signifies detriment and evil and the destruction of the things and persons of the citizens of that city or region.

And Abū Ma'shar said, for every clime, establish a planet from which the signification of the condition of the king might be taken, so that you might know what might come to kings, by the will of God.

---

[206] I believe that by "in front," Bonatti means "in a later zodiacal degree" for then the planet would probably be moving towards that malefic; "behind" must mean "in an earlier zodiacal degree." Since Saturn's signification is more like prison and Mars's is more like death, then if Saturn were "in front" and the significator were moving towards him, it would signify capture and imprisonment; likewise if Mars were in front, it would show killing.

[207] I.e., voluntary emigration (according to Bonatti, Tr. 6).

Chapter 27: On the knowledge of the planetary significators in the revolution of the year, both of the significator of the king and certain others

If the Sun were in the 10th in a revolution of the year, not removed from the cusp of the 10th house by more than 4° ahead or more than 10° after,[208] and the Lord of the bound of the degree of the 10th house were in that bound,[209] or were to aspect its own bound from a good place from the Ascendant, and from an aspect of friendship, these two, so disposed, signify kings and their affairs. For if the Sun were then free from the impediments of the malefics (and likewise the Lord of the bound of the 10th house), and in a good place from the Ascendant (and better than this if [the Lord of the bound] were in the angle, except, however for the 4th house), kings and great men fit for a kingdom, and their affairs, will be saved. If however the Sun and the Lord of the bound of the 10th house, and the places in which they were, were impeded by the presence of the malefics or their aspects–and more strongly so if the impediment were from the angle, both of the figure of the revolution and of the significators[210]–kings and the aforesaid great men, and their affairs, will be impeded and their condition will be made worse.

If however the 11th and its Lord were sound and free from the impediments of the malefics, the soldiers and allies of kings will be saved. But if they were impeded, [the soldiers and allies] will be impeded and suffer detriment.

And Abū Ma'shar said Mercury signifies scribes and business dealers, and astronomers, and learned men, and the wise. And he said this: [that] if [Mercury] and his place were fit and lasting, [the aforesaid people] will be fit. And Jupiter signifies providers and leaders; if he were fit and sound they will be made sound. And likewise Venus signifies women.

Chapter 28: On the condition of the king and on the condition of his substance, and on the condition of his own soldiers or allies

You will even look, in a revolution of the year, to see whether the significator of the king aspects the Part of Fortune. Because if he were to aspect it from an

---

208 I believe that by "ahead of," Bonatti means "in an earlier degree than the cusp's"; by "after," he means "in a later degree than the cusp's." See my Introduction.

209 But then wouldn't the significator probably be combust or under the sunbeams?

210 I.e., if the malefics were in the signs opposite or square relationship to the signs the significators are in.

aspect of friendship, or were joined corporally to it, it signifies [the king's] good and fortunate condition (and better than this if his significator were the Lord of the 10th house). You will then look for his substance and his soldiers and allies from the 11th house and its Lord: which if you were to find them well disposed, of good condition, say the condition of the soldiers and their substance will be good and fortunate.

If the Lord of the Year were the significator of the king

If however the Lord of the Year were the significator of the king, then look for his substance from the 2nd and its Lord, just as you have looked for the substance of the common people.

Indeed for his soldiers and allies, Abū Ma'shar said you will look from the Lords of the triplicity of the sign in which the significator of the king is, and judge concerning them in the revolution according to how you were to find them disposed. For if all were well disposed, judge their good condition through the whole year or revolution. If however you were to find them poorly disposed, judge the contrary. If however you were to find one well disposed, and the other poorly, judge according to that. For if the first were well disposed, judge good in the first one-third of the revolution. If the second, in the second. If the third, in the third. And if you were to find the contrary, you will judge the contrary. And always make the Lord of the bound in which the significator of the king is, a participator.

On the common people and their substance

You will judge likewise concerning the condition of the common people through the Lord of the Year, and concerning their substance through the 2nd and its Lord; and concerning the condition of each through the Part of Fortune: which if it were well disposed, it signifies good. If however it were poorly disposed, it signifies the contrary.

Again concerning the significator of the king, if his significator were Mars or Saturn

If Mars or Saturn were the significator of the king, nor were [either one] the Lord of the Ascendant, nor of the 10th, nor of any exaltation, and one of them will impede by its presence or opposition or square aspect, it introduces destruction which will come to men from the direction of their own king; and its impediment will be stronger if it were in an angle. And if it were in the

Ascendant, or in the eastern part, it will come from the direction of the east, and its arrival will hasten. If indeed it were in the 7th or in the western part, it will come from the direction of the west, and it will slow down somewhat. If however it were in the 4th or in the northern part, it will come from the direction of the north, and will slow down more. Indeed if it were in the 10th, it will come from everywhere, and will happen generally to all men; but it will come more strongly in the northern and southern parts than in the east or west; and the harshness over them will slow down, and especially in Germany and parts adjacent to them.

When a benefic is in charge

And if the significator of the king were a benefic, and were so placed just as I have told you concerning a malefic, it signifies goodness and joy, and the gladness of the citizens or inhabitants of the aforesaid areas, according to [where] it is in any of them, unless it is impeded by retrogradation or fall or descension (because if it were so, it will signify nothing good).

And Abū Ma'shar said that if there were a bad aspect to the Lord of the Ascendant or to the significator of substance, there will be oppression in the body; and [if it were] from the second, in substance; and from the third, in brothers; and from the fourth, from the direction of parents and older kin; and from the fifth, from journeys and from those things which were from his own hand; and from the sixth, from infirmity; from the seventh, from women and war; from the eighth, from the remains[211] of the dead, and contention. And if the sign (namely the eighth one) were a movable or common one, death will be feared concerning the king, if it were the significator of the king whom the malefic Lords aspect.[212] And if this aspect were from the eighth to the significator of the rustics, it will be feared concerning the rustics. And if the significator were one (namely of [both] the king and the rustics), it will be feared concerning everyone, for death will invade them. And if it were from the ninth, from the direction of pilgrimages and religious men who seek justice. And if it were from the tenth, from the direction of the king and his domination. And if it were from the eleventh, from the direction of friends. And from the twelfth, from the direction of enemies. And he said, speak likewise for the good if the aspect

---

211 Literally, from "what is left behind" by the dead (inheritances).
212 I am unsure what Lords he means.

were from a strong benefic, and the malefic were to [be cadent].[213] And he said, say likewise in the revolution of the years of nativities.

Chapter 29: On the impediments of the malefics and on their aspects, what they would signify, and how the impediments and the impeding ones might be known

In a revolution, look at the significators (namely of the king and the common people or the rustics), and see whether they are aspected by malefics or not. Indeed if the malefics were to aspect them from the opposition, and the malefics themselves were impeded, it signifies (on account of the enmity of the aspect) that impediment will come to the king and the rustics from the direction of enemies.

And Abū Ma'shar said if the aspect were a square, the impediment will be from men who are not known to be enemies. And he said [it is] because this aspect is in the middle, and does not publicize enmity. And if they were to aspect them from a sextile aspect, the impediment will come from the direction of certain people who are thought to be friends, nor however it is really certain whether they are friends or not. If however they were to aspect them from a trine aspect, the impediment will be from the direction of friends.

And Abū Ma'shar said that if the [malefics'] aspect were such a figure from their own places,[214] this is just as was said toward the significator of the rustics. And if it were toward the significator of the king, it will enter in concerning the king. And he said it is necessary that it be seen whether the rustics would help the king, or the king would help the rustics. And this is known by the complexion which there is between each of the significators and the impeding or aspecting malefics; and this according to the kind of aspect (namely whether it were a trine, or sextile, or a square, or opposition); and from out of what places or houses or dignities. Which if the malefic impeding the significator of the king or that of the common people or rustics were in its own domicile, he from whom the impediment will come will be from that clime or kingdom or region (namely of those things which are signified by those testimonies). Like if he were in domicile, he will be famous in the region, and will be of the household

---

[213] *Ceciderit.* Normally he would say *cadens fuerit*, but below in Ch. 34 he uses *ceciderit* again, explicitly in contrast to being angular.

[214] Normally this would mean "from their own domiciles" or "dignities," but in this instance it simply means the places in which they happen to be. Below he explicitly addresses the dignities.

members of the king. And if it were in exaltation, he will be noble and powerful, namely from among those who are fit for a kingdom. And if it were in triplicity, they will be from among those who are not fit for a kingdom, but are near them. And if it were in bound, he will be from among those below the afore-said, who are fit to be military companions,[215] or marquesses, and the like. And if it were in the face, it will be of the more noble people. And if he were of the nobles who are below marquesses, still they are of great soul [or magnanimous]. If however it were not in one of the aforesaid dignities, he will not be well-born nor known in the region; and men will say that they do not know where he is from, and perhaps that they will say he is born from an unknown father, or from fornication, or that a commoner is a father to him.

And Abū Ma'shar said if the significator of the king[216] were in charge,[217] he will be an enemy from the same clime, and the king will be weak in prohibiting and repelling him. And he said if the significator of the rustics were in charge, he will not be an enemy from the clime, nor from its own rulership. And he said the significator is the Lord of the Year, and the significator of the rustics; and he said, and the Moon is the significatrix of the rustics, and of all the common people, and is not in charge; for every one that is in charge, is a significator, but not the reverse; because not each significator is in charge.[218]

Chapter 30: What the retrogradation of the significator of the king and of the Lord of the Year or the significator of the rustics, signifies

If it were to happen at some time that the significator of the common people were retrograde in the revolution of the year, though it happens most rarely (still it could occur), as was said elsewhere, it would threaten a very horrible evil. For the retrogradation of the significator of the king signifies his weakness and his depression; and it will be a great thing if he were to avoid being deposed from rule, and if his kingdom were to escape destruction in that year. Likewise the

---

[215] Recall that a *comes* was originally a fighting companion (or a member of a group of them) to a chief or ruler on military expeditions (see footnote, Tr. 2, Part 3, Ch. 6, "On the 4th House and its Lord"). Vassals later came to perform administrative functions, and his comparison with marquesses suggests he means someone who has received an administrative honor.

[216] Per 1491.

[217] It is unclear what Bonatti means by "being in charge" (*praeesse*) in this context.

[218] Serious damage has been done to this last sentence. I do not know what it is trying to convey.

retrogradation of the Lord of the Year will signify destruction and the bad condition of the populace and the citizens of that region.

You will look to see in whose bound each of them were. For if it were retrograde in the bound of some malefic (and more strongly so if the bound were in the domicile of some malefic), this danger will be longer and greater than if it had been in the domicile or bound of a benefic; and likewise if the Lord of the bound were impeded, because it will increase the malice again, and multiply it. If however it were free, it subtracts something from the malice, even if not much.

If however it were retrograde in the bound of a benefic, the impediment will be decreased; and all the more so if in addition again it were the domicile of a benefic; and again something more if the benefic were well disposed.

Chapter 31: What Mars and Saturn would signify if they were badly disposed in the revolution of the year

When you revolve the year, look to see if Mars were stationary in his first station, wanting to go retrograde and be joined with Saturn–or if Saturn is so disposed that he goes towards Mars while [Mars] is standing [still], or Mars goes towards him while [Saturn] is retrograding: it signifies the austerity and hatefulness of men, so that there will not be any who wishes to obey his betters if he could avoid it, and piety will be cut off; nor will there by any who feels pity for another with zeal, but evildoers will abound, and cutters of roads, and pillagers; nor will a slave fear his master, nor a religious man one ruling him; and it will be worse if Saturn were in Libra, and worse again if he were retrograde, and worse than this if the Sun were to aspect him by his opposition, and Mars were to aspect the Sun, and [the Sun] him. And it will be worse again if Mars were peregrine, joining himself to Saturn; and it will be the ultimate evil above all others if the revolution were in the setting[219] of the Sun, or near it, namely a little bit before or after.

And Abū Ma'shar said quarrels and war will fall between the citizens of the east and west, and there will be battles in diverse places. Therefore strive to understand all of these with a very detailed investigation.

---

[219] See Ch. 44, which is dedicated to this and explains this.

Chapter 32: If the Lord of the Ascendant and the Moon and the other significators were impeded: what would follow from that

The Lord of the Ascendant and the Moon signify the matters of the common people in the revolution of the year; which if they were impeded, and were found in a place of enmity from the Ascendant, they signify impediment that is going to come over men in their persons and their things, according to the quantity of the enmity, and according to the place of enmity into which they fell.

For if they were to fall in the 6th, they signify infirmities [and] pains are going to come to men in the revolution. If however they were to fall in the 8th, they signify death, and more severely so if the 8th were a human sign. And if they were to fall in the 12th, they signify enmities and betrayals according to the substance of the sign in which they were: like if they were in Gemini, it will be because of young men and adolescents. If they were in Virgo, it will be because of young women. If they were in Libra, it will be because of men of mature age. If they were in the first half of Sagittarius or in Aquarius, it will be because of the general mass of men. If they were in Aries or Capricorn, it will be because of smaller animals. If they were in Taurus or in the last half of Sagittarius, it will be because of larger animals and those which are ridden. And if they were in Leo, it will be because of forest animals, and those rough and wild. And if they were in Cancer or Scorpio or Pisces, it will be because of animals spending time in waters.

And if the Lord of the exaltation (if the ascending sign were the exaltation of some planet) and the Moon were not impeded in the aforesaid places,[220] it signifies the same as the Lord of the Ascendant does; but it will be [below][221] the signification of the Lord of the Ascendant. And the signification or impediment of the Lord of the bound will be less than the signification of the Lord of the exaltation. And the signification of the Lord of the triplicity will be below the signification of the Lord of the bound, if one of them were impeded. And the impediment of the Lord of the face will be below the impediment of the Lord of the triplicity.

Look, however, to see how the aforesaid planets are aspected by the benefics or by the malefics: because I say the benefics decrease [impediment] unless they are impeded by combustion or retrogradation; indeed the malefics increase

---

[220] On the basis of the sentence construction, it is impossible to say whether Bonatti means (a) the Lord of the exaltation is unimpeded *and* the Moon is in the aforesaid places, or (b) the Lord of the exaltation and the Moon are not impeded *and are both* in the aforesaid places.
[221] Adding *infra* to match the rest of the paragraph.

[impediment] unless they are direct and well disposed and receive impeded planets [that are] inimical to the Ascendant.

And Abū Ma'shar said that if the impediment were from Mars, there will be a choleric fever, and sudden death. And if the impediment were from Saturn, there will be fever from black cholera, and death.

The chapters on battles are not put here, but they are found in the book on elections.[222]

Chapter 33: When war is signified in the revolution of the year: from whom it comes or will be incited

If you were to look up to see whether there were going to be battles and dissensions[223] in the year which you are revolving, and whence they would be incited and by whom, look for this matter according to the method which the ancients have handed down to us, and particular our most reverend predecessor Abū Ma'shar, who was proficient, and very astute and bold, in the science of the revolutions of years, [and] even in all other areas of astronomy. For you will then erect the figure for the revolution of the year, and establish the Ascendant and the other houses, and all the planets in the domiciles in which they were; and look at Mars, and see from whom he himself is being separated, or from whom he is then [already] separated.

For Abū Ma'shar said, because [the one from whom Mars is separating] is the one who sent him, and who incited the war (even if it were a benefic from whom Mars were separated, even if it were Jupiter); however the inciter of the war will be from among the persons who are signified by Jupiter [if it were Jupiter], and of the more powerful ones; and it will be possible that he is of the class of bishops and the like. And if he were separated from Saturn (since Saturn in such a case signifies kings), it seems that the king is the one who has incited the war, or it will be due to the advice of old and ignoble men.[224]

---

[222] This heading appears in both 1491 and 1550, and seems to be an editorial remark. It might be that the electional chapters on war (Tr. 7, Part 2, 7th House, Chs. 3-7) originally pertained to revolutions. But note that the next chapters do indeed pertain to war.

[223] *Discensiones.*

[224] According to this doctrine, a war could only be incited by Jupiterian or Saturnian men, since only those planets are slower than Mars. This implies that all or most wars are started by the counsels of old men, monied interests, and because of people with status interests to protect.

And Abū Ma'shar said there will be a war if Mars were to commit his own disposition to Saturn, and Saturn were joined with him, and were to receive him. And he said if Mars were separated from Jupiter and joined to Saturn without reception, know that he will be its provocator, and will provoke for justice, because he is of the household members of the king. If however [Mars] were not separated from Jupiter, and were joined to Saturn, the one who incited the war will be of ignoble people who are not fit for a kingdom, nor of great dignity. And if you were to see Mars separated from Saturn and joined to Jupiter, there will not be a war; and if there were, it will not be between honest men, nor Catholic nor distinguished men nor bishops or the like.

Therefore, after you were to see him from whom Mars is being separated, and from whom it seems the war ought to be incited, and him to whom [Mars] is joined, nor were you to see reception, and their conjunction were in one latitude (and if it were a conjunction of Mars and Saturn), see which of them is stronger in its own place. And the one of them who towers [over the other] is the stronger, that is, the one who goes over the other. The one who goes over the other is he who is northern of the other [in latitude], as was said above. And if Saturn were above the other, it signifies the weakness of the war. If however Mars were to go above Saturn, it signifies its strength. You may say the same if one of them were to receive the other.

And Abū Ma'shar said that, however, the first thing it is necessary for you to know in this chapter is of what kind the kingdom's strength is, and how much it is–then you might know the time of the duration of the kingdom. And if you were to know what it will be for the kingdom, and you were to see the time of its duration, look at the hour of the destruction of the one rising up from the impediment of Saturn and Jupiter and Mars, or of him from whom Mars is being separated.

And Abū Ma'shar said, know its destruction from the destruction of these three planets, because it is they who incite war. And if Mars were retrograde and the others were direct, war will appear, but its appearance will not be come to an end until Mars goes direct–for then its appearance will come to an end. And he said, if indeed the war were incited, and Mars were cadent from the Ascendant of the year, or peregrine, it will be weak.

And Abū Ma'shar said[225] if you were to see the first side received by his enemies,[226] and it were opposite the first side, or in its square aspect, this will be

---

[225] This paragraph seems to pertain to the Lords of the 1st and the 7th. But there is an ambiguity here, in part because of the reference to Jupiter and Saturn. The word I have

the "strength of the sword." If however the first side were to receive the second side, there will not be a war. If indeed [the second side] were not received, and you were to see war, and the first side were received, there will be no strength to the insurgents; and there will be a stability of men with the first king, and their inclination toward him. And he said, and likewise look for the second side, because reception is an ally and appeasement, and the strength of the received. Therefore if it did not receive, it will be peregrine, and there will be no trust in it [him?] nor will there be strength. And he said the first side in the condition of kings, and their secrets, and intentions, is the degree of Saturn. The second side is the degree of Jupiter. And he said I have already made this clear to you in the book of conjunctions.[227]

Chapter 34: Which of the planets would signify wars in the revolution of the year, and which of them is the dispositor

Abū Ma'shar said Mars disposes wars, and signifies the masters of armies and the captains of soldiers; which if he were strong in an angle, it signifies war; and if he were to be cadent, he does not signify it. And he said, indeed the Moon is

---

translated as "side" is *pars*, the word which can also mean an [Arabic] Part. In *OGC* II.5.18, Abū Ma'shar speaks of certain Parts (which he uses for different purposes), and says that "the astrologers" think the first Part is Saturn and the second one is Jupiter–which Bonatti seems here to echo, and attributes this opinion to Abū Ma'shar himself. So it seems there may be some confusion in Bonatti's use of the text. But most of the paragraph makes sense in the context of the Lords of the 1st and 7th. See also Ch. 116, the subsection "Likewise concerning the two Parts in a revolution of the years of the world."

[226] Bonatti's Latin reads, "if you were to see the side received by his first enemies." Textually and astrologically, Bonatti's line does not really make sense, so I have read *primae* for *primorum*.

[227] In the passage from *OGC* mentioned above, Abū Ma'shar does not speak of the "secret of kings," but Bonatti could be drawing on a copy of BN *lat.* 16204 (see Introduction). Al-Rijāl (pp. 408-09) describes a number of Parts, in which *he* mentions a "secret." In one set of the "two Parts," the first is taken from Saturn to Jupiter, and projected from the degree of their conjunction in a mutation conjunction (i.e., a mutation from one triplicity to another); the second is taken from Jupiter to Saturn, and projected from the degree of their conjunction in the 20-year conjunction in which one is at the time. We are to measure distance from the Parts to their Lords, and from the Part to Mars (one year per degree), and that is a timing mechanism. Then al-Rijāl cites another source (who allegedly drew on Māshā'allāh) for two Parts involving Saturn and Jupiter, which is too complicated to describe here (see *OGC*, Appendix V), but involves the calculation of a distance called "the secret." Finally, he mentions a third set of two Parts: (1) cast the Aries ingress chart for the year in which a king ascends the throne, and measure from Saturn or Jupiter ("whichever is eastern"), to the Sun; add to this amount the minor years of the planet that signifies the type of religion (as Venus for Islam). (2) Take the distance from the Sun to Saturn or Jupiter ("whichever is western"), and add to it the distance measured in (1) (not counting the minor planetary years); project this sum from the Ascendant.

the key to these: which if she were fit [or adapted], they will be achieved [or undertaken]; and if she were impeded, they will be impeded.

Again on the same topic, according to Abū Ma'shar

Abū Ma'shar said if Mars in the revolution of the year were in one of the angles of the Ascendant, whichever one it was, he will incite war according to the quantity of his own strength, and therefore[228] he incites war if he were in the square aspect of Saturn and Jupiter. And if you were to see that Mars was going to incite a war, look to see in what place from the Ascendant he were to fall, and you will see where the Part of War[229] were to fall, and over which of the houses the Part will rule, and you will see if one of the malefics (namely one or more) were to aspect the domicile of Mars or the Part of War from the opposition or square aspect, or they were in them, or they were to aspect the sign which ruled over that city or region for which you are revolving the year; or [if] the ones that rule that clime or city or region were to aspect the significator of the king or of another great man from the opposition or square aspect, or they were joined to him corporally. It signifies that if the king or a noble man were to have war with someone or some people in that revolution, that his enemies will achieve victory over him; or at least grief and sorrow will enter over him, and tribulation and distress. And if the planet which was his significator were combust, it will signify the same, and it will be feared concerning him. And if it were retrograde, the figure signifies his flight, and the strength of his enemies, and his fall and dejection; likewise if it were first in a good place from the Ascendant, and then goes down to a weak place.[230]

Again on the same topic, if one of the malefics were to rule: what would follow from thence

Abū Ma'shar said if Mars were to rule the signification of the year, and were strong, there will be war with skills and worries, and with plundering and powerful killing. And if Saturn were to rule the year or the quarter, there will be war by seductions and cleverness, and through discipline [or knowledge] and

---

[228] The last clause of the sentence does not really follow from the first, so I am unsure why Bonatti (or Abū Ma'shar) says "therefore" (*ob hoc*). Perhaps it made sense in the context of Abū Ma'shar's original work.

[229] This could be the Part of Warfare and Boldness (see below, Part 2, Ch. 16).

[230] I am not sure what Bonatti is referring to here–whether the planet is moving through the *zodiac* to a bad or weak place? If so, that would be like if the significator of the king were in the 5th sign or house, and were moving toward the 6th sign or house.

skills. And he said if one of the malefics were to rule the year, and the other malefic were the Lord of the Quarter, there will be no doubt of having wars in that quarter. And likewise if a malefic were to aspect the Lord of the Year or Quarter from the opposition or by a square aspect; or the Lord of the Quarter were in the 7th or retrograde. And he said if [a malefic] were inimical to the Lord of the Quarter, it will be in the same quarter; and likewise if it were inimical to the Lord of the Lord of the Month,[231] in the same month.

Chapter 35: When war is signified in the revolution of the year; and if it were, when victory is signified; and when flight or defeat; and when peace (or the extinction of the war)

After you were to see, in the revolution, that a future war is signified, look at the planet who signifies it: because if it were direct and of good condition, it does not permit the war to be ended. And it will endure, and be annulled from, the side of the king or chief of the region in which you are, or for which you revolved the year which you are seeking; and it will signify peace and the extinguishing of the war. Even see how the significator is aspected by the planets, and by how many of them: because a multitude of planets aspecting him (and more strongly so, if they were to have dignity in the place in which he is), will signify his strength and victory, and that he will be aided more so than his adversary, both by his own and by other people. And if it were stationary in its second station, it signifies him to be strong and powerful in war, and likewise those following him. If however it were stationary in its first station, it signifies his strength in the beginning of the war, but ultimately he will not perfect [it] well, nor will he persevere. If however it were retrograde, it signifies his flight and the rupture [of his army].

And if it were the significator of the enemy or the one wishing to war with him, just as I have told you about the significator of your kingdom, by the aforesaid conditions, you will judge the contrary of what you have judged. If however the significator were direct, as I said, nor impeded, it signifies either peace, or, if there were a fight or war, it signifies victory. And if you wanted to know from the side of whose people or whose allies his victory will be, and [what] the reason for the subduing of his enemies is, look to see which of the

---

[231] Bonatti has not explained how to find the Lord of the Month.

planets better aspects him, and from a greater dignity,[232] because that one will be the significator of those who are the cause of his victory. Like if it were the Sun or Saturn, it will be the king or another more noble person (but the Sun signifies more junior people than Saturn). If however it were Mars, they will be bellicose soldiers. And if it were Jupiter, they will be great men, nobles, and wise. And if it were Mercury, they will be literate men, both noble and common. And if it were the Moon, they will be men who act by means of merchant activities, navigation and the like. And Abū Ma'shar said if it were Venus, they will be Arabs.

Chapter 36: How it should be elected for one wanting to go to war[233]

If however someone wished to go to war, after which you were to see it was going to happen in the revolution, and you wished to elect for him the hour for doing this, look at the three superior planets to see whether they are retrograde or direct. If however they were retrograde, Abū Ma'shar said let the beginning of your hour for going to war be that of their going direct. And if they were direct, when they undertake to go retrograde, and likewise when they begin to be combust. And if they were combust, when they begin to emerge; and if they were occidental, when they become oriental; and if they were oriental, when they become occidental; or when they are changed from the signs in which they are (namely at the hour in which the planets signify war), because then the planet is said to change figure;[234] and likewise when its substance or signification is changed.[235]

If however Mars were received at the hour of the revolution (and even better if he were received by one of the benefics by domicile or exaltation), he extinguishes war in that year or revolution. And if the reception were from the

---

[232] Is this based on the dignities of the degree in which the significator is, or the dignities the aspecting planets have in *their own* places?

[233] Compare with the instructions for war elections in Tr. 7. The instructions here are simpler because the rising sign and location of the planets is determined at the ingress, so only their subsequent movements can be used. But presumably, if the revolution signifies war, one could also elect to go out to war in the usual way.

[234] *Mutare figuram.* See the fifty-fourth consideration for selecting the Lord of the Year (above), and the use of changing signs in horary (Tr. 6).

[235] The upshot of these instructions seems to be that war is disruptive and the opposite of peace; therefore if there is currently peace and one wants to go out to war, one should wait until the planetary conditions turn into their opposites.

10th, it signifies not only the extinction of war; but it even signifies peace in that year.

Chapter 37: Through what men or peoples the fight or war will come to be

If you were to look at the erected figure of the revolution of the year, and you were to find a future battle or war, look to see which side Mars seems to be allied to; for he will be allied to that side with whose significator he bears himself more amicably, and which he aspects more; and from which side of the east or west he is;[236] and from which side is the planet from which he is being separated (because that is on the side of the Ascendant, and he to whom he is joined is on the opposite side). For from whatever side Mars is, if he were direct, the war will come to be from that side, through bellicose and honest[237] men, who confidently show their faces to their enemies, nor do they show their backs to them. Indeed if he were retrograde, [the war will arise] through changeable men who want to be praised for things they are not doing, and sometimes attribute to themselves what others are doing, and speak more than they act, and threaten more than they strike, and who clamor for war with great vehemence, but do not remain firm in war, but abandon it over the shoulders of others,[238] and they exhibit themselves as having done great things, and they are predators like thieves and the cutters of roads. And if Mars were stationary, the war will be stronger just as I told you above in the other chapter when I spoke of the station of the significator.

Likewise, look at Saturn, who, even though he leads men gravely to war, still he brings strong and terrible things more so than anything else, and more pestilences; wherefore he must be looked at in this matter, because he signifies this from the side on which he is.

And Abū Ma'shar said, for Saturn signifies a harsh condition for the citizens of the same side in which he is, according to the quantity of the substance of the sign in which he is, and the bounds of his own place, after you were to follow

---

[236] In al-Rijāl this is called being "in the *haiz* of the Ascendant [or the 7th]."

[237] By "honest" (*probos*), Bonatti doesn't mean they are necessarily in the right; but their personal honor leads them to be brave and open (rather than being sneaky and working through subterfuge).

[238] *Super humeris aliorum.* Exact meaning of idiom unclear, but it evidently pertains to cowardice–perhaps it means that while they retreat, they look over their shoulders at those they leave behind?

him by succession: the Ascendant, and the house of substance, and of brothers, and the rest, up to the end of the twelve signs.[239] And he said if Saturn were retrograde, it will be how I told you with Mars, but it will be more severe. And by means of these same chapters, someone can act in questions of wars, and in the departure of hours[240] to wars, and in the taking out of *carroccios*[241] and military banners. Nor should you believe that this chapter (nor even any) contradicts the others; but distinguish the times, and harmonize the writings.

And Abū Ma'shar said a retrograde planet signifies a commingling of things, and reversal and diversity, also war and victory by the Lord of the same clime that belongs to that planet. And a stationary planet signifies the desire for evil and the repetition of what had already ceased, and killing. And [its] aspect signifies evil, and a quarrel, and seduction, and cleverness.

Chapter 38: Whether the captain of the adversary is young or old

If however you wished to know the age of the captain or leader of the other side, look at the impeding malefic; which if it did not impede, look at his place. And look at the place of the significator of the enemy. If they[242] were both oriental from the Sun, the captain or leader will be a young man, and younger than that if the Moon were oriental with them; if indeed they were occidental, they will be old men. If however one were oriental, the other occidental, he will be of mature age, not very young nor very old; but a malefic signifies one younger than the Lord of the seventh, if it were oriental; and an older man if it were occidental.

---

[239] I am not sure what this notion of following him by succession means, but it could refer to the concept of succession laid out in Ch. 26.

[240] *Horarum.* Bonatti often speaks of the hour in which one might depart to war, but I do not understand his use of *hora* here.

[241] Lat. *carochium.* A *carroccio* is a standard mounted on a car or wagon, pulled by animals: note especially the *Carocium* of Milan, which was a kind of iron tree with a cross on top. Bonatti must be thinking of emblems representing armies and cities that are paraded into battle, especially the one used by the Florentines present at the battle of Montaperti, when Bonatti's election aided the Sienese against them. This *carroccio* was red, bearing the flag of the Florentines, and drawn by oxen draped in red.

[242] Note that Bonatti says to look at the "places" (i.e, the houses or signs), but speaks only of the planets themselves. Perhaps there is an older or implicit doctrine referring to the domicile rulers of the signs these planets are in.

Chapter 39: If the significator of the war were pacified with the Lord of the Year: what will follow from thence

Abū Ma'shar said if the significator of the war were pacified with the Lord of the Year, it will be good in that year. And if it were pacified with the Lord of the semester, or with the Lord of the quarter, it will be good in that semester or in that quarter. And if it were pacified with the Lord of the month, it will be good in that same month. And if with the Lord of the day, in that same day.

I say "pacified," that is, "joined to him by body or by aspect with reception." And he said if it were pacified with the Lord of the profection,[243] it will be good in the last half of the month. You may understand the same concerning the [Lord of the] day and hour.

And[244] if the pacification were from the beginning of the sign up to its seventh degree and-a-half, it will be good in the first six months. And if it were from the seventh degree and-a-half, up to the end of the fifteenth degree, it will be good from three months up to the end of the half-year. And if it were from the fifteenth degree up to its twenty-second and-a-half degree, it will be in the last six months of the year. And if it were from the twenty-second and-a-half degree up to its end, it will be from the ninth month up to the end of the year.

You may understand the same concerning the month, day, and hour; and in those times there will be security and peace, and men will not take offence, but they will be confident, nor will it be necessary for them to fear.

Chapter 40: What the malefic planets would signify if they were in human signs in the revolution

Look in the revolution, when you revolve a year, and see if one of the malefic planets were in the human signs (namely in Gemini, or in Virgo or in Libra, or in the first half of Sagittarius, or in Aquarius), and see whether it is slow in course. Likewise, see if the other malefic is joined to him by body, or by an opposite or square aspect (whether he who is joined to him is retrograde or direct): because it signifies detriment that is going to come to men. If it were

---

[243] Does he mean, "the Lord of the month, by monthly profections using the chart of the year?"

[244] I think this paragraph is instructing us to look at the degrees of either the significator of the war or the Lord of the Year, and use the degrees of the sign they are in, treating the whole sign by longitude as representing one year.

retrograde, this will happen more quickly, and with greater wounding. And if the conjunction were from the angles, it will be harsher and more crafty.

Which if the malefic who aspected the other (and the other [is] namely the retrograde one who is joined to him) were in the 10th, there will be impediment, whether harshness or evil, which is then signified for all men generally, and in every region, unless the planet who is the Lord of the sign that rules some region, works to the contrary; and more severely and strongly, if the malefic who impeded were in the Midheaven, and the Lord of the Ascendant were the Lord of the Year–because then an obstacle will be discovered for him, and the detriment will begin from the eastern direction, and will extend up to the western one.

If however the malefic who aspects the other were in the 10th, and the retrograde one who is joined to him were in the 4th, the impediment will begin from the western direction, and be extended up to the uttermost ends of the south of Ethiopia, and those regions will be oppressed for that reason.

If however the aspecting malefic were in the 7th, and the retrograde one who is joined to him were in the 4th, the beginning of the impediment will be everywhere, and will be extended up to the west from the north. And if the two malefics were being joined, the impediment will be more severe, and appear more quickly; and there will be severe mortality in men–and more strongly so if Saturn were he who impedes, because he naturally impedes the signification of the sign in which he is.

Therefore you should see in what place the malefic were to fall from the place of the other malefic (namely the slow one), because if they were joined in a common sign (or he who is joined to the other is joined to him from a common sign), the evil will be determined by death. If however it were in a fixed or movable sign, the end of the signification will be according to the nature of that one of the two malefics who is then stronger by the place in which it were found. For if Mars were stronger, it will be determined by killing, or by hot, pestilential infirmities, according to how he was more prepared to be joined with the Lord of the 8th or with the Lord of the 6th or with a planet who transfers the light between him and one of them. If however Saturn were stronger, it will be determined[245] either through melancholic or pestilential illnesses, in accordance as he is joined (or ready to be joined) with one of them, just as I said concerning Mars.

---

[245] Reading *determinabitur* for *terminabitur*.

And Abū Ma'shar said you will commingle the strength of the death with him. And these things will happen more strongly if their conjunction were from the angles. If however it were outside the angles, their significations will be reduced, nor will they impeded so much, and they will be improved.

And Abū Ma'shar said the greater destruction will be in the side in which the impeding malefic were.[246] And he said, know therefore what there is by the sign in which the two malefics are, in terms of cities and provinces; because the aforesaid evil things will happen in them.

Chapter 41: On the matter which introduces fear in the revolution of the year, and what the malefics would signify in the angles

Sometimes some horrible things tend to appear in the revolution of the year, which introduce fear. Whence, if you were to see one of them when you revolve the year, see whether he who introduces the fear is joined to or aspects himself with Saturn or Jupiter, because they are heavier than the rest. Wherefore the fear will oppress, and one will have to fear concerning it, and more strongly so if the aforesaid planets were impeded (and especially Saturn, because he will signify that there are long-lasting pains that are going to be prolonged from that fear and death).

If however he did not aspect [Saturn or Jupiter], nor were he joined to one of them, it will harm little. If however the significator of the evil were in an angle, it will signify a multitude of evil, and its durability.

And Abū Ma'shar said if it were ahead of the angle,[247] it will be middling and brief. And he said it would help by dignity in this time, and it will help concerning good and evil.

Chapter 42: If the Lord of the sign in which the Lord of the Year is, were to aspect him, or if he did not aspect him: what it would signify

Look to see, in a revolution, in whose domicile the Lord of the Year is; and see whether it aspects him from a trine or sextile aspect, nor is it impeded: because if it were so, men will be in a good status (namely in quiet and security

---

[246] Based on the material in earlier chapters, I believe the side is determined by what side of the chart Mars is in.

[247] I believe that by "ahead of," Bonatti means "in an earlier degree than the cusp's." See my Introduction.

and peace, and joy, and tranquility and happiness). If indeed it were not impeded, nor aspected, or aspected and were impeded, judge between each.[248] If however it did not aspect him, and it were impeded, it signifies sorrow, and worry, and fear, litigation or contentions, and the complete contrary of that which it signified for the good.

And Abū Ma'shar said that this is according to the quantity of the complexion of the substance of the sign in which the significator is: because if it were in the 1st, it will be in their persons; if it were in the 2nd, it will be in substance, and understand the same concerning the rest of the houses.[249]

Chapter 43: On the revolution of the year, if it were in the setting of the Sun

You will consider the revolution of the year, whether it is toward the setting of the Sun.[250] For Abū Ma'shar said if it were so, the Sun will commit his own disposition to the Moon, who is the luminary of the night. Therefore, look at her, and see where her place is from the Ascendant: which if she were fit to take up the disposition of the revolution, look at the Lord of the sign in which she then is; and you should see how he is aspected by the planets, and judge according to how you see it; which if benefics aspect him, they signify good; indeed the malefics signify evil.

Even look to see how she is placed with Saturn, that is, in what kind of aspect, namely a trine or a sextile; and whether Saturn receives her by domicile, or by exaltation, or by two other dignities: because then Saturn will commit his own disposition to her. For if Saturn were to commit his own disposition to her, she will be made stronger, and will dispose the affairs of the revolution better. Indeed if she were to commit her disposition to him, she will not dispose

---

[248] In other words, judge a middling result.

[249] Bonatti is making Abū Ma'shar say two distinct things (though they are presented as one): (a) the "complexion of the substance of the sign," which is probably the same as the "substance of the sign," referring to whether the sign signifies humans or animals (and of what kind, etc.); (b) the people or matters signified by its house location.

[250] In Ch. 32, Bonatti said that a revolution will be in the setting of the Sun if it is a little bit before or after. But here he says *toward* its setting (*ad occasum*), which suggests being a little bit before the full setting. This is supported by the fact that the disposition will now pass to the Moon, whereas if the Sun had already set, the Moon would already have taken over.

afterwards concerning the revolution, and if she were to dispose, her disposition will be bad.[251]

And Abū Ma'shar said, look at the increase of her light, and its diminution, and whether an eclipse is going to come to her in that year. And he said, it is necessary that, in an eclipse, its place be seen, and the degrees of its fulfill-ment;[252] and in an eclipse of the Sun, its degrees and the place of the conjunction; and the *al-mubtazz* over these places, and how the planets aspecting her are aspected. The *al-mubtazz*[253] is the planet who is in charge of the degree of the conjunction or prevention by the multitude of [its] dignities or strengths.[254]

Chapter 44: If the Lord of the Ascendant were impeded in a revolution of the year: what would follow from that

Look at the Lord of the Ascendant in a revolution of the year. Which if you were to find him impeded, announce the impediment is going to be over men in that year, according to the substance of the ascending sign: like if the ascending sign were formed in the image of a human, it will happen to them in their persons. If however the ascending sign were formed in the image of another animal, it will happen to animals formed in that image. And this will happen more severely in the land which the sign rules, and which the planet rules.

And Abū Ma'shar said that it will be more from the direction of the east, and in the areas deputed to the planet which is the Lord of the ascending sign, than in the others: like if the Ascendant were Libra, and Venus were impeded, the land of Libra will suffer impediment from winds, and infirmities and headaches, and the like.

And if the Ascendant were Taurus, the land of Taurus will suffer im-pediment, and detriment from cold, and snow, and dryness, the destruction of the fruits of trees, and the impediments of cows, and crooked [or winding] things,[255] and the like, according to the nature and disposition of each region, unless Mars worked to the contrary.

---

[251] My use of "his" and "her" in the latter sentences (regarding the Moon and Saturn) are educated guesses, but they follow the logic of the paragraph and Bonatti's way of thinking.
[252] This must mean the degree of the Moon at the eclipse.
[253] Or perhaps *al-mubtazzes*.
[254] It is unclear whether this means an *al-mubtazz* by weighted or equal points.
[255] *Amfractibus* [=*anfractibus*]. I am not sure why Bonatti (or Abū Ma'shar) says this.

And if the Ascendant were Gemini, and Mercury were impeded, the land of Gemini will suffer from the blowing of winds, and from the corruption of the air, and from pains in the head and the intestines, the tongue and lungs, and in the places of the breathing-holes of the body.

And if the Ascendant were Virgo, the land of Virgo will suffer from cold and dryness, and moderate sterility, and from pains in the chest and in the area of the heart, unless Jupiter works to the contrary.

And if the Ascendant were Cancer, the Moon were impeded, the land of Cancer will suffer from rains, and from pains in the eyes and the whole head, unless Saturn works to the contrary.

And if the Ascendant were Leo, and the Sun were impeded, the land of Leo will suffer from the dryness of the air, and from the flowing down of rheum, and from illnesses of the head, and the like, unless Saturn works to the contrary in coldness and constriction.

And if the Ascendant were Scorpio, and Mars were impeded, the land of Scorpio will be impeded by waters and poisonous reptiles, and from pains in the head and the arms and the private parts, and the like.

And if the Ascendant were Aries, the land of Aries will suffer from the dryness of the air, and from the flowing down of rheum, and from pains in the head, and the like, unless Venus works to the contrary.

And if the Ascendant were Sagittarius, and Jupiter were impeded, the land of Sagittarius will be impeded by persons in the first part of the year, and in the last [part] by animals which are ridden, with illnesses of the head and the legs and the like.

If however the Ascendant were Pisces, the land of Pisces will suffer from the flooding of waters, and from illnesses of the feet, like gout, and the like, unless Mercury works to the contrary.

And if the Ascendant were Capricorn, and Saturn were impeded, then the land of Capricorn will suffer from cold, and dryness, and sterility, and from pains in the knees and the joints, and the head, and the feet and the like, unless the Moon operates to the contrary.

And if the Ascendant were Aquarius, and Saturn were impeded, the land of Aquarius will be impeded by moist winds, and from illnesses of the legs, and the neck, and the head, unless the Sun works to the contrary.

And if the Lord of the Ascendant of the revolution were in charge over other lands than [those] the [rising] sign is in charge over, they will participate with the lands of the impeding ascending sign, even if they are not impeded as much as those that are deputed to the sign. And if the ascending signs[256] were sound, and the planets free, the lands subject to them will be saved, according to the nature[257] of each.

And Abū Ma'shar said, after you have looked at the Ascendant, look at the second and third, and fourth, and fifth, and the rest of the houses, and their Lords, just as you have looked at the first, up to the end of the signs. And he said, make the angles more dignified, and their Lords, because their job and strength is to be over the rest of the signs which signify the matters of kings.[258]

Chapter 45: What will follow from the conjunction of the two malefics with the Lord of the Year, or with the significator of the king

In the revolution of the year, look at the conjunction of the Lord of the Year, and the significator of the king, with the malefics. For if the two malefics were joined with the Lord of the Year, whether they are joined to him[259] or he to them, this signifies severity which will come over the rustics or common people; and this will happen in the land or region belonging to the sign in which the malefics are. If however they were in different signs, it will happen in different regions, according to how they are deputed to the signs. If however the conjunction were with the significator of the king, it signifies that severity will come over the king from the aforesaid regions.

---

[256] I am not sure why Bonatti puts this in the plural.
[257] *Esse.*
[258] *Quoniam est eis opus & fortitudo super caetera signa quae habent significare res regum.*
[259] Reading *ipsi iungantur* for *ipse iungatur.*

And Abū Ma'shar said, the lifting up of the strength of the malefics is looked for in his journey. And he said, the testimony of Saturn and Jupiter is sought in this, according to how it is revealed in the chapter on conjunctions.[260]

Again on the same topic

Abū Ma'shar said if one of the two malefics were joined to the other, and they were in human signs (whether by body, or by opposition, or by square aspect), [so long as] they were joined together.[261] If however one of the malefics were Saturn, and he were stronger than Mars, it will signify many and serious infirmities, and they will die more from them. If however it were Mars, and he were stronger than Saturn, it will signify killings instead of the infirmities of Saturn. If however one were in a human sign, and the other in another [type of sign], each will introduce an impediment concerning the significations of the sign in which it is; however, this will be less, nor does it matter whether one or two are diurnal or nocturnal, or masculine or feminine. If however they were received, their impediment will be reduced according to the reception.

And Abū Ma'shar said those who are infirm in that same year, health and safety would be hoped for them apart from the moderate amount who will die. If however the malefics were received, there will be less death and less killing. And Abū Ma'shar said they will be commingled with each other.

Chapter 46: How the bodies of the king and the common people must be looked at in the revolution of the year

After you have looked to see what would follow from the conjunction of the malefics with the Lord of the Year and with the significator of the king. Now it remains to say in this chapter, how the condition of the common people or the rustics, and the king, must be looked at in their persons. Indeed you will look at the condition of the common people or the rustics and the king in their persons, from the Lord of the Year, and from the Lord of the Ascendant; and see what there is in the Ascendant of the revolution in terms of aspects: whether the benefics or the malefics aspect it. Because if the benefics were to aspect the Ascendant and the Lord of the Year, they signify the good condition of their

---

[260] It is unclear to me what is meant by the raising up (*sublimationem*) of their strength, or what chapter Bonatti is referring to. The chapter on conjunctions must refer to the aforementioned book of conjunctions (or perhaps *OGC?*).

[261] This reads like a chapter heading, just as in many places in Bonatti's own text (as in Tr. 6).

bodies in the revolution; and even better if in addition they were to aspect the Lord of the Ascendant; and better again if in addition they were to aspect the Moon; and more perfectly yet if the Part of Fortune were there, aspected by the benefics.

If however the malefics were to aspect the Ascendant, nor were the other significators sound, nor well located, nor the Part of Fortune, judge the contrary of that which I told you, namely instead of good, announce bad. Like if the malefics were to impede the Lord of the Year, you will judge impediment according to the substance of the impeding malefic. For Saturn signifies impediment from prolonged pains and death. Indeed, Mars signifies impediment through iron and fire, and killing, both in fleeing and otherwise.

However, you will look for the condition of the king from the Sun and from the tenth, and its Lord, not to mention from the Part of Fortune and its Lord: which if you were to find them well disposed in the trine or sextile aspect of the benefics, or in a square with reception, or in their corporal conjunction, and the benefics were to aspect the tenth, judge the soundness of the king's body, everywhere and wholly. If however you were to find the contrary, you will judge the contrary. And if you were to find the condition to be less good than I have told you, you will judge less good. And if you wanted to make Saturn a participant in the aforesaid, you will not err.

Chapter 47: Which planets would signify kings and kingdoms, and on the impediments of the four angles

Abū Ma'shar said the Sun and Saturn signify kings and kingdoms. And he said whatever kind of planet you were to find impeded out of the four angles, say evil from its substance. Whence, you must see where the Sun and Moon fall in the figure of the revolution. For if they were to fall in good places from the 10th, and stronger ones, or in the tenth itself, they signify the good condition of the king generally, and the good disposition of kingdoms.

Likewise the angles must be looked at, and their Lords. For if you were to find the angles and their Lords made fortunate (and make the Moon a participant, and the Part of Fortune)—which if you were to find them well disposed (namely made fortunate and strong), announce good generally. If however you were to find them badly disposed, announce the contrary. If however you were to find some of them well disposed, indeed others badly, announce according to what you find. For, announce good according to the significations of those well disposed, indeed announce evil according to the significations of those poorly disposed.

Again on the same topic, according to Abū Ma'shar

Abū Ma'shar said the king whose clime and citizens belong to the Lord of the Year will be the stronger among kings. After this, what follows by means of the succession of the strengths of the signs,[262] and every nativity which is under that sign, or under the sign of the Lord of the Year, will be more trustworthy for the good, and of a better rank and dignity among men, unless his nativity is impeded in its root. Whence you ought to look in the hour of the revolution to see if the Lord of the Year were the significator of the nativity or the region, or the clime over which the king rules, because that king whose kingdom is under the rulership of the Lord of the Year will be stronger than the other kings, and his kingdom will be better and longer lasting, and in a better condition than the other kingdoms.

And they who are born in the cities or regions or that kingdom in the revolution (and let the Moon be made fortunate and strong), will be more fortunate and famous; and they will be reputed better than the others who are born in other regions, provided that the planet which is the significator of some one of them is not impeded in the root of his nativity. Even if the Part of Fortune is impeded, it will complete [or furnish] what I told you concerning the Part of Fortune. If however the significator of the nativity of one of them were impeded, the native will not be so fortunate (however he will be less unfortunate than the other unfortunate people of the other regions).

Chapter 48: If the Moon or Mercury were the Lord of the Year or the significator of the king, and is aspected by the malefics: what would follow from that; and on the Part of Fortune and its Lord

If at some time it were to happen that the Moon or Mercury is the Lord of the Year or the significator of the king, and one of the malefics were joined with it, and were to impede it by aspect or conjunction, the condition of the year and of the vulgar or common people will be weakened and made harsh, if it were

---

[262] My tentative suggestion is that this means the people or king belonging to the second sign and its domicile Lord will be second-best; those belonging to the third will be third-best; and so on.

the Lord of the Year. Indeed if it[263] were the significator of the king, [the king's] condition will be weakened and made harsh, nor could this be avoided or prevented–and this, on account of the weakness of the one who is the significator, since it will not have so much virtue that it could expel the impediment introduced to it by the malefic with whom it is joined–unless the Part of Fortune (and its Lord) works to the contrary, by doing good on account of its disposition. Indeed if they[264] were impeded, they will not signify good but its contrary, according to the substance of the sign in which they are: because impediment will fall according to what is signified by that sign, and over the things signified by it; and then it will be said to be inimical to the significator.

Then look at see whether the significator of the king commits its own disposition or strength to the significator of the common people: because the disposition of the year or of the king will be worse if the significator will be impeded by a malefic, and is joined to a planet which is inimical to the Ascendant; and *vice versa*.

Chapter 49: On the committing of the disposition of the Lord of the Year to the significator of the king: what would follow from thence

Abū Ma'shar said if the Lord of the Year were to commit its own disposition to the significator of the king from a square aspect, the king will bear down upon the rustics in search of substance; and for this reason distress will enter upon them. And if it were from the trine or sextile aspect, they will turn over the *census* without his entering into the district upon the rustics. And he said, because if he were to commit the disposition without an aspect, this will be without the act of the king, and the king will think that he will not see it.[265] And he said that if the significator of the king were to commit disposition to the Lord of the Year, the king will withdraw substance in that same year. And he said, if however the Lord of the 11th were to aspect the significator of the king, this will be with his good intentions.[266]

---

263 The Moon or Mercury.

264 Bonatti must mean the Part of Fortune and its Lord, since by hypothesis the Moon or Mercury is already impeded by the malefics.

265 I believe Bonatti is saying that the king will get his money, even though–because he has not taken steps to get it–he thinks he will not get it.

266 Literally, "with his good mind/spirit" (*cum bono animo suo*).

Chapter 50: On the conjunction of the Head of the Dragon with Saturn, and on the conjunction of the Tail with Mars, and what would follow from thence

Abū Ma'shar said the conjunction of the Head of the Dragon with Saturn signifies the impediment of the substance of the sign in which they are joined, just like an eclipse of the Sun and Moon signifies, unless its malice is broken by an aspect of the benefics. Whence if Saturn were conjoined with the Head of the Dragon in Aries, it signifies impediment is going to come in that revolution, in sheep and the like, unless Mars were to aspect them by a trine or sextile aspect, and he himself were made fortunate; there will even be harm in the matters of kings, unless the significator of the king or the Lord of the 10th house were to work to the contrary.

If indeed their conjunction were in Leo, the impediment will be in forest animals living by catching [other animals], and it will harm kings somewhat, even if not much. And if their conjunction were in the first half of Sagittarius, the impediment will be in humans. If however it were in its last half, the impediment will be in large animals, but more strongly so in those which are ridden.

And if their conjunction were in Taurus, the impediment will be in cows and the like, and trees and herbs; and it will even wound sheep and boys somewhat, and the rain will be middling, and the *annona* will be reduced, unless Venus and the Moon were to work to the contrary. And if it were in Virgo, the impediment will be in women (and especially in young women), and it will touch young men somewhat; and seeds will be reduced, and things born from the earth which are turned into seed. And if it were in Capricorn, the impediment will be in goats and the like, and will wound things born from the earth somewhat (even if not as much as in Virgo); and cold will be increased, unless Mars were to work to the contrary.

If however it were in Gemini, the impediment will be in humans, and more so in young men and adolescents, less in those who are of mature age, and less again in old men. And it will be likewise in birds. And harmful winds will blow. And if it were in Libra, the impediment is in humans, and more in those who are of mature or complete age, and middle-aged; less in old men and adolescents, and those who are 45 years or less; and more winds will blow. And if it were in Aquarius, the impediment will be in humans, and more in old men and low-class people, however less in those who are of mature age, and less again in young men [and] adolescents.

If indeed their[267] conjunction were with Mars in the aforesaid signs, the impediment which Mars would signify will be much less than the impediment of Saturn, but it will be through heat and dryness, unless Jupiter or Saturn were to work to the contrary.[268]

If however their conjunction were in Cancer, the impediment will be from impeding and devastating locusts in the areas in which they are, and especially in the eastern and hot regions; and there will be rains in the regions fit for it, more so than usual. And Abū Ma'shar said things born from the earth will be increased, and those creeping upon the ground, both the wounding [kind] and the non-wounding [kind]. And if it were in Scorpio, the impediment will be in poisonous animals, both terrestrial and aquatic, and especially in scorpions. And if it were in Pisces, in animals spending time in water and especially in those which are of use to humans.

Chapter 51: On the conjunction of Mars and Saturn with the Tail

Indeed if Mars were joined with the Tail, it signifies destructions and killings, and famine, and a multitude of evil. If however the Tail were joined with Saturn, it signifies famine and a scarcity of good in whatever sign it is, and harsh destructions, and cold and the greatest fears, and the destruction of the harvests, and an overflowing of evil, and this will be in the direction [or area] in which they are.

Chapter 52: On the conjunction of the two malefics (namely Saturn and Mars) with some planet in the degree of its own exaltation: what would follow from thence[269]

Abū Ma'shar said, look at the conjunction of the malefics (namely of Saturn and Mars) in the revolution of the year, to see whether they are joined by aspect with some other planet who is in the degree of its own exaltation (and worse than that is if by square or opposition). For if [the aspecting malefic] were Saturn, it signifies evil and destruction in the region deputed to that planet.

---

267 Reading *eorum* for *eius*.

268 Bonatti probably means these sentences to apply to all signs, instead of only to the fiery, earthy, and airy signs. Why would the watery signs be exempted?

269 See also Ch. 18 on the same topic. For more on the conjoinings of the malefics, see Chs. 57, 76, and Tr. 4, Ch. 3.

And if the aspect of Saturn were from a fixed sign, the signification will be prolonged according to the quantity of degrees which there are between their bodies: up to years, or months, or weeks, or days. For if it were a signification that ought to be perfected within the year which you are revolving, it will signify months according to the number of degrees. If however it were a signification crossing past the year or revolution, it will be prolonged for years.

If however it were from a movable sign, it will signify days according to the number of degrees. And if it were not perfected in so many days, it will signify weeks.

And if it were from a common sign, they will be weeks. And if it were not completed in so many weeks, it will signify months.

If however Saturn did not aspect it, but some planet transferred their light between them, it will signify the coming of displeasing matters over men of the region of that planet; or destruction and detriment will come over them from peoples who will not be from that region. If however some planet did not transfer the light between them, and the rays of Saturn were to touch the rays of the planet located in its own exaltation, or of the planet which was fit to be able to transfer the light between them, sorrow and grief will enter over the men of that region, which they ought not to fear: for the fear will be dissolved, and will not reach actuality, by the will of God.

If however it were from an aspect of Mars, just as I said about the aspect of Saturn (and worse than that if it were a square or opposition), the aforesaid will happen just as I said for Saturn, in a similar way and for similar reasons and more, because Mars perfects the accidents he signifies by iron and fire, and the shedding of blood.

Chapter 53: On the Lord of the fourth, if it were in the house of pilgrimage at the hour of the revolution: what it would signify

If at the hour of the revolution there were incarcerated people in the city or region in which you are, just as sometimes is wont to happen, and you wished to know what is going to happen [to them] from that in the revolution, look at the Lord of the fourth from the Ascendant, and see whether it is in the ninth: because if it were in it, it signifies the pilgrimage of those who were in prisons in the city or region in which you are revolving, and the departure from their prisons in the revolution. And this will happen to them without the permission and will of the king or civil authority, or others who are in charge of that region. I say this [will be so] unless the significator of the king aspects the Lord of the 4th from a trine or sextile aspect (because then it will be from his will). If however it were from a square aspect or the opposition, then they will depart not only without his permission but even contrary to his will and orders. And if the significator of the king or the chief were in the ninth, and the Lord of the fourth were to commit its own disposition to him, it signifies that the same king or chief himself will lead the conquered people from the prisons by his own will. And if the Lord of the ninth did not receive the disposition from the Lord of the fourth in the ninth, it signifies that an enemy of the king or chief will lead the incarcerated people from the prisons.

And Abū Ma'shar said, commingle the conjunction of the planets with each other, and judge according to their commixture.

Chapter 54: What it would signify if one of the planets commits its own disposition to another in the revolution

You will even see whether one of the planets commits its own disposition to another in the revolution.[270] For if the significator of the king were to commit his own disposition to Saturn, the religious, those serving their religion, and old and decrepit men, and those doing heavy works will find good from the king; and the king will spend money on the buildings of the religious, even in their own properties.[271] And if Saturn were then above the earth, he will build a royal building. And if he were below the earth, he will build canals and ditches, and aqueducts, and will clear lands, and more so if he were in the Ascendant somewhere near [around] its end, more strongly or in the third or the ninth, and he will be occupied in heavy works.

And if he were to commit it to Jupiter, noble citizens and great men, and skilled men, famous, and bishops and the like, will achieve good from the king.

And if he were to commit it to Mars, bellicose soldiers, and the bearers of arms, and leaders of armies, and those engaging in wars, will achieve good

---

[270] Reading *revolutione* for *commissione*.
[271] *Etiam in suis propriis.*

from the king; and they will be honored by him, and he will hear them and bring them closer to himself.

And if he were to commit it to the Sun, those near [or relatives of] the king will find good from him, and especially those who are fit for a kingdom.

And if he were to commit it to Venus, women and all those of whom Venus is the significatrix, will find good from the king, and he will bring them into his household.[272]

And if he were to commit it to Mercury, then it signifies that the wise, or advisors of royal matters, scribes, sculptors, [and] painters will find useful good and favor from the king in that same year or revolution; and he will listen to them, and will bring them into his household.

If however he were to commit it to the Moon, it signifies that those who are signified by that planet to which she is joined, and to which she herself sends disposition, will find good from the king, and likewise sailors.

You may say the same about the Lord of the ninth: which if he were to commit his own disposition to the aforesaid planets in the revolution, the aforesaid people will find [good] from the Pope or from other bishops and the like, according to what was said about the significator of the king and the king.

---

[272] *Domesticabitur.* This term is related to the Greek *oikêios*, referring both to the household and what belongs to or is proper to oneself. The basic idea is that such people will have greater influence upon, and be more intimate with, the king; but it may also literally mean that they will be in the king's house.

Chapter 55: If some planet were the Lord of the Year: what it would signify in every sign, and in every triplicity, and first concerning Saturn[273]

Even though Saturn is naturally a malefic, still he can sometimes signify good and fortune accidentally, and so with every malefic. And even a benefic, even though it naturally signifies good, still it can sometimes signify evil accidentally. Therefore a malefic signifies evil and impediment through its own nature; and if it is joined with another malefic, or were to aspect him from any aspect, and he himself were impeded, he impedes [the other]. If however he were free from impediments and well disposed, and were joined with him from a trine or sextile aspect, he will not impede [the other], but will signify an adaptation to the good.

Likewise if a benefic were impeded and weak, its signification will be weakened. Whence if some impeded malefic were to aspect him, or another [planet] who was of bad condition, he will take up his malice, and will signify evil, and impediment, and the impediment will be according to the nature of the malefic impeding the benefic.

Therefore, after you have discovered the Lord of the Year, and the significator of the common people or the rustics, and it were in Aries or Leo or Sagittarius, it signifies the appearance of things at which men will have wonder in the cities and regions or lands over which the sign rules, and especially in the eastern parts; and this will be more concerning the wealthy and great men and powerful people exceeding the common magnates and nobles; and they will come to be through shrewd and ingenious men, and those hiding their own matters, and the like, and saying nothing about them.[274] And signs and wondrous portents will be shown, and this under the form of beautiful appearances and imitations.[275] You will then see whether he who rules the revolution is a benefic or a malefic.

If indeed it were a malefic, and it were Saturn, and he were free from impediments (namely made fortunate and strong), he signifies the good condition and good disposition of his own significations. If however he were impeded and

---

[273] This chapter and many of those following are based on the *Flowers*, or the texts on which the *Flowers* is based. I will not always indicate the source of the paraphrases of the *Flowers* or *OGC*, in part because there are often so many differences between the known texts of Abū Ma'shar and Bonatti, that it would be tedious and confusing to enumerate them. Readers interested in the *Flowers* may refer to the second edition of my own translation of it (2007).
[274] *Per homines…occultantes sua, & similia, & silentes illa.* I am not sure what exactly this is supposed to signify.
[275] *Hypocrisis,* lit. "false sanctity," but perhaps "surface appearances."

of bad condition in the hour of the revolution, he signifies impediment and the bad disposition of all of his significations, and those which are in his division, the which significations are the wealthy, old things, the religious, religious men living under a Rule, Jews, farmers, old men, and decrepit men, and the like. Discord will arise between men, and they will even abound in lying, and they will condemn each other.

And if Saturn were of a good condition, and well disposed in the place in which he then is, he will signify patience and subtlety, and the inquiry into all matters, both noble and common, in that year. And he signifies that the rustics will obey their masters or kings, and will be humble to them; and the empire or kingdom will be raised up, or the rulership of the region in which you are revolving the year. And its fame and name will be increased.

And if Saturn were of a bad condition, and evil or impediment were threatened in the revolution, and Jupiter were to aspect him by a trine or sextile aspect, and [Jupiter] were free, namely made fortunate and strong, he breaks the malice of Saturn, and abolishes it; nor does he determine it to harm or impede.

If however the Sun were to aspect [Saturn] from a trine or sextile aspect, nor were [the Sun] cadent from the Ascendant or from an angle (except for the 10th), nor were he otherwise made unfortunate, he will break one-third of Saturn's malice.

If however another benefic were to aspect [Saturn], and it were made fortunate and strong by the said aspects, or Jupiter [were to aspect] from a square aspect, it will break and abolish half of Saturn's malice. However, from the other aspects the benefic decreases Saturn's malice according to what its nature [or condition] is. If however a benefic (who would abolish or decrease Saturn's malice) did not aspect, it signifies the death of the wealthy and of great men, and their envy toward one another, and accusations, and their neglectfulness, and the hatred of the common people (and those subject to them) against them. It even signifies death because of waters, and impediment and fear, and death in the land or region which is signified by the sign in which he then is.

But if [Saturn] were oriental, in his own light, direct, fast in course, or in one of his own dignities, or in the dignity of some planet who is friendly to him (like Jupiter and both luminaries), and he is joined to [that planet] and receives him, and were in a good place from the Ascendant, and in his own *haym*, he signifies that men in that year or revolution will apply themselves to the disposition or heavy and laborious works, like the works of waters, the planting of trees, the collecting together and raising up of groves, and the clearing of land, and their care, the building of cities and castles and houses or palaces, and such like.

Chapter 56: On the corporal conjunction of Saturn and Jupiter

Which if Jupiter were joined to him corporally, the works which men do will be with silence, and they will work by religious means, and with the appearance of faith, and the observance of the precepts of justice. However if he were to aspect him by a trine or sextile aspect (and better than that, if it were with reception), it signifies that supremacy[276] will come over the kings and great men who are in the regions over which the sign in which Jupiter then is, is in charge (and matters over which they rejoice).

If however he were to aspect him from the opposition, it signifies that the contrary of what I told you will happen to it; because it signifies that contentions of war will come to the kings or the wealthy or great men who are in the division of the sign in which Saturn is, from the regions which are in the division of the sign in which Jupiter is[277]—from the kings or great men, or the wealthy of his regions.

And Abū Ma'shar said this will be according to the quantity of degrees which there are between Saturn and Jupiter, and the place of the conjunction, up to the hour in which the war and contrariety is. And he said if the aspect of Jupiter to Saturn were from the square aspect, instead of wars there will be differences between them in the matters [or things] which there are in the division of Saturn. And if Saturn were in Taurus, or Leo, or Sagittarius, or Pisces, or even in Aries, and Jupiter were to aspect him, it signifies the increase of the goods of the wealthy and great men and nobles in that year. And if the aspect were a trine or sextile, and he [Saturn?] were in a good place from the Ascendant, it signifies that good and joy (and what pleases them) will come to the rustics or common people from the nobles or great men.

---

[276] I believe this means that such men will enjoy greater authority, not that they will be oppressed (*dominatio* can also mean tyranny).

[277] Perhaps this is because Jupiter, being faster than Saturn will be applying his light and significations to Saturn (and not the other way around).

Chapter 57: If Mars were joined to Saturn in the revolution, and he were of good condition: what it would signify[278]

And if Saturn were the Lord of the Year or Revolution, and were of good condition, and likewise Mars, and [Mars] were to aspect him by a trine or sextile aspect, and each were to receive the other by domicile or by exaltation or by two other dignities, or both were received by one planet, it signifies that in that same year the substance of the common people or the vulgar or rustics will be increased, and their honor and reputation will be commingled with great men and the wealthy. If however Mars were to aspect him, or were to be joined to him corporally, and [Mars] were of bad condition, it signifies the destruction of the standing of the wealthy and great men in the revolution, who were in the division of Aries or Leo or Sagittarius (in short, with great delay), and those who are in the division of the sign in which each of them is. The citizens of those regions will act badly toward each other, and there will be little piety between them, and no compassion.

But if their aspect were a trine or sextile, it signifies that donations will come to the nobles or wealthy or the magnates who are in the division of Aries, Leo and Sagittarius (and likewise concerning which they rejoice and are made happy), from the citizens who are in the division of the sign in which Mars is. Even they and the other inhabitants of the regions will be of good condition, and pleasing things will come to them from the regions which are in the division of the sign in which Mars is.

If however it were by the opposition or a square aspect, without reception, it signifies the contrary of what was said. For instead of donations and other pleasing things, evils, injuries, quarrels, contentions, and contrarieties will come between the wealthy or nobles and magnates of the regions which are in the division of the sign in which Mars is, and the wealthy and the magnates of the aforesaid regions. For they will rise up in them because of battles, and they will strive against them to expel them from their cities and regions, nor will this continue through them; and the roads between them will be cut off, nor will things be permitted to be carried from these regions to those; even the whole of the citizenry in the regions which are in the division of the sign in which Mars is, will strive to wound and offend the citizens of the other, aforesaid regions.

And if Mars were joined corporally to Saturn, it signifies war, and the shedding of blood, and a multitude of fevers; it even signifies quartan fevers, and

---

[278] See also Chs. 18, 52, 76; and Tr. 4, Ch. 3.

pestilences in the eastern parts, and it signifies young men, and a battle and much killing by iron will fall between the wealthy and the magnates.

And Abū Ma'shar said the *annona* will be oppressed, and the wine; and butter[279] will be multiplied. And he said that if Mars were near the Ascendant of the year, there will be many battles, and there will be pains of the eyes, and inseparable infirmities;[280] and thunders will be multiplied, and there will be detriment in the earth of every kind, unless Jupiter and Venus were to work to the contrary; which if they were to aspect [Saturn and Mars], they will break their malice; and only Jupiter can break the malice of each and lead them back to good.

Chapter 58: If the Sun were joined to Saturn in the revolution, and they were both of good condition

If however Saturn were the Lord of the Year or Revolution, and the Sun were joined to him, and both were of good condition, it signifies that the wealthy or great men of that region will be engaged in their own affairs in the seeking of a realm, and of a high and beautiful mastery of what pertains to the nobles or the magnates. And this, even in the part turning to the side of honest and the highest pleasing things.[281] If indeed the aspect were a trine or sextile, donations will come to those who are in the division of the sign in which the Sun is.[282]

And Abū Ma'shar said, good[283] will be taken away from these parts, and things for sale; and matters will be carried away from those things which are signified by the Sun; the merriments of men will be increased, and their dignities. If however the aspect were by the opposition, instead of donations will come quarrels and war, and contrariety, nor will the things for sale be carried away from one of the regions to the other; and it will be the contrary of

---

[279] *Butyrum*. Why butter would be multiplied is unclear to me.

[280] I.e., chronic illness.

[281] *Et hoc etiam in parte declinante ad latus honestatis & placabilitatis altissimi.* I am unsure of what this signifies, especially the business about the "part turning" (*parte declinante*). *Pars* can mean "side" or "direction," but I am not sure how that improves the sentence's clarity. Perhaps this is one of Bonatti's many snide remarks about powerful people–that they will not only be pursuing their usual selfish ends, but even the ones that are honest and good?

[282] Abū Ma'shar (*Flowers*) says donations and service will come upon the wealthy who are in the division of *Saturn*, from the wealthy who are in the division of the sign of the *Sun*.

[283] The rest of the sentence suggests this should be *goods*, i.e., things for market or possessions.

what was said. And shameful and terrible rumors will come instead of the earlier happy things. Indeed if the aspect were a square, Abū Ma'shar said there will not be wars, nor will battles be multiplied, but there will be quarrels and discords between the wealthy and the magnates.

Chapter 59: If Venus were joined to Saturn in the revolution, and they were of good condition

And if Saturn were the Lord of the Year or Revolution, and Venus had joined herself to him, it signifies the seeking of venereal things like games, delights, singing, rest, the cultivation of venereal things,[284] and similar things in which men delight; and that the rustics will be commingled with the wealthy from the beginning of the revolution, but their being together in one household[285] will not last. If however Venus were to aspect him from a trine or sextile aspect, donations and sharing of households will come to the wealthy who are in the division of the sign in which Saturn is, from the citizens who are in the cities which are in the division of the sign in which Venus is; and pleasing things will come to them, and what will be conveyed to them will be of the nature of Venus.

And Abū Ma'shar said, if however she were to aspect him from the opposition, instead of donations and pleasing things there will be wars and contrarieties, and the wealthy will proceed to war with the wealthy; and what was conveyed will be cut off from those cities; and the substance from those parts will be decreased. And he said the *census* will be broken, and evil rumors will come, and the good condition will be turned into evil, and quarreling and grief, and sorrow. And the root of all of these things will be from women and because of women, and venereal things; and men will be more honest than usual—and more so if Saturn were to receive her and the revolution were at night. If however she were to aspect him from a square aspect, Abū Ma'shar said that there will not be battles appearing; but there will be diversity in the matters between the wealthy and the common people; and there will be dissensions and most ferocious discords between the citizens of those cities or regions—such that if a father were a citizen of one of those cities which are in the division of the sign in which Saturn is, and a son were a citizen of one of the others which are in the division of the sign in which Venus is, they will not

---

[284] Bonatti undoubtedly means sexual pleasure.
[285] *Domesticitas.*

agree in those things which they ought to do. Likewise they [will] quarrel and contend in their own business matters, and will talk about their business openly to others and between themselves.

Chapter 60: On Mercury, if he were joined to Saturn in the revolution, and they [were] of good condition

If however Saturn were the Lord of the Year or Revolution and Mercury had joined himself to him, it signifies that there will be men (and especially wealthy and great men) of a will to acquire pretenses,[286] and eloquence of speaking and of philosophy and astronomy and medicine and dialectics. Likewise he who was born under such a figure will apply himself in this, and it will be made fruitful, and he will succeed in them.

And Abū Ma'shar said the appearance of these things will be in this time [or season], in the wealthy and the citizens of the regions which are in his division. And if Mercury were to aspect him from a trine or sextile aspect, every good thing will come upon the wealthy from them; and merchandise for sale will be taken away from them;[287] and substance will be multiplied, and the *census* from them; and this will be praised in the cities which are in the division of Saturn and the sign in which he is; and the merchandise will often be of the aforesaid Mercurial [sort]. And they will be firm and stable in their counsels. If however he were to aspect him from the opposition, instead of donations and sharing a household there will be contrarieties and war; and these wealthy people will proceed contrary to them, in order to overcome them, and to vanquish and expel them from their own homes. And whatever good was conveyed from them to them,[288] will be cut off; and substance will be decreased from the same parts; and the *census* will be broken; and evil rumors will be heard, and the good will be hidden; and evil will appear from those cities, and more strongly so if Mercury were impeded by the malefics, or had some commingling with them. If however he were made fortunate by the benefics, then it will impede less, but it will not abolish the impediment of the opposition. If indeed the aspect were a square, it will be less than this, nor will war appear; however there will be

---

[286] *Simulationes*, which can also mean "deceits."

[287] I take this to mean they will sell their goods successfully—otherwise their money would not be multiplied, as the next clause states.

[288] I.e., through business transactions (see above). Bonatti is talking about trade wars and embargoes.

differences between these wealthy or great men, and between the wealthy and the rustics.

And Abū Ma'shar said the cause of this matter will be a Mercurial thing, just as he expounded this in his greater book,[289] according to how he himself testified. Understand this, and keep it in your mind.

Chapter 61: On the conjunction of the Moon with Saturn in the revolution, and [if] they are both of good condition

Indeed if Saturn were the Lord of the Year or Revolution, and the Moon were joined to him, there will be an appearance of legates, and rumors, and explorers, and the constituting of the affairs of boasters; and this will be among the wealthy and magnates, and even in the common people; and they will wish to be placed on an equal footing with great men in that revolution.

And if the Moon were then to aspect Saturn from a trine or sextile aspect, it signifies that donations and things over which they will rejoice, will come to great or noble men who are in the division of the sign in which the Moon is; and goods for sale and substances will be conveyed from those cities, and their *census* will be multiplied from them.

And Abū Ma'shar said these things will be brought away to the wealthy who are in the division of the sign in which Saturn is, and they will mostly be lunar things; and men will profit from planting. And he said if the aspect of the Moon and Saturn were from the opposition, it will be the contrary of what was said: for instead of donations and good things, there will be contrariety and wars; and they (namely the wealthy who are in the division of the sign in which the Moon is) will enter into their [own] harm and weakness; and what was brought from those parts to these will be destroyed; and the *census* will be broken, and the commercial roads will be cut; and evil rumors will arise and appear; and good will be destroyed and turned into evil. And if the aspect of the Moon to Saturn were a square, it will signify that war will not appear; however there will be contrariety between wealthy and great men, and the rustics or common people; and even between neighbors, because of lunar things.

---

[289] In the *Flowers*, it refers at the end of this paragraph to a "greater book of natures" (*in libro naturarum maiori*), probably Abū Ma'shar's *Great Book of Natures* (*Kitab al-taba'i' al-kabir*). The placement of this sentence suggests that Bonatti is cribbing from the *Flowers* rather than from another text for his material in this section.

Chapter 62: What Saturn would signify in every sign, and in every triplicity, and in every house, whether he were the Lord of the Year or not

If Saturn were the Lord of the Year, and were in Aries or its triplicity, it signifies the severity of the matters of great and noble men, who are in the eastern parts; but chiefly in Aries.[290]

Whence if he were in Aries, he signifies a multitude of winds, and the death of women of prayer, or of those pertaining to religion, and this in the areas of Thoracey[291] and Aiaroc;[292] also the scarcity of provisions and wine and butter, and even of oils and fats. Indeed if he were impeded, it signifies a multitude of robbers and cutters of roads, and many tribulations in the revolution. And if he were the sole significator, and were cadent from the Ascendant, not aspecting it, and he were direct, it signifies that hindrance and distress will enter over the nobles.

And Abū Ma'shar said if he were retrograde, he will destroy the houses of substances and their coffers; and more severely so if he were to receive the disposition of Mars, because then it signifies severe cold and the death of animals, in addition to what he said about battles and wars. If however he did not aspect Mars, the cold of winter will be severe, according to the disposition of the region, and animals will die in it. And he said if he were not retrograde, it signifies that there will be contention between those doing business together, and plundering, and evil, and more strongly so if Mars were to aspect him from an angle. If however he were to aspect him from a cadent, the impediment will be decreased, or rather will practically be wholly abolished.

And Māshā'allāh said[293] if [Saturn] were direct in an angle, it signifies many rains, and the contentions of the wealthy; and more strongly so, if he were to receive the rulership of Mars and his strength—for it signifies then that the rustics or common people will contend with the king. And if he were retrograde the condition of men will be burdened. And he said if [Saturn] were to receive the disposition of Mars and from the Moon at the same time, it signifies severe cold and the death of animals, and wars, and battles.

---

[290] It is unclear whether Bonatti means, "but chiefly in the areas *ruled by Aries*," or "but [the effects will be] in the *eastern parts* chiefly when Saturn is in Aries." Bonatti seems to have added this last clause himself, since the *Flowers* does not say this.

[291] Unknown.

[292] This may be Slavs or Russians (from *ar-Rus*, reading *Aiaroc* as *alaroc* with a soft *c*). See *OGC* p. 515 n.1, which also attributes the "Slavs" to Aries.

[293] *De Rev. Ann.*, Ch. 46.

Pay attention, in the revolutions of the years of the world, to see if Saturn were in a fixed sign: because then this signifies mortality, and a scarcity and decrease of things born from the earth. But in Leo [it is] stronger and more difficult and longer-lasting than in the others. Indeed in Scorpio [it is] less than in Leo; in Taurus, less than in Scorpio; in Aquarius, less than in Taurus. And by however much worse he were disposed, by that much more will his malice be increased; and more strongly so if Mars were to help him, unless Jupiter (who diminishes [Saturn's] malice according to his own disposition) were to work to the contrary.

If indeed [Saturn's] latitude were northern, it signifies the corruption of the air, and its thickness and darkness in the required and usual seasons, more so than usual. If indeed his latitude were southern, it signifies the severity of cold and a multitude of ice in its own seasons.

And if he were oriental, he signifies the griefs and sorrows of wealthy or great men, and their thoughts; and it seems that this will happen to them because of the cold [or ice]. If however he were occidental, it signifies an earthquake is going to come in that year; and you will know this by the quantity of the degrees which there are;[294] and he signifies [this] especially in the eastern parts; however, it is to be feared everywhere you revolve the year and were to find it so; but if he were oriental, it will be less than this; and less again if he were made fortunate and strong. If however he happened to be retrograde, it will be much worse.

Chapter 63: On Leo

Know that if he were in Leo, and his latitude were northern, it signifies a multitude of rains, and the corruption of the matters of great men and common men, and the destruction of the acquisitions of those doing business together.

And if he were oriental, it signifies infirmities are going to come to the rustics and low-class persons. If however he were occidental, it signifies pestilences which will come in the earth, and mortality.

Indeed if he were retrograde, it signifies hardships are going to come from the accidents which come to men, and that they will be prolonged and will be lasting. If however he were direct, it signifies their ease.

---

[294] Bonatti does not explain this point. Perhaps he means the number of degrees Saturn has transited in the sign in which he is? How does this get translated into time?

Chapter 64: On Sagittarius

And if he were in Sagittarius, and his latitude were northern, it signifies a multitude of strong waters, and the coldness of winter.[295]

And Abū Ma'shar said if he were oriental, it signifies the nearness of the wealthy from their regions.[296] And if he were occidental, it signifies battles between men (namely noble and great ones), and discords will fall between them.

And if he were retrograde, it signifies severity in the matters and goods of men, and battles and wars between them. And if he were direct, it signifies the prosperity of those journeying [or going on pilgrimages] by earth and by water.

Chapter 65: On Taurus and its triplicity

If however he were in Taurus and its triplicity, it signifies the detriment of wealthy and great men; and this will be in the southern parts in the division of the sign in which Saturn is, but chiefly in Taurus.[297]

Whence if he were in Taurus and were in an angle, direct, it signifies contentions and wars, likewise [the impediments] of quadrupeds (and especially bulls and female cattle[298]), and especially in the land deputed to the sign in which he is.

And Abū Ma'shar said if he were in an earthy sign, it signifies the destruction of those things which are from its seeds, namely a scarcity of trees, and detriment from vermin who fall in them, and locusts. And he said there will be tribulations and injury, and tremors, and earthquakes; and the destructions of cities and villages and houses.

Moreover, if Saturn were in Taurus in the hour of the revolution (whatever kind of Ascendant it is), or in Leo, or in Scorpio, or in Aquarius, it signifies battles and famine, or the dearth of things born from the earth. And if he were impeded, it signifies mortality in addition, and it will be feared concerning great men in the revolution; and this will be worse and stronger in Leo than in

---

[295] Bonatti omits Saturn in Sagittarius with southern latitude.
[296] *Proximitatem divitum de regionibus suis.* An awkward phrase, but it seems to mean that the wealthy will be close to home.
[297] See my previous footnote on Aries and its triplicity.
[298] *Bovum et vaccarum.*

Taurus; stronger in Taurus than in Scorpio; stronger in Scorpio than in Aquarius (in which these things will happen less than in any of the others).

And if Mars[299] were joined to him, and the Moon joins to them, and especially with Saturn in the [?] latitude,[300] in whatever sign this was, or from whatever one, or whatever kind of Ascendant it was, it signifies famine and mortality. Indeed if he [she?] were joined to Mars, it signifies the detriment of kings and their changes,[301] and battles in the parts of that sign in which the conjunction is deputed;[302] and many sheddings of blood, changes, and battles. And if he[303] were retrograde, it signifies in addition the destruction of the harvests; and it even signifies wars in many regions or lands and directions (especially those of the east and the south more so than in the other directions); and more severely so if he were then in the 10th: because then the evil will be more general; and there will be impediments in boys and youths.

And Abū Ma'shar said if he were removed from the angle in these signs, and were to aspect the Ascendant, and were direct, there will be what he said happened in this chapter below. Saturn in the third from it signifies the death of the king, by the testimony of the matter of years.[304]

And Māshā'allāh said[305] it will destroy seeds, and the harvests will be few. If however he did not aspect the Ascendant, the evil will be less. And if he were retrograde, it signifies the destruction of seeds, and the harvest will be small; and it will be feared for youths in that year. And if he were cadent from the Ascendant, not aspecting it, and he were direct, nor did Mars aspect him nor the Ascendant, it signifies the decreasing of the aforesaid evils, because then he could not harm much, unless Mars were to work to the contrary. And if he were retrograde, and Mars were to impede him, it signifies the destruction of the harvests, and mortality in the lands which the sign (in which he was then) rules.

---

[299] It is unclear to me whether this refers back to Saturn being in a fixed sign, or to Saturn in Taurus. This sentence is somewhat similar to a statement in Mash'allah pertaining to Saturn in the fiery triplicity, but there are enough differences that I am not sure what Bonatti's source is.

[300] Bonatti undoubtedly means either northern or southern in particular, but does not say which.

[301] *Mutationes*, i.e., regime change from one king to another.

[302] I.e., in the areas *over which* the part of the sign (in which the conjunction *is*), is deputed.

[303] I am not sure what planet Bonatti is referring to, but it must be either Saturn or Mars.

[304] I do not know what this means.

[305] *De Rev. Ann.*, Ch. 46, but Bonatti begins his own elaboration after the second sentence.

Chapter 66: If the Moon suffered eclipse

And if at that time the Moon suffered eclipse,[306] it signifies killing in the parts of the east, west, and even the south. And it signifies snow and rains in the lands in which it is used to raining. Indeed in the others, [it signifies] the alteration of the air. Indeed it signifies an abundance of seeds or harvests, and of creeping things; and the death of bulls and female cows; and there will be little wine and butter in direction of the west.

And if [Saturn's] latitude were northern, it signifies the goodness of the air, and its beauty and the goodness of its complexion. It will even signify useful and profitable rains, nor those harming seeds, and the like, but those helping them. And there will be a middling marketplace value of things born of the earth, and even [that] of other things, even if not completely [so]. If however his latitude were southern, it signifies pestilences, mortalities, and tremors and comminglings with the corruption of the air, and its worsening, and the scarcity of its goodness.

And if he were oriental, it signifies a multitude of rains, or infirmities for that reason. But if he were occidental, it signifies the fear of the wealthy and the magnates, or nobles, because of the rustics or common people; and the commingling of their matters.

If however he were retrograde, it signifies the death of magnates and nobles, and a multitude of trembling and distress between men. If indeed he were direct, it signifies long-lasting infirmities taking place in the upper parts of men.

Chapter 67: On Virgo

Indeed if Saturn were in Virgo, and his latitude were northern, it signifies the goodness of the winds, and their sweetness, and their strengthening in the times of the harvests and sowing. And if his latitude were southern, it signifies the scarcity of rains, and the wasting of the waters of fountains [or springs].

If however he were oriental, it signifies that women who are pregnant in that year will abort because of the winds; and even because of copulation after becoming pregnant. But if he were occidental, it signifies quick fevers in that year, and terrible tremblings.

---

[306] In this chapter I believe Bonatti is still talking about the condition of Saturn in Taurus in a revolution; but it is unclear whether this chapter refers to revolutions wherein the eclipse takes place at the same hour as the revolution, or one in which the Moon *will* be eclipsed.

And if he were retrograde, it signifies the fear of the king of that region from his own enemies, that they will become contrary concerning him.[307] Indeed if he were direct, it signifies gaining by that king over his enemies, and his strength against them.

Chapter 68: On Capricorn

Indeed if he were in Capricorn and his latitude were northern, it signifies the good disposition of the air, and the moderation of the rains. If however his latitude were southern, it signifies the shadowiness of the air in the winter, and its cloudiness, and cold.

And if he were oriental, it signifies the bad condition of the magnates and nobles in that revolution, and their terror, and that they will not behave well with the rustics or common people; and that they will act together poorly. If indeed he were occidental, it signifies a multitude of locusts in the usual areas, and great heat, harming and devastating the harvests.

However, if he were retrograde it signifies that the rustics or common people will be mixed together, and will grow angry with one another. If however he were direct, it signifies the good disposition of the wealthy and the magnates or nobles; and that they will behave well toward everyone and amongst themselves, and that they will love justice and rectitude, and mildness, and they will practice [mildness].

Chapter 69: On Gemini and its triplicity, if Saturn were in it

If indeed he were in Gemini or its triplicity, it signifies that whatever he signified (whether the signification were good or bad), will mostly appear in the western [parts]. But if he were in Gemini and were in an angle, direct, it signifies the severity of the northern winds, and the coldness of the winter of that year.

And Abū Ma'shar said there will be detriment and destruction in birds, and infirmities will happen to men from what is cold and dry, in whatever commixture of the hot and wet.[308] And there will be lying and contentious men, and even the shedding of blood is signified from this. And he said if [Saturn] were in

---

[307] The Latin is stated a little more forcefully, but more awkwardly: "The fear...that they will come into something contrary to him," emphasizing their action by "coming," rather than simply having contrary feelings.

[308] I do not understand how the cold and dry are related to the hot and wet in this sentence.

an airy sign, it signifies the severity of the cold, and a multitude of ice and clouds, and the corruption of the complexion of the air, and thunders, and flashings and lightning bolts, and impediment from a multitude of rains (and especially if he were from the fifth degree of the sign up to in the twenty-sixth); and there will be impediment from these lightning bolts, and from glowing sparks running to and fro in the air, below the spear-shafts.[309]

And if he were retrograde, it signifies the contrarieties of the kings and the nobles, and magnates or the wealthy; and death will be feared concerning it in that year or in that revolution, for the reason that it signifies an earthquake that is going to come in that same year.

And if he were removed from the angle, the winds (both eastern and western) will be multiplied.

And Abū Ma'shar said it even signifies the severity of the cold; and men will be in changes [from place to place]. But if in addition he were retrograde, men will likewise be in motion; and there will be infirmities from winds, and rains; and dew and hoar-frost. If however he were cadent, not regarding[310] the Ascendant, and he were direct, these things will happen in the regions which are in the division of the sign in which Saturn then is; and the winds will be multiplied from out of the southern division. If however he were direct, these things will happen by means of fortunes, without weakness;[311] and infirmities, dissolutions, ruptures, and plundering will fall among the citizens who are in the division of the aforesaid sign, and they will happen more and more strongly among the rustics and common people, and low-class persons.

And Abū Ma'shar said, if however Saturn were in the angle of the earth [the 4th], and he were the Lord of the Year in the said [airy] triplicity—or if he were not the Lord of the Year, but he were to receive the disposition of the Lord of the Ascendant of that revolution—it signifies that in that same year, and in the aforesaid places, many men will die from earthquake. Indeed, if he were to receive the disposition of the Lord of the Midheaven, it signifies battles and contrarieties in the quest for a kingdom or someone's dignity, or the destruction of the district of some city, or the land of a magnate, which he wishes to be taken away by him from another by force. And he said it signifies a multitude of waters, and the flooding of rivers, and submersions [or drownings]; even a

---

[309] *Astilibus*, from *astile*. I do not know exactly what is meant by "spear shafts," but Bonatti could be speaking about meteor showers. Perhaps the spear-shafts are long streaks of light from shooting stars or meteors?

[310] *Respiciens*, i.e., "aspecting."

[311] I am not quite sure what this means.

multitude of snow[falls], and detriment in the *annona*; and there will be a multitude of winds, and death will be signified in males.

And if his latitude were northern, it signifies the vehement blowing of winds, and the shadowiness and corruption of the air, and the changing of its color almost to black;[312] it even signifies earthquake, and especially in the areas of the sign in which he is. If however his latitude were southern, it signifies the heat of the air and its dryness; also a scarcity of rains, and a multitude of pestilences, and of pestilential [or noxious] and mortal things.

If however he were oriental, it signifies infirmities are going to come to the magnates of the land of Babylon, and to their king. Indeed if he were occidental, it signifies the dryness of the air, and a scarcity of rains—and this, if he were direct (because [if] retrograde, he will harm less).

Chapter 70: On Libra, if Saturn were in it

Abū Ma'shar said if Saturn were in Libra, and his latitude were northern, it signifies the heat of the air and its dryness; and it signifies few rains in that revolution, and the wasting[313] of waters. And if his latitude were southern, it signifies the goodness of the air, and its sweetness; nor will there be harmful winds.

And if he were oriental, it signifies the desire of shameful, criminal men. But if he were occidental, it signifies infamy is going to fall upon fornicators, and those abusing shameful sexual intercourse.

If however he were retrograde, it signifies the infirmities of male and female slaves, and of low-class people. And if he were direct, it signifies the middling quality of supplies, and particularly of barley.

And Abū Ma'shar said it signifies the rupturing of the *census* upon the king.[314]

Chapter 71: On Aquarius, if Saturn were in it

Indeed if Saturn were in Aquarius, and his latitude were northern, it signifies a multitude of rains, and the severity of cold and frost. And if his latitude were southern, it signifies a scarcity of waters, fountains, and rivers.

---

[312] *Ad latus nigredinis*, literally "to the side of blackness" or "to the surface of blackness."

[313] *Consumptionem.*

[314] *Significat confractionem census super regem.* I am not sure what this means.

If he were oriental, it signifies a scarcity of the acquisition of inheritances, and the scarcity of the substances of the rustics. And if he were occidental, it signifies a multitude of, and the strength of, burning fires.

And if he were retrograde, it signifies the severity of the same thing. And if he were direct, it signifies the death of animals which men use for their own usefulness.

Chapter 72: On Cancer and its triplicity, if Saturn were the Lord of the Revolution, and were in it or its triplicity

If however Saturn were the Lord of the Year, and were in Cancer or in its triplicity, Abū Ma'shar said whatever he were to signify (whether good or evil) will be in the northern part. But if he were in Cancer, it signifies the multiplication of waters and rains, and fishes, and locusts, and things creeping on the earth. And if Mars did not aspect him, the cold will be severe, and locusts will be multiplied; and there will be infirmities in the lands which are in the division of the sign in which Saturn is, and [in the division] of the sign which is in his opposition or square aspect. And if he were retrograde, death will be feared concerning the king of that region. If however Mars were to aspect him, without the aspect of the benefics, it signifies mortality in the aforesaid land; and evil and impediment will be multiplied. If however he did not aspect the Ascendant, rains and dew and cold will be multiplied. Indeed, if he were direct, the evil will be reduced; and more so if one of the benefics were to aspect him (unless the Moon were then in the first, because it signifies an impediment that is going to fall upon the kings and magnates of that region, and death). If however he were retrograde, and Mars were to aspect him, it signifies ruin and evil (and even locusts) in the land of the aforesaid sign and its opposition and square aspect. And if he were cadent, not aspecting the Ascendant, and he were direct, and Mars cadent from him, it signifies the security of men; and better so if he had already transited the fifteenth degree of the sign. However, there will be infirmities in the land of that sign. And if he were retrograde, and Mars were to aspect him, and the benefics were absent from him, tribulations and evils will occur to the ignoble people of those regions, and cold will be oppressive; and waters and locusts will be multiplied.

And Abū Ma'shar said there will be impediment in the water from shipwreck, and from the breaking of ships; and those on a pilgrimage by water will be endangered; aquatic animals (and those similar to them) will die. He said if indeed [Saturn] were fit, without impediment, it signifies the good of those things which I said, and the conversion of evil into good, and fitness in all of their own substances, and his signification of them.[315] And he said, look at the malefic who impedes him (which is Mars); and the Tail by conjunction and Mars by conjunction and by aspect.

And he said the peculiar signification of Saturn is over the wealthy, old things, and Jews, and religious men, and farmers, and old men, and the decrepit. Which if he were impeded at the hour of the revolution, judge destruction and impediment. And if made fortunate, judge good fortune.

And if his latitude were northern, it signifies a scarcity of waters, and the decrease of rivers and rains. If however his latitude were southern, it signifies the vigilance of men[316] in their way of life, and the smallness of their acquisition.

And if he were oriental, it signifies the corruption of the air and its shadowiness, and a multitude of cold in its own season. And if he were occidental, it signifies a multitude of rains and their corruption, and the impediment of matters from winds.

And if he were retrograde, it signifies the strength of those things which were said, and that the king of that region (which is in the division of the sign in which Saturn is) will fall into opprobrium and a very great disgrace which could not come upon him in a bigger way; and it will be compared with death. (And Māshā'allāh said[317] there will be a great battle and a powerful death). While if he were direct, it signifies the benevolent disposition of the air, and the goodness of its complexion.

Chapter 73: On Scorpio, if Saturn were in it

Indeed if Saturn were in Scorpio, and his latitude were northern, it signifies a multitude of rains, and an overflowing of waters, rivers, and their corruption. And if his latitude were southern, it signifies famine is going to come to men, and the oppressive market value of items of exchange, and especially of things born from the earth.

And if he were oriental, it signifies a multitude of wars between the wealthy and the magnates. And if he were occidental, it signifies destruction and

---

[315] Reading *et eorum significationem eius* for *et eorum significatio eius*. Meaning unclear.
[316] *Occupationem.*
[317] *De Rev. Ann.*, Ch. 46.

impediment in the sea, and of things belonging to the sea, and the occurrence of evil in them.

And if he were retrograde, it signifies pestilences in the earth, and battles. And Abū Ma'shar said if he were direct, it signifies the salvation of the clime of Babylon.

Chapter 74: If Saturn were in Pisces

And if Saturn were in Pisces, and his latitude were northern, it signifies much blowing of the northern winds, and the severity of the cold in winter. And if his latitude were southern, it signifies a tempest in the sea, and the breaking of ships for that reason; and that impediments will come to those who spend time on [or in] the water, and who work in it.

And if he were oriental, it signifies the quarrels and contrarieties of the wealthy, and mutual killings between them. But if he were occidental, it signifies that the rustics and the common people and the ignoble will be exalted, and will raise their heels[318] against the nobles and magnates, and will hurl them down and oppress them.

And if he were retrograde, it signifies the tribulations of the religious, and battles between men, and of those serving God, and of those cultivating the ways of religion, and their griefs. And Abū Ma'shar said if he were direct, he signifies the common people of the houses of religion, and of the honoring of the divine.

Chapter 75: What Saturn would signify in any house in the revolution of the year, or of the world, or of nativities, or questions, whether he is Lord of the Year or not

If Saturn were in a revolution, or in a nativity, or question:

In the first, if it were a revolution of the year of the world, it signifies the grief of many men because of something owed,[319] or because of lands. If it were a nativity or its revolution, or a question, it signifies that for the native or querent.

---

[318] This is obviously an idiom for showing disrespect.
[319] *Debiti.*

If however he were in the second, it signifies the disorder of friends in that year, and men will lose, and they will subtract from their goods.

Indeed if he were in the third, it signifies quarrels and discords that are going to come between brothers, more so than usual.

And if he were in the fourth, it signifies the destruction of buildings, and the pillaging of lands, and the detriment of seeds and treasures, and danger to come because of that; and death.

And if he were in the fifth, it signifies abortions in that year (more than usual), and the detriment of children, and griefs because of them, and contentions with heralds and legates, and that they will not exercise well what they have business with in that year.

And if he were in the sixth, it signifies the evil wills of male and female slaves against their masters, and their disobedience; and many infirmities, and the harming of small animals.

Indeed if he were in the seventh, and the sign is feminine, and its Lord a feminine planet, it signifies the evil will of women [or wives] against men [or husbands], and their disobedience. And if it were a masculine sign, or its Lord a masculine planet, it signifies the evil will of husbands against their wives; and the fraudulence of partners, and the wounding of enemies against enemies who are absent (more so than the open ones);[320] and tribulation because of lands, and often a detestable end of matters. I would tell you the same if he were so found in nativities or questions.

And if he were in the eighth, it signifies litigations because of the seeking of inheritances, or what is left by the dead, and because of the seeking of ancient things; and affliction because of death. And it signifies matters whose pain and distress or sorrow will last for a long time.

But if he were in the ninth, it signifies the destruction of faith, and the taking away of sympathy and piety, and that certain hermits or religious men will be changed from their religions, and will neglect them, and they

---

[320] *Palam.*

will even take on bad advice, and likewise with others. And certain men will be eager for low-class and horrible [matters] of alien things, like certain people who dig up the dead from their graves and rob them; and it signifies griefs and sorrows and anxieties to come to journeyers on their pilgrimages, and a long sojourn in them.

Indeed if he were in the tenth, it signifies (both in nativities or questions, and in other revolutions) grief and sorrow, and cracking down and severities on the part of the king or civil authorities,[321] and the perplexities of prison. And Abū Ma'shar said that if the Sun were the Lord of the 10th house, the king will kill him in his own prison. And if the Moon were the Lady of the 10th house, it signifies the same as the Sun, unless she is joined to Saturn. And if the Lord of the 10th house were Jupiter, the king will kill him and make him condemn himself without [there being real] guilt. And if the Lord of the 10th house were Mars, he will die because of his own fault. And if the Lady of the 10th house were Venus, it signifies prosperity and sublimity, and joy and advancement will follow from this tribulation, and the king will repent having done this, and will admit he did not act well, and he will be humbled. And if the Lord of the 10th house were Mercury, he will kill him because of an injury without explanation, when he will bear false testimony against him. And if Mercury were to aspect Mars, he will be beaten with whips. And if Mercury were with the Sun under his rays, the king will make a show of force to him, and take his substance from him, and cause the rendering of his own goods to himself. And he said, know that, among the rest of the planets, this peculiar meaning belongs to Saturn in the 10th.

And if he were in the eleventh,[322] it signifies grief and sorrow from friends, and because of friends, and the scarcity of progress in those things which one hoped, and in which one had faith concerning the good; and obstacles in matters, and their duration, and much hope in false things which profit nothing.

---

[321] Reading *potestatis* for *potestates*.

[322] Although this and the next house are designated by Arabic numerals (*11.*, *12.*), I will treat them as though they read as signs or places.

And if he were in the twelfth, he signifies impediments which will happen on the part of the king or another ruler; it even signifies that he will be captured by enemies, and one must have fear in all his affairs.

And according to how I have touched on [these matters] for you above, all of these things can be considered in revolutions of the years of the world, in revolutions of nativities, in questions, and the like, in all headings, and in anything on its own account. And what goes for Saturn is so for any other planet, both for good and for evil.

Chapter 76: On the conjunction of Saturn and Mars– what it would signify in a revolution[323]

You will even look in the revolution, when you are revolving a year (whether it is of the world or of a nativity), to see if Saturn and Mars were conjoined [corporally] in one of the twelve houses: because it signifies burdens and impediments according to the signification of the house in which they were conjoined.[324]

For if their conjunction were in the first, it signifies general evil and impediment is going to come upon the rustics and common people.

If it were in the second from the Ascendant of the revolution, it signifies the destruction of their substances and homes; and the wealthy and magnates will be forgotten by the people,[325] and will be reputed practically as being nothing, and people familiar [or close] to them will be exalted, and those serving them and their soldiers, and they will be haughty against them, nor will they wish to obey them, nor observe [their] faithfulness to them, unless only moderately or rather practically not at all.

---

[323] See also Chs. 18, 52, 57; and Tr. 4, Ch. 3.

[324] Bonatti does not specify whether this refers to (a) when Saturn and Mars are conjoined *in the hour* of the revolution, or (b) the house in which the degree of their *future* conjunction in that year.

[325] Remember that the wealthy often got much of their income through the labor of the common people and by receiving a share of legal penalties paid in court; so an affliction to their incomes would be caused by the common people's refusal to pay.

Indeed if it were in the third, Abū Ma'shar said it signifies the destruction of the houses of religion, and horrible things falling upon the religious and those cultivating God.

But if it were in the fourth, it signifies the destruction of buildings and mansions or houses.

If however it were in the fifth, it signifies destruction and impediment is going to fall upon children; and more abortions in that year than usual; and the changing of friends' wills toward each other, and even of people loving each other; and instead of love, irritation will fall amongst them, and bad will.

Indeed if it were in the sixth, it signifies impediment and detriment is going to fall upon small and great quadrupeds, and especially those which men use (like cows, horses, donkeys, camels, and the like); and on male and female slaves, and male and female servants [or attendants]; and it even signifies infirmities.

Indeed if were in the seventh, it signifies that quarrels and contentions and discords, and likewise dissensions, and many evils, will fall among partners and others participating together in something, and even between husbands and wives; and enmities will arise amongst men.

Indeed if it were in the eighth, it signifies that very many men will quit their homes and habitations in which they live, and they will go by wandering through foreign lands and regions; and ruin will fall upon them, and among men there will be worries because of what is left behind by the dead, and because of the goods which they inherit from the dead, and the money of women [or wives].

And if it were in the ninth, it signifies the detriment of the religious people of the plentiful religions, such as bishops, archbishops, cardinals, and the like. And [it signifies] cutters of roads and [the detriment] of journeys (and especially the long ones), and pilgrimages by which men go far from their habitations by seeking the great and famous houses of prayer.

If it were in the tenth, it signifies the detriment of kings and magnates, and the destruction of their condition, and the death of a great king.

Indeed if were in the eleventh, it signifies dissent and anger and quarrels and discord that is going to fall between friends. And Abū Ma'shar said every one who has a friend will be changed concerning his partner; it even signifies the evil condition of the soldiers and the household members of kings.

Indeed if it were in the twelfth, it signifies impediments which will fall upon all quadrupeds, and especially upon the aforesaid (namely cows, horses, donkeys, and the like); and detriment and worsening will fall upon every sale of beasts (and particularly the large ones), both of those for riding and those not for riding.

And Abū Ma'shar said all of these will happen in the regions which are in the division of the sign in which they were conjoined; and the planet who is the Lord of the bound in which they are conjoined will be a participator; and these will likewise happen in the cities or regions which are in the division of the sign in which [the Lord of the bound of the conjunction] is.

Chapter 77: What Jupiter would signify in a revolution, in every sign and in every triplicity (if he were the Lord of the Year), and in every house (whether he were the Lord of the Year or not)

If Jupiter were the Lord of the Year and were in Aries or in its triplicity, it signifies the appearance of religions in the eastern parts which the sign (in which he is) rules; and especially if he were in Aries it signifies their appearance, and that of sects, and the observation of divine precepts and of justice and good works in that revolution; and it signifies a multitude of winds from the area of Khorasan, and the cold of winter, and rains (but not exterminated),[326] and the flooding of rivers, and the adaptation of vineyards and trees, and that the storehouses [of grain] will be good.

And if Jupiter were then of good condition, and well disposed, it signifies the multitude of substances for the citizens of the regions which he were to rule,

---

[326] *Exterminatas.* I believe this means that the cold and rains will not end soon–literally, the winds will not be "destroyed" or "driven out."

and the goodness of their condition, and their joy, and gladness, and the delight of the common people or rustics toward the wealthy and the nobles, and the magnates.

And Abū Ma'shar said if he were impeded, or of evil condition, it signifies the contrary of those things which were said. And he said, know that the workings in the matter of Jupiter, and the aspects of the planets toward him, can be compared equally to the work in the matter of Saturn. And he said Jupiter is the significator of the nobles, and judges, and bishops, and consuls and the religious, and citizens of sects. And if he were impeded, every detriment which is his, will be suffered. And he said that if he were in the human signs, or the fiery ones, it will signify the dejection of the wealthy, and the smallness of their donations, and their observing of their rank, and their worries about their neighbors; and the destruction of the kingdom of Babylon and of the Arabs, and the smallness of substances and the desire for knowledge. And this will be over the citizens of the cities which are in the division of the sign in which Jupiter were to come down. And the practicing of lies in the broad swath of men, with an assenting to evil and injury, and infirmities of the body, and the weakness of acquisitions.

Chapter 78: On his location in Leo

And if he were in Leo, it signifies the cold of winter, and a multitude of waters, and powerful and raging winds eradicating trees; and it signifies the temperance of the air and its clarity in the last half of the winter, and cold in its end, and intemperate rains in the spring more than usual; and a scarcity of waters [and] springs, and a scarcity of fodder for animals grazing in fields in the winter; and many coughs; and it signifies a fertile year.

Chapter 79: On his location in Sagittarius

And if he were in Sagittarius, it signifies the proper mixture of the air in the beginning of winter, and cold in its middle, and in its end, severe winds; and snow and ice in the spring, and southern winds, and a multitude of fodder for field animals, and the impediment of vineyards from snow and cold, and a scarcity of fruit, and the impediment of trees.

Indeed if his latitude were northern, it signifies the good complexion of the air, and a scarcity of rains. And if his latitude were southern, it signifies the corruption of the winds, and their severity.

And if he were oriental, it signifies joy and happiness, and the good condition of wealthy and great men, and the nobles, and their joy and happiness, and that they will be [engaged] in games and dancing. And Abū Ma'shar said if he were occidental, it signifies the loftiness of the wise and the wealthy and the nobles.

And if he were retrograde, it signifies impediment in the sea; nor will it be wholly safe to sail. And if he were direct, it signifies a multitude of fishes and of animals spending time in water, and their health.

Chapter 80: What Jupiter would signify in every revolution of the year, whether of the world or a nativity or a question, whether he is the Lord of the Year or not

And if Jupiter (in a revolution or nativity or question) were in the first, if it were a revolution of a year of the world, it signifies in that year that [people] will show respect, one to another, according to how it will be fitting to show respect to everyone according to his condition; and they will observe honesty and beauty, and cleanliness and faith, and religion, and will spend their time in instruction and reason, and the purpose of their intention will be to be engaged in those things which pertain to the salvation of souls, unless Saturn and Mars were to work to the contrary. And [these things] will happen to men whom pre-eminence is suited, and the like. If however it were a nativity or question, or their revolution, it signifies something else for the native or querent.

Indeed if he were in the second, it signifies their eagerness and intention to aggregate money, and in their accumulation and attainment; and this with the restraint of a good and licit and fitting mind.

And if he were in the third, it signifies good fortune from one brother to another, and between them; and men will rejoice because of their relatives, and especially younger ones, and first or older sisters.

But if he were in the fourth, he signifies the increase of the goods of many men from what is left behind by the dead, and from inheritances and estates, or from hidden or unexpected treasures, and from ancient things; and griefs will be taken away from men, and often things about which they could be happy and rejoice will happen to them, and evil and sad thoughts will be taken away from them; even quarrels and every horrible thing will cease.

Indeed if he were in the fifth, it signifies an increase in children, and their good condition, and that there will not be abortions in that year, except perhaps some chance ones. And it signifies success because of them, and honest matters will come to be which merit praise. And it signifies the good condition of the wealthy and magnates, and of the nobles, and the usefulness of things about which men have trust in the good.

But if he were in the sixth, he signifies good and profit in quadrupeds, and especially in small ones (like sheep and the like); and he signifies the health of persons, and a scarcity of infirmities, except for in the regions and places naturally infirm (however, infirmities will be decreased in them). And it signifies usefulness from male and female slaves, and the obedience of male and female servants.

If however he were in the seventh, it signifies usefulness and good and joy from the direction of women and marriage or marriage celebrations, and good from the direction of partners, and their faithfulness; and it even signifies victory over enemies from that region; and even for a native or querent.

Indeed if he were in the eighth, it signifies the general taking away of evil, death, and suspicion in that region, if it were a revolution of a year of the world. If however it were a revolution of a nativity or question, it signifies the evil condition of the native or querent, which will come to him because of enemies; and that he himself will fall into their hands unless he watches himself well; and that burdens and impediment will follow from thence. However, ultimately it will be ended in an end that must be borne. And he will not be evil, or rather he could be praised in a certain manner.

And if he were in the ninth, it signifies profitable journeys, and especially long and useful ones in that year, and that there will be faith between men, and honesty and good; and there will be dreams, and often true ones; and the course of the dreams will take place according to the nature of the planet who is being separated from Jupiter then, or from whom he may be separated, if he were separated from one; and the dreams will have to be laid out in that revolution according to the nature of the significations; and this can even play a role in other dreams.

Indeed if he were in the tenth, it signifies the accumulation of substances, and their collection, and men will strive to be praised, and those who must be praised will be praised according to his condition, and honesty will reside among them.

If however he were in the eleventh, it signifies praise and good reputation from the direction of friends, and that men will rejoice, and they will be in gladness; and a good effecting and profiting in matters about which men will have trust, and about which they hope for good.

Indeed if he were in the twelfth, it signifies impediments which will occur from the direction of servitude; and it signifies poverty and need; and it signifies the burdens which will take place from the direction of slaves, and on the occasion of them; and even from the direction of the servitude into which men fall; and they will be saddened by accidents which will come to them on the occasion of quadrupeds, and especially large animals like horses, cows, and the like.

Chapter 81: What Mars would signify if he were the Lord of the Year, in any triplicity and in each sign; and in each house, whether he is the Lord of the Year or not

However, if Mars were the Lord of the Year and were in Aries or in its triplicity, it signifies powerful winds and many and varied mutations of the air in the eastern parts. It even signifies pains of the eyes, and a scarcity of rains; and it signifies war in the same parts, and the overflowing of the *annona*. It even signifies evil and anger and injury and quarrels that are going to be in the same parts, in the cities in which he rules, and those which are in the division of Aries. And it signifies victory in war for the citizens of those cities and the inhabitants of that region, over their enemies who have come from other parts to these in order to harm them; and [the enemies'] flight; and it signifies their

[own] and their king's engagement in martial things; and that fathers and more aged people will teach and instruct their children, and other young men, in the struggles and exercise of wars.

And if Mars were then of good condition, it signifies victory for the citizens or inhabitants of the aforesaid (or for their king) over their enemies; and that they will beat them and all who will have contended with them; and it signifies the greatness of [the king's] heart, and [that he is] quick in will and quickly changeable, and [quick] in apprehending things. It even signifies that his own rustics and subjects will love and revere him, and each of them will obey him according to his own condition.

And if Mars were the Lord of the Year, and the Lord of the Ascendant, and he were of good condition, not impeded, it signifies that there will be fertility in that same year, and it will be a rainy year, and there will be pestilences and earthquakes; and this will be moderate. And there will be joy and happiness in that same year, and workers and bearers of arms will struggle and will find good; and there will be war and contention close to the king of that region.

If however he were of bad condition, it signifies he will rarely beat his own enemies, and that it will be enough for them if they can protect themselves from them—or rather it seems more likely that the enemies will beat or overcome them. And it signifies that the king will not be very stable over the things which he ought to be engaged in, and especially over the nobles, and useful and just things; nor will he keep his own secrets well, but rather he will reveal them; and he will exercise his operations in martial matters more so than in others.

And if his latitude were northern, it signifies the heat of the air, and the scarcity of rains. If however his latitude were southern, it signifies thunderings, flashings, and lightnings.

And if he were oriental, it signifies wars that are going to fall between the wealthy, magnates, and nobles. And if he were occidental, it signifies confusions and fears that are going to come to men.

And if he were retrograde, it signifies infirmities of the eyes, and of the entire human body. And if he were direct, it signifies a multitude of hypocrites who appear in the clothing of sheep, but inwardly they will be rapacious wolves.

Chapter 82: If Mars were in Leo

If however he were in Leo, it signifies wars and contentions, and a scarcity of the *annona* in the eastern parts; and there will be death in men, and especially in young adults from 40 years to 50 years (however in boys it will be stronger).

And if his latitude were northern, it signifies a scarcity of waters. If however his latitude were southern, it signifies a multitude of waters from springs and rivers.

And if he were oriental, it signifies the impediment of animals and the like, which men use. And if he were occidental, it signifies a scarcity of fishes; and the death of animals spending time in water.

And if he were retrograde, it signifies impediment and trouble which will fall among the wealthy and magnates. And if he were direct, it signifies the blowing of the western winds; and ships at sea will be safe.

Chapter 83: If Mars were in Sagittarius

And if Mars were in Sagittarius, it signifies a war that is going to be in the western parts; and that there will be little power in those parts; and there will be an evil impediment and death in the habitations of those regions, and in those doing business; and there will be infirmities and coughing and pains of the eyes; and there will be intestinal worms killing boys, and even wounding others; and it signifies a scarcity of rains; and that cold will be generated in its own seasons, so that because of it trees and herbs and the *annona* will be devastated; and bees will suffer detriment in that revolution.

Which if he were well disposed, namely made fortunate and strong, it signifies the good condition of those responsible for wars, and their advisors, and bearers of arms, because of fighting battles and those fighting battles; and [the good condition] of those who seek injustice, and cutters of roads, just as those who work by these [methods] think their condition is good.

And Abū Ma'shar said that if Mars were in the human signs, like Gemini, Virgo, Libra, the last half of Sagittarius, and Aquarius, it signifies a multitude of wars and battles; and that men will rise up against their own king. It even signifies sudden death, and tertian fevers, and other strong and severe fevers, and a multitude of infirmities; even a multitude of cutters of roads, and the shedding of men's blood; and burning fires and lightning bolts.

Indeed if he were badly disposed, it signifies [that] the malice of all the afore-said [will be] more serious, and worse, and more harmful–unless Jupiter were to work to the contrary.

Indeed if his latitude were northern, it signifies the goodness of the air, and its excellent [or beautiful] disposition. And if his latitude were southern, it signifies the wealth of those doing business [or negotiators], and the excellence of their wealth.

And if he were oriental, it signifies peace and rest, and security; and wars will be few or practically none. And if he were occidental, it signifies the health [or saving] of trees, and a multitude of fruit.

But if he were retrograde, it signifies coughing that is going to come to men, and pains in the rear parts of the head. If however he were direct, it signifies pestilences that are going to come to animals which live next to the seashore.

Chapter 84: On another wicked signification of Mars[327]

One must even consider, in a revolution of a year of the world, whether Mars is in Gemini or not. For if Mars were in Gemini in a revolution of the year, and Gemini were the 9th house [domicile?], and the inferior planets were to follow him,[328] it signifies the Roman Church is going to take up a temporal sword in that year, and that it will wield it; and it will strive for the shedding of the blood of Christians, both of the innocent and the guilty.

[Mars in the houses or domiciles][329]

If Mars were in the first in a revolution of the year (whether he were the Lord of the Year or not), whatever kind of revolution it was, whether of the world, or a nativity–or it is a nativity or question–it signifies something horrible (and sorrow and fears, and contrarieties and contentions) is going to come to men, or to a native or querent, in that year; and men will strive to take away substance, namely one from the other; and [to take] things which do not pertain to them, with skill and cleverness, [and] not in a praiseworthy way.

---

[327] The following paragraph seems to be inserted as an afterthought; a similar paragraph on Mars in Gemini appears below.

[328] I believe this means the other planets follow him by being in earlier degrees–unlike the Sun, for whom other planets follow him by being a later degree and rising after him.

[329] I believe this is a general passage on Gemini in the houses, and that the discussion of Mars in Gemini is now ended.

And if he were in the second, it likewise signifies the taking away of substance by injustice, and without reason;[330] and it will be poverty and need inducing them to do it; and household members and ministers will be thrown into confusion against their masters (or those with whom they live or stay). Certain people wanted to say that Mars in the second is not to be denounced, for they said that he signifies mercantile dealings. But I have not found this to be proven, that I remember.

And if he were in the third, it signifies that anger and hatred, and enmity, and contrariety and contention, is going to fall between brothers and lesser blood-relatives; and that many of them will kill each other on trifling pretexts; and more strongly so if the 3rd house were Capricorn or Aquarius. And Abū Ma'shar said if the 3rd house were of the domiciles of Venus, it signifies joy from brothers and sisters. And if it were of the domiciles of Jupiter, it signifies a multitude of substances, and the acquisitions of those doing business. And if it were of the domiciles of Saturn, it signifies the robbing[331] of the dead placed in tombs; and the undermining of walls, and the taking away of other things by means of robbery. And it signifies men's engagement in making money; and in extorting money wherever they can by means of illicit domination and by false attestations, and by malicious and fraudulent words; and men will suffer dangers and tribulations. And if it were the domicile of the Moon, it signifies robberies and the undermining of walls so they may be robbed, and they will pilfer by a wicked deed; and robbers will be safe and bold in stealing. For they will steal in public and in places of doing business, not to mention at night, but even in the day. And if it were the domicile of the Sun, it signifies the cutters and cutting of roads; and pillaging in villages, and sometimes in cities and in other habitations; and even of those staying at inns, [and it signifies] public speakers and pilgrims. And Abū Ma'shar said, know that this is a peculiar feature of Mars among the rest of the planets.

---

[330] Or perhaps, "unreasonably," suggesting excess–since Bonatti proceeds to tell us the reason in the next clause.
[331] Again, *expoliationem*, "polishing."

And if he were in the fourth, it signifies death and ruin from illness; and killing by swords; and the shedding of blood, and its suspicion (and these things will come to an end in the south, from whatever direction they aspect, and in Khorasan); and from an extended tribulation; however the beginning of them will be more from the north.

And if he were in the fifth, it signifies that there will be fornications in that year, and that many children will be born from them, of which more will be considered legitimate when they are adulterous, from which their parents will profit little or nothing; but the sustenance [or provisions] of men will be suitable in that year.

And if he were in the sixth, it signifies hot illnesses, like hot fevers, and dry ones which will be motivated by corrupted blood, and from cholera that is going to some into men in that revolution. It even signifies griefs and sorrows which will arrive because of male and female slaves, and servants, and by other causes which are signified by the 6th house.

And if he were in the seventh, it signifies contentions and contrarieties, and confusion in all matters, and harm for this reason. And it signifies business transactions with fraud and deception; also grief and sorrow in it.

And if he were in the eighth, [it signifies] acquisition from the substances of the dead for some men, and this both in the revolutions of nativities or questions, and also in their questions, and in the revolutions of the years of the world; and justice will come to be for those acquiring them for this reason; and they will lose them after their acquisition; and they will fall into poverty and need; and it signifies death and mutilation, or the loss of limbs (namely hands and feet); and they will fall into disgrace and very shameful and reprehensible accusations.

And if he were in the ninth, it signifies the destruction of the status of the religious; it even signifies the seeking of horses and arms for the sake of making war and doing battle; and men will likewise seek wars; and they will strive to pitch camp and go into the army. And it signifies drinking bouts and drunkenness, and lack of self control by dishonest and illicit people; and men will be very unfaithful, and liars, and will strive to relate their dreams [to others], and relate them with lies.

And if he were in the tenth, it signifies tribulation is going to come to the rustics and common people from the direction of the king or the wealthy and powerful; and it signifies the wounds and blows of swords and whips, and distress from them, and prison, and the want or need of sustenance. And it signifies wars and contentions over matters which do not belong to those who seek them, nor pertain to them.

And if he were in the eleventh, it signifies a scarcity of wealth or profit in matters concerning which usefulness is hoped; and that they will fall into the enmity of their friends; and it signifies the destruction of substance; and men will lose hope over matters in which trust was had, and about which it was hoped–likewise [for] a native or querent.

And if he were in the twelfth, it signifies skills in thievery, and in things similar to these; and laziness and delay in these things which they ought to and are able to do; the destruction of the substances of men; and it signifies grief and sorrow is going to come because of large animals, both the ones that are ridden, and those which are not ridden, unless God averts it.

Chapter 85: On Mars in Taurus–what he would signify

And if Mars were in Taurus or in its triplicity, those things which are signified will appear in the southern parts, and especially if he were in Taurus. For then it signifies strong winds are going to come, and the destruction of fruits which are in the places from which they ought to be collected; likewise [the destruction] of trees, and this because of heat exceeding the required and natural measure. It even signifies a multitude of clouds and cloudy weather; also rains and thunder and lightnings.

And Abū Ma'shar said it signifies the death of women and cows; and it signifies wars are going to come between the citizens of the east and the citizens of the west. It even signifies pains of the eyes, and more of the left ones than the right ones; and it will abound more in women than in men; nor will the cultivation of lands be very useful; and there will be a scarcity of the *annona*.

And if his latitude were northern, it signifies a multitude of rains and the goodness of herbs, and usefulness from them. And if his latitude were southern, it signifies a multitude of northern winds.

And if he were oriental, it signifies there is going to be peace in that revolution, in the parts of Babylon and in the western parts, and the security of their citizens. And if he were occidental, it signifies a multitude of infirmities and death.

And if he were retrograde, it signifies the infirmities of boys. And Abū Ma'shar said if he were direct, it signifies the hatred of women.

Chapter 86: On Mars, if he were in Virgo

And if Mars were in Virgo, it signifies battles, and sheddings of blood in the parts of the north, and it even signifies pains of the eyes, and the abundance of the *annona* and wine and butter. And Abū Ma'shar said [it signifies] mortality in women.

And if his latitude were northern, it signifies impediment in the bodies of men; and seeds and harvest will suffer detriments. And if his latitude were southern, then it signifies the salvation of seeds.

And if he were oriental, it signifies the death of old men. And if occidental, it signifies the blowing of winds in the parts of Spain.

And if he were retrograde, it signifies battles are going to come between men. And if he were direct, it signifies the honesty and good condition of wealthy and great men.

Chapter 87: On Mars in Capricorn

And if Mars were in Capricorn, it signifies wars and pillaging, and tribulations, death in young men. Likewise tremors are going to come in the eastern parts. And it even signifies rains in the same parts, and the multiplication of the *annona* and butter and oil. And the aforesaid wars will be between the citizens of the east and the citizens of the west.

And if his latitude were northern, it signifies a multitude of snow in the required and usual seasons. And his latitude were southern, it signifies the heat of the air, and its darkness, in its own seasons.

And if he were oriental, it signifies the killing of the Emperor of the Romans;[332] and more strongly so if the Moon (since she is naturally [the Emperor's] significatrix) were in the 8th or joined to the Lord of the 8th, or Mars himself were in an angle, wherever she were joined to him. And more strongly again, if she were joined with him in the 8th, or the Lord of the 8th were to aspect her from the opposition or square aspect. And again more strongly so, and infallibly, if there were mutual reception between them (or at least the Moon were to receive the Lord of the 8th); nor could Jupiter work to the contrary, for only God could avert this. And if [Mars] were occidental, it signifies blisters, also carbuncles, and similar things that are going to befall the bodies of men.

And if he were retrograde, it signifies the scarcity of the *annona*. And if he were direct, it signifies an abundance of wine and oil.

Chapter 88: On Gemini and its triplicity

And if Mars were in Gemini or in its triplicity, it signifies that whatever he were to signify, the arrival of those signified things will be in the western parts. But if he were in Gemini, it signifies [that] impediment is going to befall men because of thunders and lightnings, and a scarcity of rains, and the severity of heat and its harmfulness. And there will be wars and contentions and robberies in the northern parts; and the king of [those parts] will be exalted in that revolution, and they will have victory over their enemies. And there will be pains of the ears, and likewise blisters, carbuncles, and the like.

And if his latitude were northern, it signifies a multitude of rains. And if his latitude were southern, it signifies a scarcity of waters, springs and rivers.

And if he were oriental, it signifies a multitude of blisters and the like; and if he were occidental, it signifies the impediment of conciliators and scribes and judges, and [the impediment] of cavalry commanders, and their hiding and flight.

And if he were retrograde, it signifies the dissent of the religious, and their diversity and sects. And if he were direct, it signifies that men will uncover secret things, both their own and others', nor will they keep them [secret].

---

332 This passage is from the *Flowers*. Bonatti (and Abū Ma'shar) undoubtedly mean the Byzantine Emperor in Constantinople (who was traditionally called the Emperor of the Romans), not the Holy Roman Emperor in the West.

Chapter 89: If Mars were in Libra

And if Mars were in Libra, it signifies winds are going to come, and infirmities and mortality in the cities or regions which are in the division of Libra. And this will be stronger in men than in women. And Abū Ma'shar said if Mars were there it signifies rains and winds, also clouds and fog [or mists]. It even signifies that there will be infirmity and mortality in the southern parts; and there will be a middling amount of wind and butter and oil. And thieves and cutters of roads will be multiplied, and there will be quarrels and evils between men; and there will be fears and tremblings or terrors in them.

And if his latitude were northern, it signifies lightning bolts and flashings which will come and appear in that year or in that revolution. And if his latitude were southern, it signifies illnesses in men on the left side.

And if he were oriental, it signifies there are going to be wars and contentions between wealthy and great men. And if he were occidental, it signifies the salvation of the wealthy and magnates, and writers of letters and the wise.

And if he were retrograde, it signifies illnesses are going to come to wealthy and great men, and to writers, and judges and the wise. And if he were direct, it signifies the wills of the wealthy and great men or the nobles, will differ amongst themselves.

Chapter 90: If Mars were in Aquarius

And if Mars were in Aquarius, it signifies burdens and tribulations that are going to come to men in that revolution; and snows will be abundant, and rains, and cold, in their own seasons. And the *annona* and wine and butter will be decreased in the western parts, and in the land which is said to belong to businessmen;[333] and it signifies the death or the change of the king or ruler of that region in which you were to revolve the year. And Abū Ma'shar said if Venus were then to aspect the Ascendant, and she were northern, it signifies a good springtime; but the wine will be of a middling amount.

And if his latitude were northern, it signifies a multitude of snows and cold in their own seasons, and in the usual regions; and locusts in its own season.

---

[333] Bonatti may be referring particularly to distinct cities or locations which acted as crossroads for trade, called fairs—like Scarborough Fair in England. But he probably means financial and business districts generally.

And if his latitude were southern, it signifies the darkness of the air, and its thickness, and the severity of the heat.

And if he were oriental, it signifies the good condition of the wealthy and great men, and the nobles; and their joy and happiness. It [also] signifies a multitude of boughs.[334]

And if he were retrograde, it signifies the severity of heat, and that impediment will fall upon trees for that reason. And if he were direct, it signifies the impediment of trees and a case of vermin in them (and more strongly so if the Head of the Dragon were there, or in Gemini).

Chapter 91: On Mars in Cancer and its triplicity

And if Mars, in the revolution of the year, were in Cancer or its triplicity (and especially in Cancer), the appearance of the things which he would signify will be in the northern parts. But in Cancer it signifies shipwrecks happening suddenly, from a strong and sudden blowing of winds; and it signifies quarreling and contention and war in the western parts; and men will be oppressed because of rendering tributes, and there will be fevers and other illnesses, and there will be pains of the throat and chest; and heat will be oppressive, and rain will be decreased. And Abū Ma'shar said it will be a dangerous year, and there will be a middling amount of oil and butter or fat; and it even signifies the death of quadrupeds (but more of horses).

And if his latitude were northern, it signifies the severity of the frost in its own season, and a scarcity of waters from springs. And if his latitude were southern, it signifies winds are going to come upon, and impediment is going to befall, trees.

And if he were oriental, it signifies pestilences are going to befall grazing animals. And if he were occidental, it signifies the worry and concern of the vulgar or rustics and common people about their own particular business matters.

And if he were retrograde, it signifies lasciviousness, and that men will love and be eager for venereal cultivations, and they will fornicate, and the like. But if he were direct, it signifies the good disposition of the air, and its fineness and clarity.

---

[334] *Ramorum.* A *ramus* generally means anything with a branch-like form (e.g., in rivers or mountain spurs), but keeping with his agricultural emphasis I have translated it as "boughs."

Chapter 92: On Mars in Scorpio

And if Mars were in Scorpio, it signifies a multitude of clouds, and the severity of the cold in winter, and the distemper of heat in the summer, and the severity of the *annona* for that reason, and even [the oppression] of trees. And there will be pains of the eyes, and robberies and cutters of roads will be multiplied, and there will be wars and pains, and other infirmities in young men. And there will be a scarcity of wine and butter and fat; and these things will happen more in the northern parts.

And if he were in Scorpio and his latitude were northern, it signifies the scarcity of waters. And if his latitude were southern, it signifies a multitude of waters from springs.

And if he were oriental, it signifies a multitude of the infirmities that befall men, and especially in the lower parts of the belly. And if he were occidental, it signifies a scarcity of men's piety toward one another.

And Abū Ma'shar said if he were retrograde, it signifies good in that revolution, and a multitude of business transactions (however, with trembling and fear). And he said if he were direct, it signifies much taking of the *census* and the destruction of the houses in which the wealthy keep their substances.[335]

Chapter 93: If Mars were in Pisces

And if Mars were in Pisces, it signifies a multitude of snow and rain, and there will be mortality in the southern parts, and more fishes will be caught in that revolution than usual; and more kingdoms will be taken apart, and it signifies the killing of kings and magnates and the wealthy and nobles (namely those who are fit for a kingdom). A scarcity of the *annona* is even signified, and wine will suffer detriment and destruction. And therefore there will be much less than men would hope for. And flying animals that impede will suffer detriment, like flies and gadflies[336] and the like. And Abū Ma'shar said if Venus[337] were to aspect the Ascendant of the year, death will abound in men, and pains of the eyes, and thunders and lightnings will be multiplied; and she will break the badness of the fruits of the earth, and they will begin to increase.

---

[335] Lit., "the destruction of the houses of the substances of the wealthy."

[336] *Taffani* (Ital. *tafano*).

[337] Perhaps this should read "Mars"?

And if his latitude were northern, it signifies the goodness of the air and its fineness or purity. And if his latitude were southern, it signifies an abundance of locusts (but they will hardly impede).

And if he were oriental, it signifies the killing of wealthy and great men. And if he were occidental, it signifies infirmities that are going to befall male and female slaves, and in male and female servants and in low-class persons.

And Abū Ma'shar said if he were retrograde, it signifies the salvation and the wealth of those doing business. And if he were direct, it signifies the guarding and saving of sheep and small quadrupeds, and of male and female slaves, and male and female servants, and low-class persons.

Those wise in this profession, and particularly our most reverend predecessor Abū Ma'shar, did not care to record [the meanings of] the latitudes except for the three superior planets', because he did not find proven truth in the other cases as he did with them. Therefore Abū Ma'shar said that he sometimes found error in [those of the inferiors]; but in no way in the superiors; whence he admonishes us to be focused on the latitudes of the superiors, and not the inferiors.

Chapter 94: On the Sun, if he were the Lord of the Year– what he would signify

However, if the Sun were the Lord of the Year or Revolution, and he were well disposed and of good condition (namely made fortunate and strong, free from impediments), it signifies the sublimities and exaltations of kings, and glory and honor, and its seeking; and that the king of that region will be exalted; and he will be worried about the increase of his kingdom–and not merely the king, but even anyone according to his own condition and according to his own nature or birth for the purpose of increasing his own status; and it signifies their usefulness and success; and that they will turn their faces away from matters displeasing to God, and from injuries, and from dishonest matters. It even signifies the good condition of the wealthy and magnates and nobles; and [the good condition] of those to whom honor is owed by men.

And if he were the Lord of the Year and the Lord of the Ascendant, and he were free from the malefics, Abū Ma'shar said kings will rejoice and they will have happiness and security; and the *annona* and quadrupeds and birds will be increased; and everything over which the Sun has signification. If however he were impeded, it signifies the impediment of all of the aforesaid. And he said if

Mercury were with Saturn or were to aspect him, and were a participant with him and were to receive disposition from him in different climes, the harvests and the rustics will suffer detriment; and robbers will be multiplied, and fear will enter in upon men, and especially in those who are of the nature of Mercury, or [in] those for whom he was the significator; and animals will be decreased in the land of the west, or in the land of the Arabs, if [Mercury] were in the figure of the quadrupedal signs, according to the substance of that sign.

And he said, look in addition to the luminary whose authority it was: because if it were made fortunate and in increased light and number, and were not impeded, it will repel a great impediment, and prohibit one from a malefic. If however there were an impediment by one of the aforesaid impediments in the hour of the revolution, the aforesaid will suffer detriment and great impediment; and there will be infirmities in the rustics or the common people. And these things will happen more strongly and terribly if it were in signs of men (which are Gemini, Virgo, Libra, the first half of Sagittarius, and Aquarius) and the authority were the Moon's; or if it were her own and [the Sun] were in Libra. And if it were in Taurus or Capricorn, it signifies the oppression of horses, cows, bulls, and gazelles.[338] And if it were in Cancer, Scorpio or Pisces, aquatic things will be oppressed. And these judgments have a place in revolutions of the years of the world, in proportion as they pertain to revolutions.

And if one of the malefics were to impede him, look to the malefic himself, and see in which signs he is, and in which house: because the impediment will be according to the significations of the house and sign in which he is.

And if the Sun were made fortunate, and one of the benefics were to aspect him, it signifies the good condition and the good disposition of all the aforesaid. For where it signifies evil, when he is impeded, there it signifies good when he is freed. And where falsity, it will signify truth concerning the same things; where injustice, there justice; where depression, there exaltation; where need, there abundance. And concentrate your mind so that you understand this well, lest you fall into error concerning them.

And Abū Ma'shar said if the Sun were in Aries or its triplicity, it will be in the eastern part.

And if the Sun were of good condition in his own place, it signifies the rectitude of the wealthy, and their justice and their achievement, and victory over their enemies, and over those who contend with him. And he said, if indeed he were of bad condition in his own place, it signifies the appearance of the

---

[338] Reading *bubalorum* as *bubalinorum*.

wealthy and great men; and the scarcity of their achievement over their enemies, and the fall of their honor in those cities.

And he said, if it were in Taurus or its triplicity,[339] the appearance of their comings (which I spoke of) will be from the parts of the south and from the cities which that sign rules; and that which belongs to it from the substance of the earth, seeds, and trees. And he said if he were in Gemini or its triplicity, it signifies the appearance of those things (of the events which I said), and in all those things which belong to it concerning high matters, will be in the parts of the west. And he said if he were in Cancer or its triplicity, the appearance of those things (of the events), will be in the parts of the north, of the animals which are signified by it.

And he said the operation in the matter of the Sun in the aspect of the planets to him will be just like the operation in the matter of Saturn in this, equally concerning good and evil.

Chapter 95: What the Sun would signify in every house in a revolution of years, nativities, and years of the world, and in nativities, whether he is the Lord of the Year or not

If the Sun were in Aries or in the first in the revolution of a nativity or a year of the world, it signifies the preeminence and sublimity and greatness of the matters of the native, and the same in a revolution; likewise in a revolution of the years of the world it signifies the status and increase of the good of the citizens of the revolution in which the year were revolved (unless Saturn and Mars, or either of them, were to work to the contrary, and [the Sun] were appearing[340] maliciously).

And if he were in the second, it signifies delight between men, and their proper condition; however there will be some deformities in the eyes.

And in the third, it signifies the mutation from one region into another, and that the king of that region will perfect his own matters, and [those] of his own subjects for the good and in a good direction; likewise a native his own matters from the direction of the king.

---

[339] This must mean we can do monthly ingresses, or else the Sun could never be in Taurus in an typical revolution.

[340] *Existens*. Usually Bonatti uses this term to designate the house location of a planet. But perhaps he means the Sun's location by sign—perhaps in Libra, where he is in his own fall.

However, in the fourth, it signifies praise between men, and their sublimity and honor. And matters will appear which had long stood hidden nor
appeared. And it even signifies the discovery of treasures or their aggrega-
tion or acquisition.

In the fifth, however, it signifies the change of the status of many men
because of children; and a native will change his own status because of his
own children; and that he will be revered by the common people; and the
common people will revere those greater than they, and they will honor
them; there will even be joy because of donations.

Indeed in the sixth, it signifies infirmities and detriments because of slaves
and other people who are signified by the 6th house, and that the rustics
or the ignoble will envy those greater than they (and likewise for a native).

And in the seventh, it signifies contrariety which will happen to the vulgar
from noble or great men or kings. Likewise these same things will happen
to a native.

In the eighth, it signifies the depression of the wealthy and of great men
or nobles, and the powerful, and their destruction and death and reproach.

In the ninth, it signifies the good disposition of men's minds toward one
another, and in thoughts pleasing to God, and in those things which
pertain to faith.

In the tenth, it signifies the honor of kings and their exaltation, and their
glory and advancement.

In the eleventh, it signifies men's joy and happiness because of friends
and mutual love between them, and [because of] things about which trust
in the good is had (likewise this will happen to a native from these things);
and good from great men who are below kings.

Indeed in the twelfth, it signifies the destruction and depression of the wealthy and magnates, also nobles–and their death; and the taking away of their dignities, and injuries to them that are going to be introduced by the ignoble; and it signifies contrarieties which will happen to a native from his enemies, and even from others (and more from low-class people than from great men).

Chapter 96: On Venus, if she were the Lady of the Year– what she would signify

If Venus were the Lady of the Year, and of good condition and well disposed, it signifies the good disposition and good condition of women, both of adults and girls, both of ones corrupted and virgins, and likewise eunuchs. And if she were the Lady of the Year and Lady of the Ascendant, and were free from impediments and from the malefics, it signifies a year of security and rest, and matters will be appropriate. There will be good in honors, and justice, and abundance, and rectitude, and peace. If however she were received, the rustics will find good from kings and the wealthy and great men, and the rustics will love their king and obey him; and marriage celebrations will be multiplied, and there will be joy and gladness in women.

If however she were impeded, it signifies little good in that year, and there will be earthquakes in diverse lands, because of which buildings will fall; and there will be war, even if [only] a medium-sized one; and the king of that region will be saddened. And these things will happen in the deputed region and her clime. Indeed if she were impeded in the hour of the revolution, it signifies impediment and the bad condition of all of the aforesaid.

And Abū Ma'shar said if she were in human signs, whatever belongs to her in terms of men will be impeded. If she were in earthy signs, whatever belongs to her in terms of the substance of the earth will be destroyed. If she were in airy signs, whatever belongs to her in terms of the substance of the air will be destroyed. If she were in a watery sign, whatever belongs to her in terms of the substance of water will be destroyed. And he said if there were a benefic instead of [an impeding] malefic, turn your opinion around, and instead of evil say good; instead of injustice, justice. And he said, also look to the planet impeding her, to see in what kind of sign it is, and commingle them: and speak about him according to what was revealed to you in the matter of Saturn.

Chapter 97: What Venus would signify in every house in a revolution of the year, whether she were Lady of the Year or not

If Venus, in a revolution, were in the first, and of good condition and well disposed, then it signifies that men and likewise a native will be in delights and joys and enjoyments, and they will delight in edibles and drinking bouts, and they will be eager for living in a beautiful way, both in victuals and clothing, and in the appearance and displaying of clothing or ornaments of the body, and the use of rings and necklaces, and the like; and good-smelling things and the appearance of honest things, and in all things in which men delight.

And if she were in the second, it signifies usefulness and acquisition because of women, and from women, and success because of that acquisition.

But if she were in the third, it signifies the forgetting of religion, and that few men will care about it (and likewise a native); and lack of self-control in venereal pursuits, and anger which they pursue because of that; and that many bad deeds will be perpetrated from that, and that friends will help friends to commit them.

Indeed if she were in the fourth, Abū Ma'shar said it signifies undeserved grief and the sorrow of things from the direction of mothers, and the end will be praiseworthy.

Indeed in the fifth, it signifies detriment because of children in the beginning of the revolution, but it will be praised, and the end and grief will be turned into joy.

However, in the sixth, Abū Ma'shar said it signifies infirmities and tribulations from the direction of male and female slaves, and even from mothers, and it signifies widowed [or bereft] women. Whence if the Lord of the sixth were of good condition, it will be well for them, and *vice versa*. And he said, the Lord of a question will not attain everything which he seeks of things. And he said, if it were a question about a sick person, he will be freed from his infirmity. And he said the reason for his liberation will be according to what I put down for you in the matter of Saturn in the beginning of the book. And he said, know that if a benefic were in the house of infirmity, the infirmity will be alleviated; but if a malefic were there, it will grow worse.

And he said if she were in the seventh it signifies marriage and joy from the direction of women, and from every quaesited matter by participation.[341] And every matter which he wished, will be accomplished for him.

---

[341] I believe this means, "from every matter in which the querent is a partner/participator," or perhaps "from every quaested matter, because of [someone's] participation."

Indeed in the eighth, it signifies the death of older partners and mothers and nursemaids.

However in the ninth, it signifies the change of the religious from one residence to another, and the truth of dreams. And it signifies faraway pilgrimages.

Indeed in the tenth, it signifies joy from the king and from the direction of the king.

Indeed in the eleventh, it signifies joy and happiness from good things which happen to them, and trust and good hope from the direction of friends, and good fortune from them.

But if she were in the twelfth, it signifies tribulation and enmity from women, and often from low-class women (likewise it will happen from [or because of] the native).

Chapter 98: What Venus would signify in every sign in a revolution

[Aries]

If Venus were in Aries in a revolution, and she were Lady of the Year and of good condition, namely made fortunate and strong, free from impediments, it signifies the good condition of the wealthy and of magnates and nobles; it even signifies the good mixture of the air and its peace in the eastern parts; and it signifies soft and temperate rains, not harmful ones, and the extinction of wars in those parts; and the good condition of the Arabs; and an abundance of their supplies [or provisions], and calm between men, and rest and tranquility and games and dancing in the lands which are in the division of Aries; and the engaging of their citizens in venereal matters. If however she were impeded, it signifies impediment, namely that she will not do good things, nor would she be able to resist the malefics [or evils].

[Leo]

But if she were in Leo, it signifies the extinction of wars and contentions, or at least their mitigation and weakness, and mortalities in the parts of the east; and there will be gladnesses and delights in venereal matters, and especially in the wealthy and magnates and the nobles (unless Mars were to work to the contrary).

[Sagittarius]

And if she were in Sagittarius, and well disposed, it signifies quiet and tranquility, and the extinction of wars in the parts of the west, and in the land of the Arabs; and the goodness and salvation of the bodies of the citizens of those regions; and the wealth of their businessmen, and the health of their children (unless Mars were to work to the contrary). And rains will be abundant somewhat more than what they ought to be; the cold of their winter will be tempered; and their honey and wine will bring profit, and it signifies the little wealth of bearers of arms in those parts (unless Mars were to oppress Venus, or she were otherwise very impeded or badly disposed).

[Taurus]

And if Venus were in Taurus in a revolution of the year, and of good condition, it signifies the appearance of those things which she signified in the parts of the south, generally speaking; they will even appear in the areas of Jerusalem, and in the right-hand side of the east, or in the land of the Turks, and in the land of the Romans.[342] It even signifies winds that are going to come in those parts (however not harmful ones); and the saving of the fruits of the trees; and this will happen because of[343] her benign nature. And it signifies the goodness of the air, and the salvation of women and cows in those parts; even the salvation of the *annona*; and likewise the citizens of the lands will be useful (unless Mars were to work to the contrary, or she were impeded or badly disposed).

[Virgo]

And if she were in Virgo, and were well disposed, it signifies tranquility and a good condition in the northern parts; and an abundance of wine and the *annona* and butter, and fat; nor will there by mortality in them unless Mars were to work to the contrary.

[Capricorn]

And if Venus were in Capricorn, it signifies a scarcity of wars and robberies and pillaging and cutting of roads and tribulations; and the salvation [or good

---

[342] Undoubtedly this means "the Byzantines."
[343] *Ex parte.*

health] of young men; and a scarcity of rains in the parts of the east and south; and an abundance of *annona*, wine and butter. And there will be tranquility between the eastern and southern [parts]. But if she were impeded or Mars worked to the contrary, her signification will be abolished, nor would she be able to do good.

[Gemini]

And if Venus were in Gemini in a revolution of the year, and of good condition, it signifies the appearance of the coming of her significations in the parts of the west; likewise in the land of the Arabs and in the parts of the north; and it signifies the salvation of men in those parts; and the fit mixture of the air and rains; and the breaking up of wars and contrarieties; and the increase of gladnesses in the northern parts.

[Libra]

And if Venus were in Libra, and of good condition and free from impediments, it signifies the salvation of the citizens of the regions which are in the division of Libra; and men will be saved more than women; and it signifies the salvation of men in the southern parts (unless Saturn were to work to the contrary); and there will be wine and butter and fat in those parts; and robberies and the cutting of roads and pillaging and contentions will be mitigated (unless Mars were to work to the contrary, or she were impeded).

[Aquarius]

And if she were in Aquarius and of good condition and well disposed, it signifies the good condition of men, and the taking away (or at least the decrease) of burdens and tribulations which are going to come to men in that revolution; and the decrease of snows and rains and cold in winter; and the saving of the wine and butter in the parts of the west and in Alexandria; and in the whole land which is said to be of those doing business;[344] and the safekeeping of the king of that region in which you are revolving the year. Which if she were to aspect the Ascendant and she were northern, it signifies a scarcity of

---

[344] Again, Bonatti may be speaking of regions of Europe in which the market "fairs" were held–regions to which people would travel from far away for extensive trading. For instance, Scarborough Fair was a 45-day trading event.

wine–however the spring will be good and useful and sweet (unless Mars were to work to the contrary, or she were otherwise badly disposed).

[Cancer]

And if Venus were in Cancer in a revolution of the year, it signifies there will be an appearance of those things which it signified in the northern parts. It signifies the salvation of those sailing, and peace between men in the western parts; and alleviation from things rendered and from tributes, more so than usual; and there will be a diminution of fevers and other illnesses, and heat will be diminished; and there will be rains; and dangers that are going to come will be alleviated in that year or in the revolution; likewise the death of quadrupeds [will be alleviated], and especially that of horses (unless Mars were to work to the contrary, or she were otherwise badly disposed).

[Scorpio]

And if she were in Scorpio, free from impediments, it signifies the diminishment of clouds, and the good disposition of the air, and the alleviation of the cold of winter, and of the heat of summer, and the salvation of the *annona* and trees. And illnesses will be decreased (and particularly pains of the eyes), and especially in youths; and robberies and the cutting of roads, and wars [will be decreased]; and wine and butter will be saved; and these will happen more in the northern parts than in others.

[Pisces]

And if she were in Pisces, it signifies the diminishing of snows and rains; and mortalities in the parts of the south; and the catching of fish; and the kingdoms in their parts[345] (and the wealthy and nobles and magnates) will be saved; and the *annona* will be saved so that it does not suffer serious detriment (likewise wine). Which if she were impeded and badly disposed, and were to aspect the Ascendant, it signifies thunders and flashings, and death in men, and pains of the eyes; however, things born of the earth will be increased (unless Saturn were to work to the contrary).

---

[345] I believe this refers to lands in the southern parts (see earlier in the sentence).

Chapter 99: On Mercury, if he were the Lord of the Year– what he would signify

If Mercury were the Lord of the Year or Revolution, and of good condition, and well disposed, free from impediments, it signifies the good condition of those doing business, of the wise, and writers, and those of great works, and arithmeticians, and of those using number by means of teaching, and geometers; it even signifies the good condition of boys, according to how he is joined with the planets. For if he were joined with a masculine planet, this will happen in males; if with a feminine one, this will happen in females; and better than this if the Lord of his own domicile were to receive him.

But if he himself were the Lord of the Year, and he were the Lord of the Ascendant, free from impediments,[346] and one of the benefics were to aspect him, men will find good from the king. And anyone will find good from his own rulers; and he will be heard by them, and he will find honor and praise and a good and praiseworthy status from them; and the year will be useful for [these] said persons. If however he were impeded, nor were he received, it signifies the contrary of what was said: because men will find difficulties from kings and their rulers, and be pressed down by them; and the year will be contrary to boys, the wise, and those doing business, and the other aforesaid people.

And Abū Ma'shar said, if however a malefic were to aspect him in addition, his condition will be destroyed from the position which I said. And he said if the Moon were free from the malefics, rains and cold will be multiplied, and legates will rejoice and find good; and better and more dignified that that, if she were received: because then they will find a position of dignity from a king or kings, and it will rain in its own season when it is necessary. If however he were of a bad condition, and badly disposed, it signifies the impediment and bad condition of the aforesaid, and their evil disposition, of each one according to his position.[347] If however he were joined[348] to masculine and feminine ones at the same time, it signifies that this will happen generally in boys and girls. And

---

346 I would normally have translated this sentence as, "But if he were the Lord of the Year, and the Lord of the Ascendant were free from impediments," indicating two different planets. Each version is equally faithful to the text. But the previous chapters that parallel this one show that Bonatti is interested to see when a planet is *both* Lord of the Year *and* the Lord of the Ascendant. Therefore I have changed the emphasis of the sentence in order to align it with the previous chapters.

347 *Subiectum*, lit. "field" or "subject."

348 Omitting *non*, which would make it read "if he were *not* joined."

Abū Ma'shar said whatever belongs to him will suffer detriment from this. Second, the the narration will be on those things which pertain to him, and on the human, earthy, airy, and watery, and bestial figure [he is in]; also on the aspect of the malefics and the benefics to him, and his being clothed[349] by them. And he said the narration of all of these will be in the way I made clear to you equally so[350] in the chapter on Saturn.

[Aries]

Which if he were in Aries or its triplicity (and especially in Aries), it signifies an abundance of waters or much rain; and a scarcity of the *annona* in the parts of the west, and the detriment of wine, and it signifies there are going to be powerful winds in that revolution, and dew and fine and soft clouds, and the death of boys, as I said. If however the Moon were joined to him, it signifies a multitude of fishes. If however he were joined to the Sun, it signifies an abundance of wine, and the salvation of women; and more strongly so, if Mars and Venus were then with the Sun when Mercury is joined to him. If however it were Saturn instead of Venus, it signifies the multiplication of waters. Indeed, if Mars alone were with him, it signifies pains of the eyes, and a multitude of battles and wars.

[Leo]

And if he were[351] in Leo, it signifies the severity of the summer in its own times, and [the severity] of the summer winds. And if he were beyond the 10th house, up to the 7th, it signifies impediments in that direction, and a scarcity of the *annona*, but not one totally ruined. And if one of the benefics were to aspect him, the malice will be abolished; and it signifies a scarcity of wine and fat (however, dates will abound in the parts in which they grew); and there will be pains of the eyes, and there will be death in wolves and other quadrupeds living by preying.

---

[349] *Indumentum*. Although this word means "clothing," the passage from the *Flowers* on which this seems to be based, refers to Mercury being "clothed" or *influenced* by the malefics and benefics.

[350] *Aequalitate*, lit. "with equality." But the passage from the *Flowers* refers to another book of Abū Ma'shar's.

[351] Reading *fuerit* for *fuerint*.

And Abū Ma'shar said the condition of the nobles will worsen in Khorasan.[352] And the aspect of the malefics increases evil, and the aspect of the benefics spares and restrains, with the aid of God.

[Sagittarius]

If however he were in Sagittarius, it signifies there are going to be snows in that revolution, in their customary times, and a diversity of air and its inconstancy, and the scarcity of the *annona* and produce, trees, and lands, and a scarcity of waters; however there will be wine and butter and oil and fat, and there will be battles and wars in the parts of the west.

[Taurus]

Abū Ma'shar said if Mercury were in Taurus, it signifies a multitude of waters, and the destruction of the harvests and the detriment of wine, and this could happen because of the diversity of the air, and its diverse alteration; and a scarcity of butter and oil or fat, and pains of the eyes from the direction of the east, and the death of nobles (namely princes and great men, or the wealthy), unless Jupiter and Venus were to work against it (because if they were to aspect the Ascendant of the revolution, they will abolish all malice and every impediment that Mercury would have signified). Indeed if Mars were to aspect the Ascendant of the revolution, it signifies the severity of war, and it even signifies the death of cows. And this will happen more in the parts of the south.

[Virgo]

And if he were in Virgo, Abū Ma'shar said rains and harvests will be multiplied, and pains of the eyes will be abundant; and death in the parts of Animarot.[353]

[Capricorn]

And if he were in Capricorn, it signifies battles and tribulations are going to come in the parts of Khorasan. And Abū Ma'shar said, if however he were

---

[352] *Curasen.*
[353] Unknown.

conjoined to Venus and Mars, there will be a war in Khorasan from the men of
Abagir.[354]

[Gemini]

And Abū Ma'shar said if Mercury were in Gemini, it signifies battles on the
part of the Latins, from the citizens of Khorasan and great men; and a multitude
of snows, and detriment in the harvests and oils and butter; and there will be a
multitude of wine; and it signifies pestilence and death in women, and a
multitude of blisters and inflammations beneath the skin; it even signifies dew
and the humidity of the air. And Abū Ma'shar said if the Sun and Jupiter were
to aspect the Ascendant of the year, pestilences and death will be decreased; and
men will be stronger than usual in the parts of the east, and wealthier, and they
will make more wealth, and be successful.

[Libra]

And if he were in Libra, it signifies the scarcity of wine and the *annona*; and it
signifies powerful and severe winds are going to come in that revolution. And if
Saturn were to aspect or be joined to him, it signifies pains of the head and belly
are going to come to men. But if the Sun were to aspect Saturn them, it will
repel the malice, and abolish it, nor will it impede.

[Aquarius]

And if he were in Aquarius, it signifies a multitude of locusts in the parts in
which they are accustomed to being; and a scarcity of rains; and it signifies
itching and blisters happening to men from the corruption of the air and from
its diversity. And if he were then corporally joined with Venus, it signifies an
earthquake is going to come in that revolution (and more strongly so if they
were joined with the Sun; and again more strongly if Mars or Saturn were to
aspect them from the opposition or square aspect). And there will be pestilences, and robbers will be multiplied, and from the conjunction of Saturn it
signifies an abundance of rains.

---

[354] Unknown, but perhaps Azerbaijan?

[Cancer]

Indeed if he were in Cancer, it signifies killing is going to come in the western parts; and even in Animarot.[355] And [it signifies] the scarcity of the *annona* and of fat and butter; and that impediment will fall upon trees and likewise in seeds, and in wine. And there will be infirmities (and especially around the parts of the neck and throat because of inflammation[356] [to the mucous membranes], like sore throats and the like). And if he were conjoined to Mars and Venus at the same time, it signifies the killing of the wealthy and magnates or nobles in the parts of the west, unless Venus and the Moon were to work to the contrary– which if they were to aspect, they will abolish the malice and repel it.

[Scorpio]

And if he were in Scorpio, it signifies a multitude of snows and rains in their own seasons, in the usual regions; and it signifies battles and wars in the parts of the west and north, even if perhaps more slackened; which if Mars were to aspect, the northern ones will be stronger than the western ones. And there will be more robbers and cutters of roads than usual; and there will be pestilences in the parts of the north, and fevers with strong cold; and there will be abscesses and pains of the eyes with inflammation and redness and opthalmia.[357]

[Pisces]

If however he were in Pisces, it signifies winds and rain, and these will happen more often in the parts of the north. And Abū Ma'shar said there will be death in the parts of Animarot; and crawling things and fishes will be multiplied. For all of these will come to be if Mercury were the sole significator. But if planets were to aspect him, the things signified will be according to the disposition of the planets and their aspects toward him.

Nor should you wonder if I have put down for you [Mercury's] position in the signs, because revolutions do not come to be only according to the entrance of the Sun into Aries, but rather they come to be according to his entrance into

---

[355] Reading *Animarot* for *Animaror*.

[356] *Reumatica.*

[357] In modern medicine, "opthalmia" includes all sorts of eye infections causing redness (like "pinkeye" or conjunctivitis), but since the earlier phrases already speak of inflammation, I am not sure if *opthalmiae* here has some other technical meaning for Bonatti.

every movable sign, namely when the revolutions are according to halves or according to quarters, as often happens.[358] And then it could be what I said, even if not always.

Chapter 100: What Mercury would signify in every house in a revolution of the world, whether in a nativity or in the revolution of a nativity, whether he is the Lord of the Year or not

If Mercury were the Lord of the Year, and were in the first in a revolution or in a nativity, [then] if it were a revolution of a year of the world it signifies the training of men, for whom wisdom, and likewise writing and instruction matter; and that they will be more eloquent in disputations and in the sciences of the *quadrivium* than usual. If however it were a nativity or revolution, it signifies that the native will be wise in literature, eloquent in disputations, and learned in numbers, measures, harmonies, and in the motions of the celestial bodies, and what happens because of them.

And if he were in the second, it signifies wealth and profit and the increase of substance, and the increase of honor and a good reputation with the king and from the king; and a good status and good condition between men, both for the native and others.

And if he were in the third, it signifies the good condition of siblings from brothers and sisters, and of friends from friends.[359] For a native it signifies an abundance of brothers and sisters according to natural possibility; and a multitude of the friends of the native[360] and of people in the household and of those loving him.

And if he were in the fourth, it signifies exchanges of words between men more so than usual; also contentions and sorrows or griefs that are going to fall between men.

---

[358] Bonatti is pointing out that that because ingress charts may be cast for any of the Sun's four ingresses into the cardinal signs, we can have delineations for Mercury (who is never farther from the Sun than 27°) in many different signs. But this is not quite satisfactory, since in an Aries ingress, Mercury could not be in Taurus (since that is farther than 27° from the beginning of Aries). But Bonatti also occasionally suggests that we can do monthly ingresses, so perhaps there is no problem here.

[359] Bonatti's use of *ex* instead of *a* is unusual and suggests that a subset of siblings or friends will benefit. But the point is not emphasized enough to make much of it; it could simply be a stylistic variation.

[360] Reading *nati* (sing.) instead of *natorum* (pl.).

And if he were in the fifth, it signifies fortune from children; and from the direction of children, and gladness and from rumors arriving from some other place; and men will rejoice from dances or games and delightful things; and that sorrows that already had been, will leave them; and matters over which they will rejoice and be happy, will come over them. The same thing will happen to a native both in a nativity and in a revolution, if Mercury were then so found.

And if he were in the sixth, it signifies contentions which will come to men, and likewise to a native, from the direction of ignoble people, and deceptions from the direction of male and female slaves; and likewise that of male and female servants, and small animals, and the worsening and breaking apart of matters and honor.

And if he were in the seventh, it signifies playfulness and delight from the direction of women and from women, and contentions because of that.

And if he were in the eighth, it signifies contentions which fall between men because of things already past, which will be renewed between them. And if it were a nativity or the revolution of a nativity, it signifies that enmities will happen to the native from neighbors and from the direction of neighbors, which he could hardly or never avoid; and they will speak lies against him, and contentions will happen to him because of that, and because of substances which were left to him by the dead or because of a very antiquated thing.

And if he were in the ninth, it signifies mutual praise between men, and honesty. And for a native it signifies wisdom, learning; and if he were to adhere to the *quadrivium*, he will advance well in it, and particularly in astronomy, and even in the other sciences; and that he will be praised for it by people known to him and even by others.

And if he were in the tenth, it signifies that a native will acquire a magistracy and dignities and great honors because of literature and writings; and the *quadrivium* [is] of arithmetic, [geometry], music, and astronomy. It signifies the same in the revolution of the world for those who are experienced in those sciences.

But if he were in the eleventh, it signifies mutual friendship between men is going to come; and in a nativity and in the revolution of a nativity it signifies a multitude of friends, and joy because of nobles and from nobles.

Indeed if he were in the twelfth, it signifies (in a revolution of the year of the world) the absurdity of men in the revolution, and their ignorance. If however it were in a nativity or in the revolution of a nativity, it signifies the stupidity of the native, and the diversity of his mind, and the lack of knowledge or sense, his imbecility and drunkenness and shallowness and impudence, and ineptitude in going and returning and asking about unfit matters, and the matters have no basis. And if it occurred to him to know or understand or discern something, this will be more in beasts than in other matters.[361]

Chapter 101: On the Moon, if she were the Lady of the Year– what she would signify

However, if the Moon were the Lady of the Year or Revolution, and of good condition (namely made fortunate and strong, free of impediments), it signifies the good condition of the vulgar generally; and even the good condition of sailors and mothers, *lectatorum*[362] also, and gourmands[363] or gluttons, and their diurnal rest;[364] and the goodness of their way of life. If however she were impeded, it signifies the contrary of these things which I have said, and the bad condition of the aforesaid, and of all of their significations.

And if she were in human signs, there will be impediment in men according to the sex of the sign in which she is. And if she were in fiery signs, impediment will fall upon everything that she were to signify of fiery things. If however she were in earthy ones, it will fall upon all that she were to signify of earthy things. If indeed she were in airy signs, it will fall upon all that she were to signify of airy things. Likewise if she were in watery signs, it will fall upon all that she were to signify of watery things. And if she were in a sign formed in the image of some other animal, it will fall upon animals shaped in the image of that sign.

And Abū Ma'shar said, [see] in what kind of sign [the planets] are being aspected: the narration will be about all of this in the way I revealed to you in the chapter on Saturn. And he said, know this, and understand well, because all of these belong to the secrets of the science of the stars. And he said there will be nothing in them which would be hidden from you, with the aid of God.

---

[361] I take this to mean that he will learn about large animals and livestock instead of more intellectual disciplines.

[362] Unknown word. Possibly a paronym of the many *lect-* words pertaining to reading. But it is more likely from *lectum* (or *lectus*), "couch, bed." This would make sense in light of terms for gluttony that follow, making the word mean something like "those who lay around in bed."

[363] *Guliardorum.* I read this tentatively as "gourmands" from *gulo*, to be a gourmand or glutton (and to match the following "or gluttons"); but it could also be read (as Zoller does) as *goliardorum* or "goliards," i.e., wandering minstrels or *bon vivants*. Both the eating and the wandering are fitting for the Moon.

[364] *Diurnalem quietudinem.* This must mean they rest all the time–i.e., for the whole day and night, and not just during daytime hours (which would be *diurnam quietudinem*).

However, you can attend to a certain thing whose basis I have not found, nor even was it said by any sage: that whatever kind of revolution of the year it was, or of whatever kind its Lord was, if it were to rain noticeably on the eleventh day of the entrance into June,[365] that evil and detriment and impediment will fall in fruits and things born of the earth, and their destruction by one-sixth. And if the Lord of the hour of the Ascendant of the revolution were impeded, detriment will be suffered by one-fifth. Indeed if the Moon were then impeded, it will happen to one-fourth. Indeed if the Lord of the Ascendant of the revolution were impeded, one-third of the aforesaid will be destroyed.

Again, you will consider whether it rains on the sixth day of the entrance into October[366] or not: because if it rains by means of rain,[367] you will judge there are going to be harmful rains; and more strongly and more harmfully so, if the conjunction of the Sun and Moon or their opposition were to be present on that day; and more strongly so if the conjunction were in a moist mansion [of the Moon].[368]

Chapter 102: What the Moon would signify in a revolution of the year of the world or [in a] nativity in every house, or in the revolution of a nativity, whether she is Lady of the Year or not

If the Moon were in the first in a revolution of the year of the world, whether she is Lady of the Year or not, it signifies fast changes of men in that revolution–from place to place, from one thing to another, from one proposal to another; and it signifies the effecting of things into which men introduce themselves. And it signifies preeminence and dignities for those for whom it is appropriate, and even that men will acquire good from their elders [or those greater than them]; and those who have mothers will acquire good from them; and men will rejoice over women. And if it were a nativity, good will happen to the native. The same in his revolution.

If however she were in the second, it signifies grief and sorrow which happen to the native because of substance, and that they will lose their goods in that revolution; likewise for a native it will be destroyed [or diminished].

---

[365] When the Sun is at approximately 20° Gemini.
[366] When the Sun is at approximately 12° Libra.
[367] I am not sure what distinction Bonatti is drawing here.
[368] See Tr. 10 on astrometeorology.

And if she were in the third, it signifies that men will be friendly to one another, and especially in lands which are in the division of the sign in which the Moon then is; likewise it will happen between brothers, for their love will be increased. And if there were enmity between them, it will be decreased; and men will perfect the matters which they begin, and for the perfection of which they strive; and they will even acquire good from the wealthy and the magnates; and dignities from kings and nobles and wealthy and great men who are fit for a kingdom. And pilgrimages will be suitable and useful (unless Saturn or Mars were to work against it). You may say the same about the affairs of a native, and that he will strive to be with nobles and wealthy people who are not slaves to money.

But if she were in the fourth, and the revolution were diurnal, it signifies its beginning to be evil, and impediment; however the end will be praiseworthy. If however it were nocturnal, neither the beginning nor end will be praised; men's affairs will be restricted,[369] and even persons will suffer detriment, unless Jupiter were to work to the contrary. And if it were a nativity or its revolution, the same will happen to the native. And if it were a question, the querent will be saddened because of it. And he will be happy just as was said about the diurnal or nocturnal revolution. Abū Ma'shar said [this will be so] unless it was a question about an acquired treasure or a buried thing (because it is the best in this, for the thing will appear and be uncovered).

And if she were in the fifth, it signifies having children in that revolution. And if it were a nativity, it signifies a multitude of children. And if it were the revolution of a nativity, it signifies having children in it, if [the native's] nature were fit to be able to do this. And this signifies masculinity in a nocturnal matter; if however it were diurnal, it signifies femininity. You may say the same in nativities and their revolutions, and questions; nor will many horrible things appear. And Abū Ma'shar said it signifies the arrival of rumors from faraway parts, about which men will rejoice, and particularly parents whose children are absent. And he said if you wished to know what the rumors were, look at the planet from which the Moon is being separated, because the rumors will be according to its nature. And if you wished to know whether the rumors were written on paper, or a legate had brought them by mouth, look at the Moon and Mercury to see if she is joined to him or is being separated from him. And if she were separated from the Lord of the seventh and were joined to Mercury, the

---

[369] Reading *minuentur* for *minuetur*.

rumors will be written on paper. Indeed if she were separated from Mercury or from his[370] Lord, the legate relates his own rumors.

And if she were in the sixth, Abū Ma'shar said it signifies quarrels and contention from the direction of fathers, and wealth from quadrupeds, and the health of the body.

And if she were in the seventh, he said it signifies wealth from the direction of women and marriage, and success because of them.

And he said if she were in the eighth, it signifies the ruin, and being finished, and the deposing, of the king (or his death); and confusion in works, and men will testify falsely, namely one against another; and they will quarrel with each other, and one will strive to chase away the other and eject him from his own place. And there will be tribulations and anxieties in men, and infirmities of the spirit or mind, like those which happen to raging people who are not in their right minds[371] (who are called lunatics by the vulgar). For it signifies enchanters and enchantresses pretending to know enchantments of this kind, for the reason that they might extort something from some people, because of which enchantments certain people in tunics falsely blaspheme astrologers. And there will be evil thoughts in the hearts of men. And if it were a nativity, the native will apply himself to these. It will signify the same in the revolution of a nativity.

And Abū Ma'shar said if she were in the ninth it signifies taking part in journeys, and evil thoughts, and the changing [over] of the king from region to region,[372] and the aid of women, and the knowledge of the dispensation of the kingdom and other things. And he said if the ninth domicile were of the domiciles of Mercury, it signifies wisdom of the stars. And if it were of the domiciles of Venus, it signifies the loftiness of the sciences and singing.[373] And if were of the domiciles of Mars, it signifies the mastery of instruments and the work or arms. And if it were of the domiciles of Jupiter, it signifies the divine cult and knowledge in the law, and the preeminence of judges. And if it were of the domiciles of Saturn, it signifies the science of alchemy and engagement in it. For men will be eager for this in that revolution. Likewise [for] a native in whose nativity the Moon were in the ninth, or in a revolution.

---

[370] *Eius.* It is impossible to say whether this means Mercury's Lord, the Lord of the seventh, or the Moon's Lord. According to Bonatti's style, one would expect Mercury's Lord. But Mercury's Lord has not been mentioned, only the Lord of the seventh.

[371] *Veris.*

[372] Bonatti is probably speaking of something more substantial than travel. His use of *mutatio* is typically used in reference to a planet changing signs or a political regime change. But he does not say there will be another king. Perhaps it means the king will change residence?

[373] *Cantilena.* The word literally means "gossip," but Bonatti uses it in relation to singing.

And if there were a benefic,[374] not impeded, in the 2nd or in the 4th, wealth will follow[375] from that; lacking this, however, it will not. But if a malefic were there, harm will follow from that. And if the malefic were impeded, the destructions of substance will follow, and it signifies many and diverse masteries.

And if [the ninth] were the domicile of the Sun, it signifies knowledge and foresight in all *quadrivial* disciplines. And if it were her own domicile, it signifies the general knowledge of all things which are taken from the waters or which proceed from them. And he said, know that the Moon has these particular [meanings] amongst the other planets.

And Abū Ma'shar said if she were in the tenth, it signifies the effecting of matters in [horary] questions, but there will be a command of the king in this, if it were in the day. If indeed it were in the night, it signifies the effecting of matters from the direction of the king and women, and this will be quick. And he said, but a matter in each of the times (namely in the day and in the night) will not be durable. Likewise if a king were to undertake to rule in it, he will be deposed quickly; because this place is a winning one in the signification of the Sun; indeed the Moon is not sufficient except in a middling way in this signification.

And if she were in the eleventh, it signifies that one friend will follow from another; it even signifies the attainment of things which men hope for, and in which they have trust. Likewise for a native, both in a nativity and in a revolution.

Indeed in the twelfth, it signifies impediment and duress, and the instability of things, and quarrels and prisons from the direction of enemies.

And Abū Ma'shar said, if you were asked about some matter, when it will be, and the Moon were your significatrix, and she were in the twelfth, this will be at the hour of the Moon's exit from that same place: for the matter will be perfected through this, and the absent person will be and will come, and especially if this were and the end of the lunar month. And if the Moon were impeded by Saturn, then judge something horrible and evil, and you should not have doubt in this, if God wills.[376]

---

374 Reading *fortuna* for *fortunate* ("if she were made fortunate").

375 Reading *sequetur* for *sequentur*.

376 Bonatti usually uses *dubito* to mean fear, so he could mean, "you should not have fear in this, if God wills." But why should we not fear something "horrible and evil"?

Chapter 103: What the Head and Tail and comets would signify in a revolution of the year, both of the world and of nativities

It was spoken above about the significations of the seven planets—what each one of them would signify in every sign and in every house in the revolutions of years, both of the world and of nativities, or in nativities themselves. Now it remains to speak about the Head of the Dragon (what it would signify in revolutions themselves) and its Tail, and about comets—what hairy or tailed stars would signify,[377] and how many there are, just as will be spoken of in its own particular chapter.

Abū Ma'shar said, know that if the Head of the Dragon were in Aries, it signifies the loftiness of great and noble men, and the dejection of low-class or ignoble ones. And if the Tail were there, it signifies the bad disposition and bad condition of kings and nobles, and their injuries from the rustics or common people. And if one of the comets were there, it signifies the evil and detriment of the wealthy and the magnates and nobles in the parts of the east and Babylon; and a multitude of sorrows with the rustics. And he said if its appearance were in the parts of the east,[378] its work will be faster. Indeed if it were to appear out of the direction of the west, it will be slower, *etc.*

And if the Head were in Taurus, it signifies the killing of wealthy and great men in the northern parts; and it signifies a multitude of differences between the wealthy and magnates and the rustics of the western parts. And if the Tail were there, it signifies a scarcity of piety and sympathy in the hearts of men; and there will be useless pilgrimages in those parts, of little wealth and much labor. And if one of the comets were to appear in its direction,[379] it signifies the bad condition of men and a scarcity of their good, and injuries of rebels against those who are in those regions; which if it were to appear[380] in the parts of the east, its work will be faster. And if it were to appear in the west, it will be slower, *etc.*

And if the Head were in Gemini, it signifies infirmities are going to come to the wealthy and to magnates, and this will happen because of winds and earthquakes, and the filthy smokiness of the land, and wars taking place between middle class men and the wealthy (or nobles and magnates); and a case of

---

[377] The word for "comet" in Latin (deriving from the Greek) is *stella cometa*, literally a "star with hair." They are so called because their streaky tails sometimes look like hair.

[378] This must mean "if it appeared in Aries in the eastern part *of the chart for the revolution.*"

[379] *In directo eius*, probably referring to the direction of Taurus–i.e., if it is in Taurus.

[380] Reading *apparuerit* for *apparuerint*.

vermin in trees. If however the Tail were there, it signifies that the rustics will be exalted and will be stubborn and facetious against the king, and that they will fool him; and they will rise up against his soldiers and the wealthy (or his representatives). But if one of the comets were to appear in its direction, it signifies the appearance of pleasures and fornications, and unclean venereal cultivation in men; and the religious and those serving God will be thrown down and despised. And if were to appear in the parts of the east, its work will be faster; and if it were to appear in the parts of the west, it will be slower.

And if the Head were in Cancer, it signifies the goodness of the king's deeds toward the rustics and common people, and the largesse [of those works] toward them, and that they will collect the substance of the king (and after it was collected in its own places, they will disperse it). And if the Tail were there, it signifies a multitude of pestilence and mortality, and sudden deaths, and fornications, and the abuse of venereal cultivation, and a scarcity of justice, and the breaking and loss of the *census*; and the destruction of houses, of substances, and the change of the wealthy and magnates from place to place, and their pilgrimage; and the bad condition of the great workings of their own hands, and of writers and other things signified by Mercury.[381] And if one of the comets were to appear there, it signifies a multitude of locusts destroying the harvests; and a case of vermin in grain and in trees, and a scarcity of produce, and a multitude of vermin in them. And if it were to appear in the parts of the east, its work will be faster. And if it were to appear in the parts of the west, its work will be slower, and it signifies the goodness of the king toward[382] the rustics, and his piety concerning them.

And if the Head were in Leo, it signifies a multitude of rivers and the appearance of fires in the air, many injuries, and evil and killing. And if the Tail were there, it signifies a multitude of obscurity [darkness] in the air, and earthquakes; and the increase of waters and the detriment of trees, and the destruction of the harvests. And if one of the comets were to appear there, it signifies an infestation of wolves, and impediment to men from them; and a case of vermin in the grain, and the destruction of houses and of substances. And if its appearance were in the parts of the east, its work will be faster. And if it were in the parts of the west, its work will be slower.

And if the Head were in Virgo, it signifies the destruction of the harvests and the rest of the produce; and a scarcity of all things which are measured, and a

---

[381] Why Mercury, if the Tail is in Cancer?
[382] *In.*

case of vermin in trees, and the detriment of those who remain from the first destruction, even after they were restored in the places in which they will be believed to be saved or guarded. And if the Tail were there, it signifies the hatred that is going to fall upon the wealthy and magnates; and there will be fights and dissensions, and battles between them; and churches and the great houses of religions will suffer detriment; and there will be diversities and controversies between men, and debates and dissensions in faith. And if one of the comets were to appear there, it signifies the taking away of certain things from the household members of kings and magnates, and their changing from place to place, or from region to region; and they will be led practically as captives or deported people, or sent over to the borders. And there will be a taking away of their goods without their having it again,[383] nor will they be recovered by them or through them. And if its appearance were in the parts of the east, its work will be faster. If however it were in the west, its work will be slower.

And if the Head were in Libra, it signifies that kings and the wealthy and the nobles or magnates will make use of their own men upon the rustics, contrary to justice, and especially against those whom they will rule; and they will strive to extort from them what they ought not to; and they will accuse them and say they have offended them concerning something which will not be their fault; and they will think they have taken from them something which they have not taken, [and] because of this they will inveigh against them. And they will afflict them with punishments so much, that for that reason they will come into poverty and need; and they will fool them. But if the Tail were there, it signifies the mortality and detriment of quadrupeds; and there will be dryness and a heaviness of frost in their own seasons, destroying harvests in the fields, and herbs, and seeds, and trees, so that little produce will be collected from them. And if one of the comets were to appear there, it signifies robbers and cutters of roads, [and] pillagers who openly send their own men to the people, and they will plunder all whom they are able; and men's thoughts will be in fear lest they fall into poverty; and they will expect harms, and they will fear at one time because of cold, at another because of heat, and this will last a long time in their hearts. And if its appearance were in the parts of the east, its work will be faster. If however it were in the parts of the west, it will be slower.

And if the Head were in Scorpio, Abū Ma'shar said it signifies good and joy in middle-class men, and evil and sorrow in great men; and it signifies wars and

---

[383] *Rehabitio.*

battles and wounds; a multiplication of fornication with deception. And he said [it signifies] their falling into the hands of the king in addition to what will happen to them in terms of grief and sorrow. And he said if the Tail were there, it signifies a case of fevers in men, and infirmities happening in the chest; and a multitude of catarrhs [or inflammations] in the throat, with the joy of the wealthy in that time; and their happiness through much peace, and a multitude of wars; and the collection of substances, and the destruction of their homes. And if one of the comets were to appear there, it signifies a multitude of battles and wars and rebels against the king; and the change of soldiers between them;[384] and its investigation by them in addition to what is not in their hands, nor their power; for they will seek impossible things. And if its appearance were in the parts of the east, its work will be faster. Indeed if it were in the parts of the west, it will be slower.

And if the Head were in Sagittarius, it signifies the affliction of the rustics of Babylon by their own king; and that he will oppress them with injuries and torments; and that all of their quadrupeds will be impeded (and particularly horses and other animals which those making war, and bearers of arms, use)— and more strongly so if it were in the last half of Sagittarius. And there will be impediments in the instruments of wars, and their falling apart. It even signifies the heaviness of the air, and darkness with much corruption; and the heat will be oppressive in its own seasons. And if the Tail were there, it signifies the dejection of the nobles and great men, and their bad condition; and the exaltation of low-class people and the ignoble; and more strongly so if it were in the first half of Sagittarius. And the wise and scribes and doctors of the law, and consuls or advisors will be saddened, or hidden impediments will come to them, because of which they will be saddened. And if one of the comets were to appear there, it signifies the depression of the aforesaid, and tribulation falling upon them (and particularly scribes); their annihilation with the loss of substance because of a concealment. And if it were to appear in the direction of the east, its work will be faster. If however it were in the west, it will be slower.

And if the Head were in Capricorn, it signifies the gladness and loftiness and joy of the wealthy and of great men, or nobles, and their exaltation; and the fall of low-class and ignoble people who are called "tails" by certain people.[385] But if

---

[384] I believe this means there will be shifting loyalties among the soldiers, between the rebels and the king.

[385] *Qui a quibusdam caudae appellantur.* A *cauda* is not only a tail (as with the southern node of the Moon), but is also used in the context of mockery ("having a tail" or *caudam trahere* being equivalent to looking like a fool).

the Tail were there, it signifies harmful earthquakes in certain parts of the earth, and especially in the southern ones. And if one of the comets were to appear there, it signifies fornication in men in those times. And if its appearance were in the east, its work will be faster. If however it were in the west, it will be slower.

And if the Head were in Aquarius, it signifies the detriment of the religious, and of the faith of sectarians; and the death of certain ones of them, and of judges and doctors of the law. And if the Tail were there, Abū Ma'shar said it signifies the investigation of the king against the lords of inheritances in which they ought not to [have them]; and their being misleading in the *census*, and injuries and afflictions which he will administer against them, with their capture and whipping. And if one of the comets were to appear there, it signifies a multitude of battles, and killings, and tortures in the same season. And if its appearance were in the direction of the east, its work will be faster. If however it were in the west, it will be slower.

And if the Head were in Pisces, Abū Ma'shar said it signifies the loftiness of the nobles, and the excelling of each man in his own rank more than he would excel according to his nature, and the collection of substances in the houses of substance.[386] And if the Tail were there, it signifies the reaching of the soldiers over the king, and the multitude of the wealthy and the change of more[387] of the wealthy from their habitations because of sins, with much talking in a sect, and the appearance of novelties. And if one of the comets were to appear in the same place, there will be the greatest war over the relations of the king;[388] and they will kill each other,[389] and there will be enmities in the others, and a taking away of their hand from obedience.[390] If however its appearance were in the

---

[386] I have substituted Abū Ma'shar's version of this sentence as found in the *Flowers*, since Bonatti's version is both incomplete and confusing (and seems to have an incorrect verb). The meaning seems to be that people will advance socially beyond what their natural standing would dictate, and banks will be filled with tax revenues.

[387] *Quam plurimorum.*

[388] Following the *Flowers* by adding "of the king."

[389] The *Flowers* adds, "and they will be killed by others who are elevated above them."

[390] Reading *ab obedentia* with the *Flowers*, instead of *ad obedentiam* ("toward obedience"). Likewise, *OGC* (vol. I, p. 322-23) reads: the "opposition of the *qai'ids* and knights towards the king, their removal from obedience in serving [him]." I believe this reference to "hands" comes from the early feudal ceremony involving the placing of the hands into those of one to whom one makes fealty or homage. Moreover, by the 11th Century, contracts of homage or fealty used *miles* (soldier) interchangeably with *vassus* or *vassalus* (vassal). Thus I believe this sentence means that vassals of all sorts will break their promises to support their king.

direction of the east, it will be faster in this which it signifies. And if it were in the direction of the west, its work will be slower in this which it signifies.

However, if you wished to see the direction in which what the comet signifies will come, it will be in which part its tail is. Because in that same direction will be what it signified in terms of tribulation and pestilence. Indeed the hour which I told you, in the remaining works, in this book, in which everything that was said [will be], will be when [the Sun] will have come to the sign which was of the substance of those things which I told you; or to the planet whose nature is in the operation just like the nature of the effect which appeared to you would be in the same year.[391] And he said, know this and consider it, because it is of the secrets of the science of the stars, and its truth; of which work it is a precept that it be hidden,[392] and it not be seen except by you, according to how I have expounded it to you.

Chapter 104: On Comets

However, Ptolemy says[393] there are nine types of comets, of which the first is called a javelin, the second a *tenaculum*,[394] the third a measuring-rod,[395] the fourth a *miles*,[396] the fifth the lord of *ascona*,[397] the sixth a morning or dawn comet, the

---

[391] I have used mainly the *Flowers* for this sentence, since it is marginally more clear than Bonatti's own; but I have added "the Sun" in brackets because that is what Bonatti himself writes. Bonatti's sentence runs: "Indeed in the remaining works (which were said), Abū Ma'shar said the hour will be when the Sun will have come to the sign which is of their substance (which I told you), or the planet whose nature is in the work, just like the nature of what is to come, which were to appear to you to be going to happen in that year." My sense is that Bonatti must have made a bad paraphrase of this sentence from the compiler of the *Flowers*, and not the other way around.

[392] The *Flowers* says, "This is of the secrets of astronomy which is worth the trouble to be hidden." I believe that Bonatti mistakenly read the manuscript abbreviation *precium* ("worth, price") as that of *praeceptum* ("precept").

[393] According to Thorndike (1949, p. 29), a pseudo-Ptolemy has written a list of the nine types, and they are obviously the basis of Bonatti's text. I have not yet seen this text. Below I will list pseudo-Ptolemy's versions where appropriate.

[394] Following pseudo-Ptolemy for Bonatti's *coenaculum* ("dining room"). A *tenaculum* is an instrument for holding something (from *teneo*, to hold). By the description below, perhaps it is a kind of tray.

[395] Reading *pertica* with pseudo-Ptolemy for Bonatti's *partica*. A *pertica* is a measuring rod used to measure grants of land (and it is said below to pertain to agricultural predictions); so perhaps it looks like two long rods.

[396] *Miles*. This word usually means "soldier," but can also mean a woman who is giving birth for the first time. Below, it is said to be of the nature of Venus and is related to people trying to bring new things into being. Since there is no English equivalent of *miles*, I will retain the Latin.

seventh silver, the eighth rosy, the ninth black. And he said that the first four of these are likened to stars. And all signify wars and terrors and great events in the world. And he said that from their color will be known the evil that is to be, and from the nature of the sign in which they first appear; and it will be known when the evil will be, for if it were to appear in the east or north and it were to go toward the south, it will be speedy; and if in the west, [the evil] will be delayed.

Indeed that which is called a javelin is horrible to see, and proceeds near the Sun, and appears during the day; which when it appears, signifies changes and the destruction of produce, trees, and things born of the earth; and the mortality of kings and of the wealthy, and of those who are fit for a realm.

Indeed, that which is called a *tenaculum* is practically of the color of Mars, and has beneath it a ray like the smoke under ashes; which when it appears, signifies scarcity, but not in an excessive way–but not famine. And it signifies battles concerning which the religious interject themselves beyond the degree to which they are competent [to carry out].

That which is called a measuring-rod has a thick ray and it drags a measuring-rod behind it, and is not very bright; which when it appears, it signifies dryness and a scarcity of waters, and the smallness of the *annona*; which if it were joined with one of the planets, it signifies other things according to the nature and disposition [of that] to which it is corporally joined. Like if it were joined with Saturn, there will be mortality, and much of it in old men and Jews and the religious and those who are dressed in Saturnian clothes. However, if it were joined with Jupiter, its significations will appear in kings and magnates according to good and evil, in proportion to how [Jupiter] were disposed (made fortunate and strong, or made unfortunate and weak). Indeed if it were joined with Mars, it signifies even more battles, and mortalities by the sword and the shedding of blood, and the burning of fire. However, with the Sun it cannot appear. But if it were joined with Venus, it signifies dryness and a great diminution of waters. Indeed if with Mercury, it signifies the death of youths and the wise and scribes. If indeed with the Moon, it signifies mortality what is going to fall between the common people and other low-class persons.

---

[397] 1491 reads: *astonae*, and Thorndike's pseudo-Ptolemy reads *ascone*. Could this be a misread for *acontiae*? *Acontiae* (Gr. *akontiai*) are meteors or shooting stars with dartlike trains–but Bonatti has already used a synonym (*veru*) for his first comet called a javelin. And his description below, describing rays like wings, does not seem like *acontiae*–and why the "lord" of *asconae*?

That which is called a *miles* is of the nature of Venus and inclines greatly toward the manner of the Moon; and it has a long ray, and likewise hair, and extends [the ray or hair] behind itself; which if it were to appear, it travels the twelve signs; and it signifies the harming of kings and of nobles and magnates, and that men will rise up in the world who wish to change the laws and ancient things, and lead new things [into being]; and its worse signification will appear from the part toward which it extends its tail and hair.

The lord of *ascona* is said to be of the condition of Mercury, and its color is blue. And it appears small in comparison with the other comets; and it has a long tail, and extends its rays to one side or another in the manner of a wing having heads underneath it, bringing it down to one place. Which if it were to appear, it signifies the death of kings or magnates and nobles who are fit for a realm; and especially toward the part into which it extends its tail or rays; and it signifies battles. And I saw one appear in the 663rd year of the era of the Arabs, in which Pope Alexander died; and not long afterwards King Manfred was killed by a certain brother of the king of France named Charles; and again, not long after that Conradin was killed by this same Charles in the kingdom of Apulia (and many dukes and many barons with him), and this was in [the year] 665 of the era of the Arabs. And there were many battles and dissensions from the time of the appearance of this comet, and they lasted a long time.[398]

That which is called morning or dawn, is red. And it has a long tail, but less than that of the lord of *asconae*. And it is of the nature of Mars, for it has his significations; which if it were to appear out of the part of the east, having its head below it, [it signifies] battles and the burning of fire, and pestilences and famine in the land of Babylon and in the lands of the Arabs and the Phormati; and dryness in Egypt and a scarcity of waters; and this will be extended up to the western parts.

Indeed, that which is called silver, has a ray in the likeness of the purest silver, whose clarity exceeds the clarity of all nocturnal stars; which if it were to appear while Jupiter is located in Pisces or Cancer, it signifies an abundance of grain and produce in the parts in which it were to appear. Indeed if Jupiter were in Scorpio, these things will happen, but somewhat less than this.

---

[398] Pope Alexander IV died in May 1261, but the comet was also said to herald the death of Urban IV (which happened on September 9, 1264). King Manfred of Sicily was killed in battle against Charles I of Anjou on February 26 or 27, 1266. Charles I of Anjou executed the teenage Conradin (then the popular King of Sicily and Jerusalem, and the last of the legitimate Hohenstaufens) in on October 29, 1268. In the East as well, there were many changes and upheavals in the Crusades.

Indeed that which is called rosy, is big and round, and the face of a human can be observed in it, the color of which is in between gold and silver; which if it were to appear, signifies the death of kings and magnates and the wealthy and nobles, and of those who are fit for a kingdom; and an event of great matters and of an appearance of those things themselves, and of the causes of ancient things; but they will change for the better.

That which is called black is of the nature of Saturn, practically of a similar color to him; which if it were to appear, signifies mortality through natural death and death by the sword and by beheadings.

Chapter 105: What the Head of the Dragon and the Tail would signify in every house, both in revolutions and in nativities or questions

In the preceding chapter it was stated what the Head of the Dragon and its Tail signify in every sign; in this one must be stated what they signify in every house. Whence in any revolution you must consider in which house either of them is found.

And Abū Ma'shar said if the Head of the Dragon were in the first in any revolution or nativity or question, it signifies increase and strength and loftiness in that revolution, and this according to its conjunction with the planets. For if the Head were joined with benefics, it signifies the increase of good. If however it were joined with a malefic, it signifies the increase of evil (since its nature is to increase).

And if it were in the second, it signifies good fortune in substance, and its increase; it signifies the same in a nativity or question if it were in the second.

And if it were in the third, it signifies that the native will be an interpreter of dreams, and will be of good faith. And there will be useful, short journeys in that revolution, and acquisitions and profits (likewise for a native).

And if it were in the fourth, and the fourth house [domicile?] were Aries or Leo or Sagittarius or Gemini or Libra or Aquarius, it signifies the increase of good and profit from lands and vineyards, and from other immovable things. If however the 4th house [domicile?] were Taurus or Virgo or Capricorn or Cancer or Scorpio or Pisces, it signifies harm and the decrease of profit.

If it were in the fifth, it signifies the fortune of children and from children, and their increase and good and joy, and freedom from contrary and displeasing things.

And if it were in the sixth, it signifies the increase of small animals which are not ridden; and of slaves. And there will be strong and harmful infirmities.

And if it were in the seventh, it signifies the increase of partners, and good from women, and an increase of sexual intercourse, and the strength of enemies (both of a native or querent, and generally).

And if it were in the eighth, it signifies the good condition of men in their persons, and the strength of a native or querent in a nativity or question; and it signifies the taking away of grief (and its scarcity).

And if it were in the ninth, and were joined with benefics, it signifies religion and good pilgrimages, and useful and profitable long journeys. If however it were joined with malefics, it signifies the contrary of what was said.

And if it were in the tenth, it signifies that men will apply themselves to the investigation of divine and hidden things, and the scrutiny of the truth of the Most High God. It even signifies loftiness and reverence and veneration, and strength and fortune in dignities or masteries and honors.

And if it were in the eleventh, Abū Ma'shar said that there is no virtue of the Head or Tail in it–for good or evil.[399]

And if it were in the twelfth, it signifies the increase of evil and scarcity of good.

Chapter 106: What the Tail would signify in the houses [domiciles?]

If the Tail were in the first in a revolution or question, it signifies the detriment of men and the native, and the separating away of the good, and eradication and dangers and tribulations. And if a son were to remain rich after his father's passing away, he will be reduced to poverty. And if he were to remain a pauper, he will persevere in it.

And if it were in the second, it signifies the destruction of all substances, and the poverty of a native, and his being in need, and his being occupied with evils,[400] and his fall from his own station; and this will happen to him from a direction from which he will not have fear, nor will it be suspected.

And if it were in the third, it signifies the detriment of brothers, and from brothers and sisters, and because of them and their burden. And if the third house [domicile?] were a masculine sign, this will happen to brothers. And if it

---

[399] Non est in eo virtus capiti seu caudae boni vel mali.

[400] Occupationem in malis. This might also mean that he is engaged in evil things, but that does not seem to be the sense of the whole paragraph.

were a feminine one, this will happen in sisters. And perhaps that they will die from them,[401] since [the Tail's] nature is to destroy [or diminish]; or a quarrel will happen to him from his brothers, or with others of his lesser blood-relatives, or with friends or neighbors.

If however it were in the fourth, it signifies the poverty and need, enmity and labor which they will sustain in the investigation of matters, without usefulness.

And if it were in the fifth, it signifies the destruction of fortune and its expulsion, and a case of horrible things upon children; and that those who have children will be saddened because of it, and they will be in need; and that men will carry their own old clothes.

And if it were in the sixth, it signifies the laziness and weakness of male and female slaves, and small animals, and their decrease (and if it were a nativity, the native will not have fortune in them), and a decrease of infirmities. And if there were infirmities they will be decreasing and diminishing, and decimating[402] or exterminating the bodies of the sick.[403]

And if it were in the seventh, it signifies that men will not rejoice with their wives like they are used to rejoicing with them in other revolutions; and there will be quarrels and contentions between them, and this will happen more in the rustics and the common people than in others. And if it were a nativity, it signifies that the native will not rejoice with wives, nor from wives, nor even from other women, but he will have quarreling and contentions with them (unless perhaps from those mattering to him), nor [will he rejoice] because of partners. And it signifies the strength of his enemies. You may say the same in his revolutions. However, he will not have many enemies, even if some.

And if it were in the eighth, it signifies the loss of things because of death, and that those who are supposed to inherit goods from the dead, will lose many of them. You can say the same, that it will happen to a native.

And if it were in the ninth, it signifies change from place to place (however, not exile); and the destruction [or decrease] of faith and religion, and long, useless journeys; but more likely harmful ones than lucrative ones.

And if it were in the tenth, it signifies the impediment of kings and nobles or magnates, and the destruction [or diminution] of their honor or dignities. And

---

401 This undoubtedly means, "from their detriment and burdens."

402 Reading *decimantes* for *demacantes*.

403 There seems to be a strain here between (a) the power of the Tail to decrease things, and (b) its malefic influence on what it touches–if infirmities are so decreased, why will they decimate and exterminate the bodies of the sick?

Abū Ma'shar said it signifies deposing and dangers, and a pilgrimage or fall [or mishap]. It signifies the same for a native.

And if it were in the eleventh, Abū Ma'shar said that there is no operation for [the Tail] in it.

And if it were in the twelfth, it signifies the detriment of large animals and the destruction[404] of them and of enemies; and few will be incarcerated in that revolution. And if they were incarcerated, the prisons will be emptied of them. The same will happen in nativities or in their revolutions, if the Tail were in the twelfth. Indeed Abū Ma'shar said if the Tail were in the twelfth, it signifies a scarcity of good fortune, and a scarcity of evils. And he said, concerning the significations of the planets and of the Head and Tail in the twelve houses, if they were in a better condition, say better; indeed if they were in a bad condition, change the content and say the contrary of the good (namely, the bad), and speak boldly, and do not fear, nor should you dismiss what I have told you; nor should you say otherwise, and you will discover [it], if God does not oppose [you].

Chapter 107: What the [malefic] fixed stars would signify in revolutions of years, and nativities, and what they would do in them

Having spoken of the revolutions of years, and of the things signified by the planets, and of the Head of the Dragon and its Tail (what they would signify in every house and in every sign), it now remains to speak of certain fixed stars which are found in every sign—of which certain ones signify serious evil and impediment, certain ones signify good. And this is a matter with which it is very necessary to concern oneself, because much concerning the judgments of revolutions and nativities and questions, and elections, depends on them and from them. For revolutions and nativities and questions and their judgments are changed by them with a powerful change, much more strongly than by the planets. And in this, many of the honest astrologers are often deceived, because they do not consider them in their judgments, but only the planets and the Parts. And this is the reason why they are sometimes deceived, and the contrary of what they judge happens in them, both in the good and in evil; and they are rebuked and held in slight esteem because of ignorance, when they are not to be rebuked. Nevertheless, I cannot excuse them from laziness or negligence—you

---

[404] *Diminutionem.*

however, if you were to consider them well in judgments, both of revolutions and nativities, and questions, you will not go astray, if God does not prevent it.

If however you were to calculate for every revolution or nativity or question, and you were to erect its figure, you will consider all the houses from the 1st to the 12th, and you will see whether one of the fixed stars written below is found in the degree of the cusp of some angle; and you will judge good or evil according to the nature of the one which you were to find in it, according to what I will tell you. And I will have told them to you just as I have found certain ones of them to be understood by the sayings of the wise, and certain ones by experienced and established reason.[405]

And Abū Ma'shar said, know that in the head of Aries are two stars, of which one is in the thirteenth degree and forty-fifth minute, and the other in the fourteenth degree and forty-fifth minute, which are of the nature of Mars and Saturn. And their peculiar nature is to harm, and they are on the northern side.

Indeed another is in the ninth degree of Taurus and the fifty-fifth minute, which is called the Pleiades. And another in the thirteenth degree of the same [sign]. And both are northern. And another is in its fourteenth degree and forty-fifth minute, and it is called the Devil.[406] And another is in the fifteenth [degree] of the same [sign], which is called the Head of the Devil or Gorgon.[407] And another is in its nineteenth degree and fifteenth minute, which is called Aldebaran; and all are of the nature of Mars. But Mercury and the Moon participate in the Pleiades.

Indeed another is in Gemini in the eighth degree, which is called the Shoulder of the Dog,[408] and it is of the nature of Mars and Saturn. And another is in its tenth degree and fifteenth minute, which is called Bella-trix, and is of the nature of Mars. Another is in its seventeenth degree and fifty-fifth minute, and its latitude is in the south. Another is in its eight-eenth degree and fifty-second minute, which is called the Witch,[409] and it is of the nature of the Sun and Mars and Saturn.

---

[405] Unfortunately, he does not tell us which ones he knows by his own experience.
[406] *Diabolus.*
[407] *Caput diaboli vel gorgonis.* Caput Algol.
[408] *Humerus Canis.*
[409] *Malefica.*

Another is in Cancer, in its second degree and third minute, which is called the Camel,[410] and it is of the nature of Saturn and the Moon. And another is in its seventh degree and fifty-fifth minute. And another is in its thirteenth degree, of the nature of the Sun and Moon, which is called Killing the Camel.[411] And another which is called the Foot of the Dog,[412] in the same degree, of the nature of Saturn; and another in the seventeenth degree and fifty-fifth minute, which are both northern, of the nature of Saturn.

Indeed in Leo is one star in the fifteenth degree and fifty-fifth minute, of the nature of Saturn.

However, in Virgo are two stars, of which one is in the seventh degree and eleventh minute of the same, and is of the nature of Mars. The other is in the fifteenth degree, of the nature of Saturn.

Indeed in Libra is one star in the twenty-sixth degree, and it is of the nature of Saturn.

However, in Scorpio are three stars, of which one is in its first degree and third minute; and the other in the eighth degree and seventh minute; and another in the ninth degree. And all are of the nature of Mars.

In Sagittarius are two small stars, of which one is in the nineteenth degree and second minute, another in the twenty-first degree and first minute, and they are of the nature of Saturn.

In Capricorn are two stars, of which one is in its twenty-seventh degree and second minute, and it is named The Evil One.[413] And the other is in its twenty-ninth degree and fifth minute. And both are of the nature of Saturn.

---

[410] *Camelus.*

[411] *Occidens Camelum.* Perhaps "The One Killing the Camel." But this star might belong in Capricorn, and mean the star that "Sets the Camel," i.e., it sets when the Camel rises.

[412] *Pes Canis.* Probably Mirzam (β Canis Major), in the paw.

[413] *Mala.* If singular, it refers to a feminine evil thing or person. But it could also be "Evils." Note that it is opposite a star in Cancer called "The Good One" (see below).

In Aquarius is one star in the ninth degree and fourth minute, of the nature of Mars and Saturn.[414]

Indeed in Pisces is one star in its fourth degree and seventh minute, and it is of the nature of Mars and Mercury.

Chapter 108: On the peculiar nature of the aforesaid [malefic] stars in every house[415]

If you were to see the Lord of the Year or Revolution, or of the nativity or question, joined with one of the aforesaid fixed stars in the same degree in the revolution of the year of the world, know that evil and impediment will fall upon the kings and the wealthy or nobles and magnates. You may say the same about the affairs of a native in nativities and questions and in the revolutions of nativities. And griefs and sorrows and malign thoughts will fall upon them, and infirmities from headaches, and fevers and death. And more strongly so if this were in Aries. And by how much their conjunction were less than one degree, by that much greater will its impediment be, until the conjunction then reaches to one minute. And if their conjunction were in one and the same minute, it will not only signify their impediment, but it will even signify their destruction and death. The same thing will happen if one of the aforesaid stars were to fall in the degree of the Ascendant of the revolution and of a nativity or question, by coming down up to one minute by means of the aforesaid conditions. And if one of the aforesaid stars were in the degree of the Ascendant of some nativity, the native will be unfortunate, bad, afflicted, and full of labor, and of many illnesses; and he will never rejoice in his own life; and his infirmities will more often by from headache; and more strongly so if the Ascendant of the nativity were the Ascendant of the year in which one of those stars was in the Ascendant of the revolution.

But if one of those stars were to fall in the 2nd from the from the Ascendant of the revolution, or the Lord of the 2nd were with one of them in the same degree (as was said) it signifies impediment is going to fall in the substance of men, and the destruction [or diminution] of them; and especially [that] of the

---

[414] Note that he says below there is a benefic fixed star exactly opposite this one (in Leo), of the nature of the benefics.
[415] Both 1491 and 1550 use *domus* for these houses.

wealthy and great or noble men; and dullness of mind will fall upon them; and they will weep from need and poverty, and will believe everything has forsaken them. And for this reason they will fall into sorrow and blaming; and the infirmities of that revolution will be from the impediment of the ears, neck and throat (like inflammation and dry catarrh, and the like); and more strongly so if this were in Taurus. And if one of the aforesaid stars were in the 2nd in some-one's nativity, or if [the nativity's] Ascendant were the 2nd from the Ascendant of the revolution, or the Lord of the 2nd of the nativity were joined with one of the stars, it signifies that the native will be of bad condition, a pauper, of little wealth, and will lose what he will earn. Nor will his own substance be capable of growing because of his own wealth. He will be dull, lazy, of little skill, and will be reputed very little, or rather as virtually nothing in relation to his birth status. And if he were wealthy, he will be impoverished, and his substance will run through his hands, with him not knowing how. Even with him wanting and trying to keep or guard it, it would fly away.[416] And he will have many illnesses, and often his illnesses will be in the ears and throat and neck and shoulder; and more strongly so, if the 2nd house were Taurus.

And if one of the stars were to fall in the 3rd from the Ascendant of a revolu-tion, or the Lord of the 3rd were with one of them in the same degree (as was said about the 1st and the 2nd) it signifies the evil and impediment of the houses of oration [or prayer], and that short journeys will not be useful in that revolu-tion; and that there will be quarrels and contentions between brothers, and one will be saddened because of the other, without a reason why it should be so; and there will be severe and chronic infirmities in men; and they will be more often of the shoulder blades and shoulders and arms; and more strongly so if this were in Gemini. And if one of the aforesaid stars were in the 3rd in someone's nativity, or his Ascendant were the 3rd from the Ascendant of a revolution, or the Lord of the 3rd of the nativity were joined with one of the stars, it signifies that the native will be evil to his own brothers and to those who give one [brother] preferment over him, and who think him to be a friend of theirs, and to his own lesser blood-relatives and neighbors. And he will be inclined to see another person as evil,[417] and he will rejoice if he were to see adversity or impediment happen to someone; and he will be intent on acting badly, and his thought will not be on the good. Nor will he see good for himself, or useful-ness, from his own journeys (and especially the short ones); and if he were to

---

[416] Reading *volet* for *valeat*.
[417] *Malum alienum.*

strive to go abroad on the aforesaid pilgrimages,[418] he will lose his own substance in them; however it will not[419] be a great matter for him to lose his substance, only if he were not to lose his person with it. And the greatest proportion of his illnesses will be of shoulder blades and arms.

And if one of the aforesaid stars were in the 4th from the Ascendant of the revolution, or the Lord of the 4th were with one of them in the same degree, as was said regarding the other houses, it signifies evil and the impediment of farmers and harvests and things born of the earth; and it even signifies battles between cities and estates, and among other habitations; and that there will likewise be quarrels between fathers and sons, and disputes and envy, and one will be saddened because of the other, and *vice versa*. And the end of those things which men will do, or which will come in that year, will be to the bad. And if someone were to buy land or another estate or inheritance, he will not see from it what he believed [he would], or what he hoped or intended. And there will be many infirmities of men in the chest or of the lungs, and from the parts adjacent to them (and more strongly so, if this were in Cancer). And if one of the aforesaid stars were in the 4th in someone's nativity, or [the nativity's] Ascendant were the 4th of the revolution, or the Lord of the 4th of the nativity were joined with one of the stars in the same degree, as was said regarding the others, it signifies evil for his parents, and that he will hate them. And the end of all things about which he interjects himself, will be bad; nor will the works which he himself accomplishes be praised, even if they were good and things to be praised; and his infirmities will often be of the chest and lungs, and of the parts adjacent to them.

But if one of the aforesaid stars were to fall in the 5th from the Ascendant of the revolution, or the Lord of the 5th were in the same degree with one of them, as was said regarding the other houses, it signifies evil and impediment which will fall upon children, and hate which parents will have for them, and it signifies the detriment and decrease of sexual intercourse in that revolution; and that discord or litigation and impediment will fall between lovers and between those who loved each other at first; and between whom there was domestic relations[420] because of donations and other delightful things. And the infirmities

---

[418] *Et si nisus fuerit peregrinari peregrinationibus praedictis.*

[419] Adding *non*.

[420] *Domesticitates.* This does not make sense when compared with the *Flowers*. The *Flowers* says only that there will be impediment between people who are loved, and that those who give money will not be paid back–skipping *domesticitas* altogether and not linking it with "donations."

which happen to men in that revolution will often be in the their bellies and stomachs, and in parts prohibiting venereal worship.[421] And if one of the aforesaid were in the 5th of someone's nativity, or the Ascendant of the nativity were the 5th of the revolution, or the Lord of the 5th of the nativity were joined with one of those stars (as was said regarding the others), it signifies that the parents of that native will hate him, and this according to the substance of the sign which is the 5th of the nativity, or in which the Lord of the 5th of the nativity is; for if this sign were masculine, the father will hate him more, and the mother less; and if it were a feminine sign, his mother will hate him more, and his father less. Nor will the native be obedient to his parents, nor will he persevere in loving someone who loves him, nor even [in loving] other people. And if he were to undertake to be good, he will not persevere in his goodness, nor will he be fortunate in children (if one of [the stars] were in the 5th), nor in these things which are signified by the 5th house. And perhaps that he will avoid having children altogether. And his infirmities will more often be of the chest and stomach, and because of them (and more so if the 5th were Leo).

If however one of the aforesaid stars were to fall in the 6th from the Ascendant of the revolution, or the Lord of the 6th were with one of them in the same degree, as was said regarding the other houses, it signifies impediment is going to fall upon quadrupeds (and especially upon small ones). And Abū Ma'shar said this even signifies [impediment] upon the body of the king, and upon his male and female slaves; likewise upon other slaves; and in male and female servants; and upon low-class people, paupers or persons in the nature [or substance] of that sign. And there will not be wealth for those wishing to engage in the trade of slaves or animals (and particularly small ones). And Abū Ma'shar said, for him who flees in that same year, he will find impediment; and certain ones of them will not be returned; and infirmities will abound in men, and the majority of them from an overflowing of choler abounding in the intestines. And if one of them were to fall in someone's nativity, in the 6th of the nativity, or the Ascendant of the nativity were the 6th of the revolution, or the Lord of the 6th of the nativity were joined with one of those stars in the same degree (just as was said in the others), it signifies that the native will not rejoice from male or females slaves and male or female servants; nor will he be fortunate in them; nor will he care to own one of them, even if he were to use them; nor will he be fortunate in them nor because of them nor because of those things which are

---

[421] *In partibus prohibentibus cultum venereum.* The *Flowers* is rather clearer, saying that the infirmities themselves (in body parts like the stomach) will prevent sexual intercourse.

signified by the 6th house, if one of those stars were in the 6th of his own nativity. And Abū Ma'shar said, from his childhood he will want to flee from his parents, nor will he see good from quadrupeds, but rather evil (and worse from small ones than from others), for they will die in his possession and in his harm. And the majority of his infirmities will be in the lower parts of his body (and more strongly so, if the 6th were Virgo).

And if one of the stars were in the 7th, or the Lord of the 7th were with one of them in the same degree, as was said regarding the other houses, it signifies a multitude of battles and those making war upon the king of that region, or its greater magnate, and there will likewise be fights and quarrels, and contentions between kings; and there will be a subsiding and contentions between partners and those participating together, and many men will drive out their wives in that revolution, and will quarrel with them. And it even signifies that kings and magnates will grow angry with their subjects and with their household members, and against them; and the hearts of men will harden. Nor will piety reside in them, nor empathy, nor will men care to celebrate nuptials, nor will they be satisfied to contract marriage; and faith and legality will recede from them. And if someone were to accept something mutually from another, or someone else's possession were to reach him, he will deny the truth, nor will he want to return it to him; nor will men care to exercise their arts nor their sciences, nor their professions. And Abū Ma'shar said there will be more infirmities of men in the bladder and kidneys and hips and rear parts. And if one of the aforesaid stars were to fall in the 7th in someone's nativity, or the Ascendant of the nativity were the 7th of that revolution, or the Lord of the 7th of the nativity were joined with one of those stars, the native will not rejoice from wives or from other women, nor will he see good from them, nor from partners, nor from those cooperating with him, nor concerning things which he is in charge of, nor concerning any matter which is signified by the 7th house. And more often he will lose his fights, and his battles, and his lawsuits or contentions; and likewise others' possessions which he is in charge of. And if he were skilled in the law, he will not be fortunate in his advocacies. And Abū Ma'shar said his infirmities will be more from the throat and from the kidneys and legs and rear parts (and the more so if the 7th were Libra).

If however one of the aforesaid stars were in the 8th, or the Lord of the 8th of the revolution were with one of the aforesaid in the same degree, as was said regarding the other houses, it signifies impediment and evil is going to fall upon those who were used to going here and there, by injuring some of them by means of robbery, and [it signifies] their return to the places in which they are used to staying, from their robberies or from their thefts. And it signifies the taking away of some things of the region in which you were to revolve the year, and belonging to the civil authorities of that city or community (if another king were not in charge of it), or belonging to him who had the direction of the community or the city; nor will the lost thing be found again. And it signifies quarrels or discords falling between those who inherited the goods of the dead; nor will they agree with each other, unless by the interposition of others. And it signifies the death of low-class persons and of those who are forced to eat the bread of suffering (namely something averse) by need forcing [them],[422] according to the nature [or substance] of the sign that is the 8th house [domicile?], or in which the Lord of the 8th is: like if it were a masculine sign, it will be more in males; if however it were a feminine one, it will be more in females. And if the 8th were a masculine sign, and the Lord of the 8th in a masculine sign, it will be only in males. And if the 8th were a feminine sign, and the Lord of the 8th were in a feminine sign, it will be only in females. And if one were masculine and the other feminine, it will be in each, however more according to the nature [or substance] of the 8th than of that in which the Lord of the 8th is; and there will be pestilences in them. And Abū Ma'shar said impediment will be multiplied upon the substances of those contending with a greater king (of the kings of the clime). And he said they will need the aid of the greater king (namely of Babylon and of the Romans and the Indians). And there will be more infirmities of men and women in the genitive organs and in the private parts, and around the parts adjacent to them. And if one of those stars were to fall in the 8th in someone's nativity, or the Ascendant of that nativity were the 8th of the revolution, or the Lord of the 8th were joined with one of them in the same degree, just as was said with the others, Abū Ma'shar said that the native will be wandering, a fugitive, not turning aside toward a place to stay, nor will he enter under a roof. And he said he will be of those who collect people inimical to him, and seek to be with demons; and love being alone, and will not see in himself that he is loved for his labor and his pilgrimage,[423] and this will be more in the places of the dead and in a place of stinking corpses; nor will he rejoice in those things which are signified by the 8th house. And more infirmities will be

---

[422] *Scilicet alienum indigentia cogente.*

[423] The impression here is that such a native will be alienated, confused, and not even know what his own value is. But the *Flowers* says differently: "nor will good be seen in him for his own labor and pilgrimage"—in other words, *others* will not see value in *him*.

because of the private parts and around the private parts and the areas adjacent to them (and more strongly so if the 8th were Scorpio).

And if one of the aforesaid stars were in the 9th, or the Lord of the 9th of the revolution were with one of them in the same degree (just as was said regarding the other houses), it signifies impediment and destruction and evil is going to fall upon bishops and upon other religious men, and those cultivating God, and especially those who are signified by the planet disposed worse: like if it were Jupiter, it will fall upon bishops and the like; if it were Saturn, it will fall upon those wearing rough clothing. And by how much more powerful and more famous the religion is, by that much more will the impediment fall upon its cultivators; and the sects or religions approved of by the Roman Church will be diminished and pressed down, and even the other religions of men; and dullness and ruin will fall upon them, and the forgetting of those serving God and his praises; and they will recede from it, and certain of them will deny him, and will desist from His commands; and doubt will fall in them, and they will believe something else is better than that which they believe or observe. And detriment and sorrow will even fall upon pilgrims on faraway pilgrimages, and long journeys will go contrary to journeyers, nor will good happen to them from thence, but their thoughts will be empty and of a bad end. And certain people will rise up and reveal their own severity, and they will machinate to bring about the ruin of the king of Babylon, however they will not be able to perpetrate the evil deed they have planned in that year; and fights and battles will be broken up. And there will be more infirmities of men next to the thighs and the hips. And if one of the aforesaid stars were to fall in the 9th in someone's nativity, or the Ascendant of the nativity were the 9th of that revolution, or the Lord of the 9th of the nativity were joined with one of those stars in the same degree (as was said with the others), Abū Ma'shar said the native will be practically stupefied in his affairs, and in his own care,[424] nor will a pilgrimage and changing [from one place to another] agree with him. And his infirmities will be more because of the thighs and hips (and more than this if the 9th were Sagittarius).

But if one of the aforesaid stars were in the 10th, or the Lord of the 10th of the revolution were joined with one of them (namely in the same degree), just as was said regarding the other houses, it signifies that dejection and evil and impediment is going to fall upon kings and the wealthy, and the nobles and magnates or powerful people ([that is,] upon those who are preferred above other men); and there will be weakness in them, and discord and contention and

---

[424] *Cultura.*

mutual envy will fall between them; and impediment will fall on their substances and matters; and their complaint will be puny,[425] and little money will be given to them as tribute, except perhaps for what they might extort from people by violence or by another reprehensible method; nor will men revere them in the usual or required way; and they will suppress their dignities and professions and kingdoms, and the rustics or common people will be elevated, and they will resist against them, and will condemn and deride and despise them; and they will change their names with derision. And they will do this, not to mention [the fact that] if the magnates were to cross through villages or plains, there will not be even one base man from the crowd who will not deride them. And these things will happen to them throughout the entire revolution. And there will be more infirmities of men from the knees and from the parts adjacent to them. And if one of the aforesaid stars were to fall in the 10th in someone's nativity, or the Ascendant of the nativity were the 10th of that revolution, or the Lord of the 10th of the nativity were joined with one of them in the same degree, just as was said for the others, it signifies the low position of the native, and his dejection, and he will be despised among those who ought to exalt him, if they can, and particularly among those close to him; and he will be laborious in his life, and have little wealth (less so than he does expenses); nor will he earn wealth in those things about which he were to have trust in the good, and that which he does earn will not be turned to his own usefulness, unless by accident; and it will be middling [in amount]. And Abū Ma'shar said, what I have told you will be according to his nature. And his infirmities will be more from the knees and those [parts] adjacent to them (and the more so if the 10th were Capricorn).

Indeed if one of the aforesaid stars were in the 11th, or the Lord of the 11th of the revolution were joined with one of them in the same degree (just as was said regarding the other houses), it signifies discord and anxiety is going to fall between friends. And one will strive to overthrow[426] or despise the other; and he will be eager for his wounding or harm. And the trust of men will be annihilated; nor will what they intend, follow from those things in which they have hope. And the substances of kings and the wealthy or magnates will be diminished; and they will suffer detriment—likewise the soldiers of the king of the region, and his ministers, and his allies; nor will they have good faith toward him, nor a good will; nor will they use arms to his benefit, nor in his aid, if he were to need it; but they will be unfaithful. And the infirmities of men will be

---

[425] *Et paucus erit eorum conquestus.*
[426] Reading *supplantare* for *suppeditare* ("to supply in abundance")

more because of the legs and around the legs. And if one of the aforesaid stars were to fall in the 11th in someone's nativity, or the Ascendant of the nativity were the 11th of the revolution, or the Lord of the 11th of the nativity were joined with one of them in the same degree (just as was said for the others), it signifies the native is going to be of middling trust, so that he will not believe something is able to profit him; and something good will hardly or never happen to him. And if it were to happen to him, it will be middling; and it signifies him to be hateful and despised by the common people; and so great will be the worthlessness of his heart, that he will not believe himself able to avoid anything evil or any contrary, dangerous thing. Nor will his thoughts be on anything good; and he will rejoice when he sees an unlucky stranger.[427] And his intention will be to do evil, even if he cannot perfect it; he will not praise anyone, nor will he be praised by anyone. Nor will he be advanced to any secular or clerical dignity, unless perhaps to the sort which redounds to his harm or the contrary. And his infirmities will be often because of the legs (and more strongly so, if the 11th were Aquarius).

Indeed if one of the aforesaid were to fall in the 12th, or the Lord of the 12th were joined with one of them in the same degree (just as was said in the other houses [domiciles?]), it signifies a multitude of robbers and of cutters of roads. It even signifies the fraud of male and female slaves against their masters; and fall and detriment; the destruction of those dejected and of low-class persons; for they will be thrown down, and it will go badly for them, and likewise for the incarcerated; and prisons will be emptied with the detriment of the incarcerated. And larger quadrupeds will suffer detriment. And kings and nobles or the wealthy and magnates, and the rational and the wise, will be raised up; and they will be raised up over the vulgar and the common people and the rustics and the ignoble, and over all who earlier had derided them to their detriment and seizure.[428] And the infirmities of men will be more because of the feet. And if one of the those stars were to fall in the 12th in someone's nativity, or the Ascendant of the nativity were the 12th of the revolution, or the Lord of the 12th of the nativity were joined with one of them in the same degree (just as was said for the others), it signifies that the native will be evil, crafty with an evil cleverness, laborious, ingenious with a fraudulent skill, having many anxieties and hardships, and many enemies; and many men will hate him, both without cause and with cause. And Abū Ma'shar said, for every one who sees him will

---

[427] *Alienum malum.*
[428] *Deprehensionem.*

hate him, from his childhood up to old age. And his infirmities will be more because of the feet–and more strongly so, if the 12th were Pisces.

And Abū Ma'shar said[429] if Jupiter [or Venus] were to aspect [these places] from out of the place of the image,[430] and were to project his [or her] own rays to that degree, and he [or she] were strong in his [or her] own place, it signifies the [breaking of the] strength of those stars. And if Venus [or Jupiter] were weak in her [or his] own place, something of her own works that should appear, will not work.[431] And he said the multitude of [the fixed star's] evil will be according to the quantity of the strength or weakness of the [benefic] planet [aspecting it]. And if [the benefic] were to aspect from a place of enmity and contrariety,[432] it will not repel any of the evil, especially if it were weak in its own place. But it will strive to repel the evil, however it will not repel any of it.

And he said, if however a malefic were to aspect in it from a place of dejection,[433] everything that I told you of the matters of the planets will be evil; and its [evil] work will hasten and one [evil] will follow another. And he said if [the malefic] were to aspect out of a place of enmity and contrariety, everything which I said will be evil, and [there will be] contrariety from the beginning of the evil's coming, [and] anticipation up to its end.[434]

Indeed if the Sun were to aspect the place itself, he will reveal the evil itself, and will act to lay it bare.[435] And he said every one who strives to conceal what will happen, will not be able to conceal it. And he said, this will be general for the same generation and the cities.

And he said if Saturn were to aspect, tribulation will descend one after the other.

---

[429] The rest of this chapter is derived from the *Flowers*, §6. Bonatti's paraphrase is loose, so I have provided supporting words in brackets.

[430] Bonatti's Abū Ma'shar does not explain what image (i.e., sign) he is talking about. It may be from either whatever sign Jupiter (or Venus) happens to be in, or (more probably) a sign in which he has dignity.

[431] *Flowers*: "[Venus and Jupiter] will not work anything of their own operations which would have force."

[432] This may mean "from the sign of its own detriment," but then it speaks of being "weak" in its own place (which would seem redundant).

[433] Reading *ex loco deiectionis* (with the *Flowers*) for Bonatti's *in loco directionis* ("instead of a direction").

[434] *Flowers*: "all that I said regarding the event will be from the beginning [of the year] up to its end."

[435] Reading *opponere* for *apponere*.

And he said if Mercury were to aspect, this will be commingled and colored.[436]

And he said if the Moon were to aspect, her operation will be [what was said] concerning the operation of the Sun. And he said it will be a little less and faster in every thing that she does, on account of the quickness of her course.

And he said, know that everything which I have told you, will be in the city which is in the division of that same sign. And he said, therefore consider this, because you will not go astray, if God wills.

Chapter 109: What the fortunate fixed stars would signify in nativities and questions and the revolutions of years

Having spoken of the misfortunes which are introduced by the unfortunate fixed stars into inferior things, now we must speak about the fortunes which the fortunate fixed stars confer in them. For just as some unfortunate fixed stars are found in every sign, so in every one of them some fortunate fixed stars are found, which are causes of contrary things (namely of fortunate ones).

Therefore, know that in the fifteenth[437] degree of Aries and its sixth minute, is a certain star of the nature of Jupiter and Venus, and its latitude is southern; and its peculiar nature is to be useful and to aid. Indeed another one is in its twenty-sixth degree and first minute, of the nature of Jupiter.

In Taurus is one star in its first degree and third minute. Another in its eighth degree, seventh minute. A third is in its ninth degree and first minute–all of which are of the nature of Venus.

Indeed in Gemini is one star in its nineteenth degree and second minute. And another in its twenty-first degree and third minute–which are of the nature of Jupiter and are of the second magnitude.

---

436 This is an addition by Bonatti. The *Flowers* does not mention the Moon at all, and treats what Bonatti says about the Moon as a property of Mercury's aspect. But Bonatti may actually be right, or perhaps he had access to a better manuscript of the *Flowers* than was used for the printed edition.

437 In this section Bonatti spells out the ordinal numbers, so there is no question in which degrees and minutes the stars fall.

In Cancer is one star which is called The Good One, in its twenty-seventh degree and second minute.[438] Another in its twenty-ninth degree and fifth minute. And they are both of the nature of Jupiter, and do good.

In Leo is one star of the nature of Jupiter and Venus, [in] its ninth degree and fourth minute, and it is called Goodwill.[439]

In Virgo is a certain star in its fourth degree and seventh minute, of the nature of Venus and the Moon.

In Libra is a certain star of the nature of Jupiter and Venus in its thirteenth degree and forty-fifth minute. And another in the fourteenth degree and forty-fifth minute of the aforesaid nature. And they are both southern and aiding.

And in Scorpio is one star in its ninth degree and fifty-fifth minute. And another is in its thirteenth degree and first minute. And another in its fourteenth degree and forty-fifth minute. And another is in its nineteenth degree and fifteenth minute, all of which are southern [and] of the nature of Jupiter.

In Sagittarius is one star in its tenth degree and fifteenth minute, which is called Peacemaker,[440] and is of the nature of Venus. Indeed another is in its seventeenth degree and fifty-fifth minute, and it is northern, of the nature of Jupiter.

In Capricorn is one star in its second degree and third minute, which is called Cow,[441] and it is of the nature of Jupiter. And another is in its seventh degree and fifty-fifth minute. And another is in its seventeenth degree and fifty-fifth minute, which are both[442] southern and are of the nature of Jupiter.

---

[438] Recall that in Capricorn there is a star called The Evil One directly opposite this star (see above).

[439] *Benevola.* This seems to be Bonatti's name for the star; if he had simply meant "benevolent," he would have used *benevolens.*

[440] *Pacifica.* I am going to assume this is a name and not merely an adjective (though *pacificus* is an adjective meaning the same thing).

[441] *Bos.*

[442] Presumably, the latter two of the three listed.

In Aquarius is one star in its fifteenth degree and fifty-fifth minute, and it is of the nature of Jupiter.

In Pisces is one star in its seventh degree and eleventh minute, and it is of the nature of Jupiter himself.

Chapter 110: On the peculiar nature of these [benefic] fixed stars in the twelve houses

And if you were to see the Lord of the Year or Revolution or of the nativity or the question joined with one of the aforesaid stars in the same degree, in the revolution of a year of the world, you would know that good and fortune will come to kings and the wealthy or nobles and magnates. You may say the same in nativities concerning the affairs of natives, and in questions and the revolutions of nativities. And joys and gladness and soundness of mind, and the safety of the body will come to them. And by how much their conjunction were less than one degree, up to one minute, by that much will their status be better and more suitable. And if one of the aforesaid stars were to fall in the ascending degree of someone's nativity, or the Lord of the nativity were joined with one of them in the same degree, the native will be fortunate and good; and he will lead his life in rest and joy and tranquility and every good status (and the more strongly so, if the Ascendant were Aries).

And if one of the stars were to fall in the 2nd from the Ascendant of the revolution, or the Lord of the 2nd of the revolution were with one of them in the same degree (just as was said), it signifies the increase of the matters and substances of men, and especially of the wealthy and great or noble men (and more strongly so if Taurus were the 2nd house). And if one of the aforesaid stars were to fall in the 2nd in someone's nativity, or his Ascendant were the 2nd of the revolution, or the Lord of the 2nd of the nativity were joined with one of them in the same degree (just as was said in the 1st house), it signifies that the native will be of good condition and of good status, wealthy, and of much *census* and wealth. And he will retain what is acquired, and his own substance; and he will be of good skill and engaged in his own business dealings, and will have repute among other men; and they will listen to his words, and [his words] will be pondered (and the more so if Taurus were the 2nd house).

But if one of the stars were to fall in the 3rd from the Ascendant of the revolution, or the Lord of the 3rd were with one of them in the same degree (just as was said in the others), it signifies the good condition of the houses of oration [or prayer], and that short journeys will be agreeable and useful to those journeying, and that brothers will behave well toward one another; and one brother will be made happy because of the other; and they will be in healthy bodies, and will be of sound mind (and the more so if Gemini were the 3rd house). And if one of the aforesaid stars were to fall in the 3rd in someone's nativity, or the Ascendant of the nativity were the 3rd of the revolution, or the Lord of the 3rd of the nativity were joined with one of the aforesaid stars, it signifies that he will be useful and benevolent to his brothers and his own lesser blood-relatives, and neighbors, and to those who place him above themselves, or who think of him as a friend. Nor will he be inclined to look at an unlucky stranger,[443] and he will be compassionate to whose to whom evils have come; and his intention will often be benign, and not to the contrary; and his journeys will be useful (and especially short ones), and they will be safe and advantageous, both in the affairs and in his person; and he will be sound of body, and especially around the shoulder blades and arms (and more so if Gemini were the 3rd house).

But if one of the aforesaid stars were in the 4th from the Ascendant of the revolution, or the Lord of the 4th were with one of them in the same degree (as was said regarding the other houses), it signifies the good condition of farmers and of harvests and things born from the earth. It even signifies peace and tranquility in cities and between cities and other habitations. And fathers will behave well with sons and toward sons, and one will rejoice and be made happy with the other, and on account of the other. And the end of things undertaken (which were to happen in that year or in the revolution) will be to the good. And if someone were to buy land or another estate or some inheritance, what he intends [to happen] will follow from it. And many men will be healthy, and especially around the chest and lungs (and more so if Cancer were the 4th house). And if one of the aforesaid stars were in the 4th in someone's nativity, or the 4th of the revolution were the Ascendant of someone's nativity, or the Lord of the 4th of the nativity were joined with one of those stars in the same degree, it signifies that the native is going to be good to his parents (namely his father, grandfather, father-in-law, and other more ancient ones), and that he will love

---

[443] *Malum alienum.* This stands in parallel with the section above on malefic stars in the 11th. There, someone rejoices when seeing another person suffering.

them, and that he will be obedient and favorable to them; and the end of those things about which he will have interjected himself will be praiseworthy. And his works will be praised, even if sometimes he were to do less well; however he will be praised by men, and he will be sound in body, and his health will remain, especially around the chest and lungs, and the lower parts of the chest.

But if one of the said stars were to fall in the 5th from the Ascendant of the revolution, or the Lord of the 5th were with one of them (just as was said regarding the other houses), it signifies good and fortune that will happen to children; and the love which their parents will have for them; and it signifies the increase of licit sexual intercourse, and delight in it in the revolution; for delight and good will be increased between those loving each other. And the sharing of households[444] and donations between them will be more than usual; and there will be health in their bellies and around the lower parts of the chest, and around the spine and back, more so than usual (and the more so if Leo were the 5th house). And if one of the aforesaid stars were in the 5th of the nativity, or the Ascendant of the nativity were the 5th of the revolution, or the Lord of the 5th of the nativity were joined with one of those stars, it signifies that the parents of the native will love him, but he whose nature is the sign of the 5th house will love him more; and he will be obedient to his own parents, nor will he ignore their commands. And he will be loving him,[445] and will persevere in the good, and he will be fortunate in children and in those things which are signified by the 5th house; and he will be sound of body, and especially around the chest and stomach and back, and around the genital parts (and the more so if the 5th house were Leo).

If however one of the aforesaid stars were to fall in the 6th from the Ascendant of the revolution, or the Lord of the 6th were with one of them in the same degree, just as was said in the other houses, it signifies increase and good is going to come onto quadrupeds (and especially smaller ones). And Abū Ma'shar said it signifies this even in the king and in his male and female slaves; and likewise in other slaves and in male and female servants. And the status of low-class persons will be good, according to its nature (like if it were masculine or feminine). And there will be wealth for those wishing to trade in slaves or smaller animals, and it will be well for those wishing to run away; and infirmities will be decreased, and especially those which customarily come from choler abounding in the intestines. But if one of the stars were to fall in someone's

---

[444] *Domesticitates.*
[445] Whom?

nativity in the 6th of his nativity, or the Ascendant of the nativity were the 6th of the revolution, or the Lord of the 6th of the nativity were joined with one of them in the same degree, just as was said in the others, it signifies that it will be well for that native in slaves and from male and female slaves, and in male and female servants. And he will be fortunate in them and in those things which are signified by the 6th house; and he will stay willingly with his own parents, and he will be often healthy in the lower parts of his body (and more strongly so if the 6th house were Virgo).

And if one of the stars were in the 7th, or the Lord of the 7th were with one of them in the same degree (as was said regarding the other houses), it signifies tranquility and good and the breaking apart of fights and battles; and there will be tranquility and quiet between partners and those participating together, and between other men; and there will be good will between husbands and wives, and little quarreling (less than usual). And kings and magnates will be reconciled to and humbled by their own subjects, and they will obey them more freely than usual; and piety will remain in men, and they will be intent to celebrate nuptials and to contract marriages; and faith and legality will remain in them, and they will employ truth somewhat more than usual; and they will be content to practice their arts and their professions; and health will thrive in men (and especially around the bladder and kidneys, and the hips and the hind parts). And if one of the aforesaid stars were to fall in the 7th in someone's nativity, or the Ascendant of the nativity were the 7th of the revolution, or the Lord of the 7th of the nativity were with one of them, the native will rejoice because of wives and other women, and he will see good from them and from partners and those participating with him, and from all those who are signified by the 7th house; and he will win in his lawsuits. And if he were a lawyer or versed in law it will go well for him in his advocacies; and there will be health in his throat and kidneys and legs and rear parts (and more so if the 7th house were Libra).

If however one of the aforesaid were in the 8th, or the Lord of the 8th of the revolution were with one of them in the same degree (just as was said in the other houses), it signifies the good condition of those wandering, namely of those who are used to going here and there, harming others by means of robbery; and something of their malice will be mitigated. It even signifies staying in places in which they are used to living more than usual, nor will they employ whatever evil people are able to of their robberies. It even signifies the guarding of the king of that region in which you are revolving the year, or of the ruler or civil authority of that place, or of him who must guide the republic. And if he were to lose something of his things, what is lost will be recovered. It even signifies concord between those who have inherited the goods of the dead. It even signifies the safeguarding of the life of low-class persons according to the substance of the sign;[446] nor will there be those who strive to defraud the substances of greater kings (namely the king of the Romans and the king of Babylon and the king of the Indians); and there will be health in men and women, and especially around the genital parts and around the private parts and the parts adjacent to them. And if one of those stars were to fall in the 8th of someone's nativity, or the Ascendant of the nativity were the 8th of the revolution, or the Lord of the 8th of the nativity were joined with one of them in the same degree (just as was said regarding the others), it signifies that the native will be of those who freely associate with men, and who flee solitude, and who live readily with good things. And he will see in his own person what he wants, and will rejoice regarding them and in those things which are signified by the 8th house. And he will be sound in body, and especially around the private parts and the parts adjacent to them (and more so if the 8th house were Scorpio).

And if one of the aforesaid stars were in the 9th, or the Lord of the 9th of the revolution were with one of them in the same degree (just as was said regarding the other houses [domiciles?]), it signifies joy and happiness and the good status of bishops and other religious men, and those serving God, as the planet signifying them were better disposed: like if it were Jupiter, it will be more in bishops and other clerics who are called secular. If it were Saturn, this will be more in religious men wearing rough clothing, and more likely in blacker clothing, and in more renowned men. And the sects or religions approved by the Roman Church will be increased; and they will be serving God and praising Him. And pilgrimages or long journeys will be useful and profitable; and the citizens of Babylon will be obedient to their king; and men will be healthy, and especially around the thighs and hips (and more so if the 9th house were Sagittarius). And if one of the aforesaid stars were to fall in the 9th in someone's nativity, or the Ascendant of the nativity were the 9th of the revolution, or the Lord of the 9th of the nativity were joined with one of them in the same degree (just as was said regarding the others), the native will attend closely to his own matters, and choose the better part regarding his own affairs, and even over strangers; and pilgrimages and long journeys will be useful to him; and his health

---

[446] Usually Bonatti means that if the sign is feminine, women will benefit more; if masculine, men.

will thrive around the thighs and hips–and more so if the 9th house were Sagittarius.

And if one of the aforesaid stars were to fall in the 10th, or the Lord of the 10th were joined with one of them in the same degree (just as was said regarding the other houses [domiciles?]), it signifies good and the increase of good is going to come to kings and great men who are fit for a kingdom; and there will be strength in them for the good; and there will be quiet and security between them, and it will be well for them; and the *census* will be rendered to them without contention and without impediment; and men will revere them, and their dignities and professions or realms will be exalted; and health will thrive in men, and especially around the knees and the parts adjacent to them. And if one of the aforesaid were to fall in the 10th in someone's nativity, or the Ascendant of the nativity were the 10th of the revolution, or the Lord of the 10th of the nativity were joined with one of them in the same degree (just as was said regarding the others), it signifies the goodness of the native and the greatness of his mind, and the increase of honor for him; and he will be honored by his own [people] and even by strangers, and he will lead his life without great labor, and he will live as though at rest; and he will be a man of wealth or advantage, and that which he earns will be turned to his usefulness; and there will even be the health of his body, and especially around the knees and around the parts adjacent to them–and the more so if the 10th house were Capricorn.

Indeed if one of the aforesaid stars were in the 11th, or the Lord of the 11th of the revolution were joined with one of them in the same degree (just as was said regarding the other houses), it signifies good and fortune is going to come between friends, and one will strive to support the other and exalt [him]; and one will be eager to aid and help the other. And the substances of kings and the wealthy or magnates will likewise be increased. And the soldiers of the king of that region, and his ministers, and his allies, will have good faith and a good will toward him. And they will gladly employ arms for his usefulness; and they will be faithful to him. And men will be healthy in the legs and around the legs (and the more so if the 11th house were Aquarius). And if one of the aforesaid stars were to fall in the 11th in someone's nativity, or the Ascendant of the nativity were the 11th of the revolution, or the Lord of the 11th of the nativity were joined with one of them in the same degree (just as was said in the others), it signifies that the native will have great confidence, indeed so that, regarding everyone concerning whom he gets involved, he will hope that good and usefulness will be able to follow. The contrary of those things which he hopes and about which he gets involved, will hardly happen to him; and he will be loved by the vulgar, and he will have so much trust and so much boldness, that he will not believe something evil or something contrary could happen to him. His thoughts will be on the good, and he will have pity for those for whom things go adversely. And his intention will be in doing well; for he will be praised by others and he will praise them. And he will be inclined to have an office or honors, he will be promoted to them, and his health will thrive in the legs and around the legs (and the more so if the 11th house were Aquarius).

Indeed if one of the aforesaid were to fall in the 12th, or the Lord of the 12th were joined with one of the aforesaid in the same degree (just as was said concerning all the others), it signifies the decrease of robbers and cutters of roads, and their detriment; it even signifies the obedience of male and female slaves toward their masters; and it signifies the good condition of low-class persons, and the easing [of the condition] of those incarcerated. And larger quadrupeds will be saved. And it even signifies that kings or magnates and nobles will behave themselves well toward the rustics or common people. And there will be health in men, and especially in the feet and around the feet (and the more so if the 12th house were Pisces). And if one of those stars were to fall in the 12th in someone's nativity, or the Ascendant of someone's nativity were the 12th of the revolution, or the Lord of the 12th of the nativity were joined with one of them in the same degree (just as was said in the others), it signifies that the native will be good, ingenious with a good and licit and praiseworthy skill, having little labor, and few anxieties and few worries and few needs, few enemies (and especially hidden ones), but rather he will be loved by men–as a boy, youth, and when he is an old man. And health will thrive in him, and especially in the feet and around the feet (and more strongly so if the 12th house were Pisces).

And if Jupiter were to aspect the degree in which the star then was (and [Jupiter] is in good condition), or the Head of the Dragon were there, their fortune will be increased. Indeed if Saturn were to aspect (or the Tail were there), it will be decreased. Indeed if Venus were to aspect, it will increase a little, practically unnoticeably. Indeed for the rest they will work nothing that may be sensed. However, if the Sun were to aspect the place, he will make what the fixed star signified come to act more quickly. And if the Moon were to aspect, it will hasten more again.

Chapter 111: On the varieties of manners[447]

Abū Ma'shar put this chapter in his book of revolutions, which it does not seem we should omit, since I have followed in his footsteps in this (even though I have made a longer speech than he had). And he said that in the circle[448] there are ways of life which are not likened to other ways of life. For he said, in the king is a way of life which is not likened to the way of life of the household members; and in the household members is a way of life that is not likened to the way of life of kings. And in a kingdom is a manner which is not likened to the manner of nativities. And in nativities is a use which is not likened to the use of a question.

Chapter 112: On the impediments which the Lord of the ascending sign of the revolution introduces, if it were impeded (whether it is the Lord of the Year or not)

If the Lord of the Ascendant of the revolution of a year of the world were impeded in the hour of the revolution (whether he is the Lord of the Year or not—because if another were the Lord of the Year, he is his participator in these things; and the significations are taken more naturally from them, even if they are taken from the Lord of the Year), and the impediment were in one of the angles, he will send in tribulation upon men. For if he were combust in the 10th, the impediment will be because of the kingdom or because of a kingdom of equal significance. And if the Sun were in the Midheaven, or otherwise were the Lord of the 10th, it signifies that sorrow will occur to men, or restriction, by the king or because of him. If however the combustion were in the 4th (and this closer to the cusp than near the end of the 4th), mortality will be feared in that same revolution—and this according to the nature [or substance] of the ascending sign and of the planet who is its Lord. Like if it were a feminine sign, it will be more in females; and if in addition its Lord were a feminine planet, it will be wholly in females. If however the sign were masculine, and in addition its Lord were a masculine planet, it will be wholly in males.

---

[447] This word (*consuetudo*) means "habit, custom, use." I believe the message of this chapter is that, while the general methods of delineation are similar no matter the branch of astrology or the object of concern (cities, people, questions), we must tailor the details of our delineations to the situation at hand. I have translated this word as "way of life, manner, use" as has seemed fit in this chapter.

[448] I believe he is speaking of the circle of the houses, but see below: he will speak of different branches of astrology, too.

And if the Lord of the Ascendant were Mercury, it will be more in boys up to the beginning of adolescence. And if the Lord of the Ascendant were Saturn, it will be more in old men and decrepit people, and in those who are signified by Saturn. And if the Lord of the Ascendant were Jupiter, it will be more in the wise and in those trained in law, and in men whose youth has been completed. And if the Lord of the Ascendant were Mars, it will be more in youths from the twenty-first year up to the forty-fifth. And if the Lady of the Ascendant were Venus or the Moon, it will be more in women. Indeed if the signification belonged to Venus and she had escaped from combustion, and were outside the rays of the Sun, and were oriental, it signifies that this will happen in young women.[449] And if she were occidental, it will happen in those of greater age. And if the signification belonged to the Moon, and she were from the New Moon up to the first quarter, it signifies young women up to thirty. And if she were from the first quarter up to the full amount of her light [the Full Moon], it will be in those who are from the thirtieth year up to the forty-fifth. And if she were from the fullness of her light up to the third quarter, it will be in those who, from thence up to now have already begun to grow old. And if she were in the fourth quarter, this will be in old women or little old ladies. And if by chance it were to happen in men, she signifies their ages by means of the same method.

On the signification of the Lord of the Ascendant, if it were combust in the 7th or the Ascendant

And if the Lord of the Ascendant were combust in the 7th, it signifies battles and plunderings and contentions are going to fall between men. If however he were combust in the 1st, his impediment will be harmful. You will even see of what nature the sign of the Ascendant is: because impediment will fall in the substance which is signified by that sign. Like if it were Aries or Capricorn, it will be in smaller animals. If however it were Taurus or the last half of Sagittarius, it will be in larger animals, and especially in cows and the like. And if it were Gemini, Libra or Aquarius, or the first part of Sagittarius, it will be in men. And if it were Cancer or Pisces, it will be in animals of the water which men use for their own usefulness. If however it were Scorpio, it will be in poisonous animals, both terrestrial and aquatic. And if it were Leo, it will be in wild animals who prey on living things, like lions, wolves, and the like. And if it were in

---

449 *In mulieribus iuvenculis.* This sounds like "teenagers."

Virgo, it will be in seeds and things born of the earth, and in girls who are not corrupted. And know that if the impeded planet were received by a strong, unimpeded planet, that the reception cancels the malice, and destroys it. If however the malefics were to aspect him without perfect reception, they increase [the malice], and the more strongly so if the aspect were a square or opposition.

Chapter 113: On the impediments which the Lord of the Midheaven will introduce, if he were impeded in the revolution

After you looked at the Lord of the Ascendant of the revolution and you were to see his significations, it remains for you to look at what is signified by the Lord of the Midheaven. For if he were combust in one of the angles, it signifies destruction which will happen to the king in that revolution: like if he were combust in the first, and the Sun were the Lord of the first, it signifies that the rustics or common people or subjects are going to kill the king in that revolution, and at least they will conspire to ruin him and betray him. Whence, for this purpose, so that your judgment might profit him, and discretion may triumph, and so that the will might be believed to be free, and that you could avert the evil that (according to the stars) is going to come, counsel him that he should not believe the common people nor be assured of them.[450]

And Abū Ma'shar said if you wished to know in what sort of way it should be feared for him, see which of the planets aspects the Sun at the hour of the revolution. And if Mars were to aspect him or were joined to him corporally, it signifies the killing of the king, which will happen to him by means of the advice of vulgar or common people, from everyday robbers and murderers and cutters of roads (who kill men for a price).[451] If however Saturn were to aspect him, or were joined to him corporally, a fearful infirmity will be feared concerning the king, or perhaps that he will be poisoned. And he said, if the Sun were to burn up the Lord of the Ascendant of the year, even what I said will be feared for him, in the same way by which I described it. And he said, but what there would be of this will be in his own region in which he is, nor will he go out of another

---

[450] I think Bonatti is trying to walk a fine line between believing in the inevitability of the predicted events, and trusting that the king has the free will to deal with the problem. For if the predicted event were wholly inevitable, then no advice to the king would matter. But Bonatti is hoping that his advice could at least stimulate the king to hunt down wrongdoers before they get too far in their plans.

[451] In other words, the common people will hire killers to assassinate the king.

land to it. But if the Lord of the 10th were combust in the 4th or in the 7th, these things will happen because of those coming from another land to the one in which he himself is. And it signifies that the aforesaid will come according to what was said above. And again he said, speak of evil things according to what I said in the chapter of the Sun for the king and his rustics, except that in the chapter on the malefics you will look in this matter to the revolution of the year.[452] And he said that if the Lord of the Midheaven were conjoined to a malefic in an angle, in the way he said in the first chapter, and the aspect were from the opposition or square aspect of the malefics in this place, it is more severe than the conjunction. And he said if the Sun were the significator of the king, and were to aspect Jupiter from the opposition in the revolution, the king will be inimical to the nature [or substance] of that same planet, and he will destroy it[453] just like [the Sun] does Jupiter.

On the significations of Mars in the revolution

Abū Ma'shar said, know that if Mars were in Gemini at the hour of the revolution,[454] and he were in the Midheaven, it signifies that in that revolution many men will be tortured. And if he were in the 1st or in the 7th, the hands of many people will be cut off, and many will be mutilated. And if he were in the 4th (namely in the angle of the earth) it signifies the cutting off of many hands and feet. And he said, say likewise in the entrance of two great men [or] kings in their rule. Say the same in the entrance of some position of authority or any other rule. It can be said that many malefactors will arrive whom it will be necessary to deal with. Know this and do not give it over to forgetfulness.

Chapter 114: How evil or horrible accidents that are going to come in that year, may be known at the hour of the revolution

If you wished to know the severe and horrible accidents which are going to come in the year which you are revolving, know that the accidents will be according to the disposition of the two malefics (namely Saturn and Mars). Which if they were found in the superior circle (that is, in the northern half), and with it being located above the earth (and more strongly if they were

---

[452] I am unsure of what this means.

[453] Reading *eam* for *eum*. But reading *eum* would probably make the phrase, "It will destroy *him*," i.e., the king.

[454] Note the earlier chapter on significations of Mars, which concentrate primarily on Gemini.

northern),[455] it signifies harshness and horrible things are going to come in that year. And by how much more they were elevated above the earth (and particularly Saturn), by that much more will their signification be extended to faraway and diverse regions.

And Abū Ma'shar said, know that the condition of the year will be more oppressive if the two malefics were in the high circle where the pole is, in the images themselves which, if they were going out to the end of the circle, will return;[456] and they signify destructions. Therefore if you were to see the two malefics in that part of the superior circle at the hour of the revolution, you may know then that the condition of the year or revolution will be made oppressive, and there will be severe and horrible accidents. And if one were in the square aspect of the other, their condition will be worse, for then they will signify a lack of activity in every living thing,[457] and tribulations will appear in every subject which is on the earth, and this will be prolonged and will slow down; and more strongly if Saturn were then in Virgo and Mars in Gemini, and the revolution were nocturnal, and Mars were to commit his own disposition to Saturn, and he were to receive him,[458] and each were retrograde (or at least one of them). But Saturn has greater harm, wherefore then it will signify things exceeding proper measure in malice, both in burnings and killings; nor could Jupiter break their malice, unless perhaps one of them were in Cancer in the trine or sextile aspect of Jupiter, with [Jupiter] being of good condition and well disposed. For then [Jupiter] could break the malice of the one whom he aspected, or at least he would diminish its noticeable destruction. And the weakening of the king of the region (in which you are revolving the year) will be signified, and that of the other great men and the wealthy or nobles. And kings and magnates will seek help from the common people; and religion will decreased; and piety will be taken away from men; nor will sympathy be found in them; and this will be prolonged until one of them (namely Saturn or Mars) arrives at the degree which was the cusp of the 10th house at the hour of the revolution; or it will

---

[455] I think this means, if they are (a) in northern declination (Aries through Virgo), and (b) in northern ecliptical latitude, and (c) above the earth in the chart.

[456] This is an astronomical consideration that I do not understand.

[457] In traditional thought, living beings are characterized by activity—so this is akin to saying that living things will cease to live.

[458] The only way reception could occur in this situation is if Mars were to receive Saturn while Saturn is between 21°–27° 59' Virgo, since Saturn would then be in the triplicity and term of Mars. However, this could merely be one of the typical mitigating or aggravating conditions that the medievals (in this case, Abū Ma'shar) tended to pile onto one of their best- and worst-case scenarios.

begin then and will last even after much, at least through one transit of Mars through the zodiac. If however Saturn were then in Virgo, and Mars were to commit disposition from Gemini, just as was said, and the Moon were to commit disposition to Saturn, with her in Sagittarius, then it will signify the most horrible of horrible things, the pestilence of pestilences, and it will signify the destruction of kingdoms and of kings, and the transmutation of certain kingdoms from certain kings to certain other kings.

Moreover, if the Moon were to commit her own disposition to Saturn, if she were joined to him or in his square aspect or opposition, and the Lord of the sign in which she is[459] were impeded when her conjunction were perfected with Saturn, degree by degree, and minute by minute, it signifies many diverse impediments are going to come in that revolution. And if the Moon had suffered eclipse in the most recent prevention, or she were supposed to suffer it in the next prevention, the signification of the malefic will be prolonged by as many months as the eclipse of the Moon lasted by hours.

But if the Part of Fortune were impeded, and the Lord of the sign in which she is were impeded when the conjunction of the Moon [with Saturn] is perfected (whether it is perfected by conjunction or by aspect), then the conjunction signifies the increase of impediment and destruction.

And Abū Ma'shar said, look at the Sun and his condition, and his aspect to the impeding malefic, and the Lord of the malefic in the way I told you regarding the Moon, and the perfection and the Lord of the perfection.[460]

And[461] make the Part of Fortune and its Lord participants with [the luminaries], and [make them] give aid by the dignities of the seven planets who are aided and signify the time.[462] And he said if the significator were in an angle, the evil will be prolonged (and shortened [if] in the other [houses]). Likewise, even look at the Sun to see if he had suffered eclipse in the preceding conjunction, or will suffer it in the following; because what is signified by the malefic will be prolonged by how many years as his eclipse will have lasted by hours. And he said, the Lord of the course and of the perfection signifies according to what the significator signified in terms of good and evil. And likewise the Lord of the

---

459 This probably means the Lord of the sign in which she is at the time of the perfected aspect or conjunction.

460 Again, this would be the Lord of the sign the Sun is in, when his aspect or conjunction with the malefic is perfected.

461 This paragraph is one of several garbled quotations or paraphrases from a Latin translation of Abū Ma'shar. Bonatti's style and paraphrases are not generally like this.

462 *Et face eis participem partem fortunae ac dominum eius; & auxiliare per dignitates septem planetarum qui auxiliantur & significant tempus.* I am not sure what Bonatti's Abū Ma'shar means by this.

Ascendant and the Lord of the domicile of the division: if he were to receive the Moon from Saturn in an optimal place of the circle, in a strong place, he will signify the repulsing of evil with the help of God, and the prohibiting of the destruction of evil by its fortune. And he said, likewise in nativities, if the Moon were in the place of the testifying of the Ascendant, and were aiding, and she were made fortunate by the Lord of the Ascendant, and [it was] a good complexion,[463] it signifies the long length of life and kingdom. And he said, the native will be wise and he will be fortunate. And he said, the benefics dissolve the evil of the one pushed[464] if it were strong and in an opportune place, and it were directly his testimony.[465] Indeed if it were to the contrary, they will be weakened and they will not perfect.

On the kasmīmī[466] of the Sun, according to Abū Ma'shar

Abū Ma'shar said if a star were united under the rays of the Sun, and especially Mercury, it will be strength and rule for him, unless if [the Sun] were with Saturn (whose nature is the contrary of the nature of the Sun). And if there were 15° between Mercury and the Sun, he will be in a praiseworthy place, if he were received.

When planets go out from under the rays of the Sun, according to Abū Ma'shar

Abū Ma'shar said, make sure that a significator (or some planet) has gone out from combustion, [and] that a malefic does not aspect him, because then he will be like a delicate boy. If however a malefic were to aspect him, he will lose him and it will end.[467] And likewise if it were to enter into combustion or were joined to him, he will be [like] a decrepit old man who suffers some illness.

On the condition of the higher planets in the revolution of a year of the world, and particularly of Saturn

You will look ahead to the condition of the higher planets of the revolution of a year of the world, if you were to revolve it, and see where they were to fall

---

[463] Does this mean, "and the mixture of the natures of the Moon and the Lord of the Ascendant is good"?

[464] This must refer to one of Abū Ma'shar's senses of "pushing," either "pushing power" or "pushing nature.", but in this context I am not sure what it means.

[465] *Fueritque eius testimonium directe.* Unclear meaning.

[466] *Zamini.*

[467] *Perdet eum et finiet.* Meaning uncertain.

in the circle, beginning from Saturn: which if he were to fall in the degree of his own exaltation, and he were to receive the disposition of Venus, he will be the dispositor and significator of a great matter; for he will signify there is going to be a great matter in that revolution (and principally in the Roman Empire,[468] secondarily in the empire of Babylon); and it will be to the detriment of men and in [things normally contributing to] their usefulness. And if it were so, even though it is most rare (still, if it were), it will be the greatest signification, practically exceeding measure in the exaltation and increase of the kingdom or empire, and it will be a thing to last for a long time. And it could be perceived from the substance of the sign in which Venus is, and from the bound of her place. Because if she were occidental from the Sun, direct, namely made fortunate and strong, in the bound of a benefic, free from impediments, recently having gone out from under the rays of the Sun, then she signifies it ought to happen thus; or if some planet were to aspect her[469] who received her[470] from two dignities, and commits his own strength to her, with him free, made fortunate, and strong, and well disposed, of which nothing bad may be said, he will be a participant; indeed if it were otherwise, such signification will be something else, namely may God avert it.

[On Jupiter]

You will even see if Jupiter were to fall in the degree of his own exaltation and were made fortunate and strong, free from impediments; because it will signify the greatest changes are going to come in that revolution, in that kingdom and empire, and for the good–and more strongly and fully so, if the Moon were to aspect him (with her free, namely made fortunate and strong), and another planet who receives him, and commits its own strength to him (with it being free from impediments)–and [the third planet] will be a participator. Indeed if it were otherwise, he will not observe his promise, unless according to how he is disposed.[471]

---

[468] This probably means the Byzantine Empire, and not the empire of the German Holy Roman Emperor.

[469] Reading *eam* ("her") for *eum* ("him").

[470] See above footnote.

[471] I think the "he" means "Jupiter," i.e., not being able to produce what he would normally promise by nature.

On Mars

Then look at Mars: which if he were to fall in the degree of his own exaltation, it signifies great changes (but they will be less than the aforesaid) which will be of his nature, namely they are battles, burnings, fires, the cutting of roads, shedding of blood, and the like–unless Saturn were to aspect him from a trine or sextile aspect, with [Saturn] being made fortunate and strong, free from impediments, so that nothing bad may be said about him; or [if] another who received [Mars] were to aspect him, and commit his own disposition to [Mars], with [the other planet] being free from impediments, made fortunate and strong, so that if it were otherwise, the malice of Mars will be increased, and it will happen worse.

On the other planets

Concerning the Sun, nothing needs to be said, because it is impossible for him to be in the degree of his own exaltation in any revolution.

Of the inferiors, I have not found anything said by the ancient sages, except what Abū Ma'shar said about Mercury, saying you will look at Mercury in the revolution to see if there were some planet in his exaltation who receives him, and receives from him his disposition: it will be the master of the nature of his signification which I told you (with the help of God), because he comes together with his exaltation in a revolution of years and quarters. Indeed if there were a planet in his exaltation who receives, him, it will be similar to him.[472]

And he said, concerning the nature of the malefics in the conjunction of him who is in his own exaltation in the conjunction of the malefics, and their aspects, the which planet is in the degree of his own exaltation according to how it was revealed. And he said if the Moon were made peaceful, and the Sun were strong in his own place in a revolution of the night, the Sun commits his rulership and regency to the Moon.[473]

---

[472] In this paragraph I believe Bonatti is speaking of a planet who is in *Mercury's* exaltation, which would then make it "similar" to Mercury and a participant in his significations. The reason it is unclear is because Bonatti usually uses *suus* to mean a planet's *own* domicile, etc.
[473] Again, this paragraph's strange vocabulary and awkward construction is either a result of an early Latin translation of Abū Ma'shar, or a good translation of Abū Ma'shar's own style. At this time it is difficult to say which.

Chapter 115: What the planets would signify in a revolution of the year in which an eclipse of the Sun or Moon is supposed to take place

When you are revolving a year of the world, see whether there is going to be an eclipse of the Sun or Moon in that year. Because if an eclipse was not going to come, the judgment of the revolution will not be changed, but will remain in its own being. If however one were going to come, see in which sign its arrival is. Then you will calculate the planets and the houses for the hour of the middle of the eclipse, and then look at the sign and its Lord, and see how it behaves with the Lord of the Ascendant of the eclipse, and how it behaves with the Lord of the Year (or with its significator), and how it behaves with the significator of the king, and how it aspects with them, and with the other planets.

Abū Ma'shar said that if some planet who is impeded were to aspect the hidden [luminary] at the time of the eclipse, [and] afterwards the malefics were to aspect him, what it signifies will be oppressive, and impediment will be multiplied–and the more severely so if the significator of the king were the Lord of the sign in which the eclipse were made; because if it were so, and one of the malefics were to aspect him, and the malefic were Mars, the death of the king will be feared in that revolution. And if it were Saturn, severe infirmity will be feared for him, or another very serious accident; and this will be when the Sun arrives at the degree which was the cusp of the Midheaven at the hour of the middle of the eclipse. And if the Lord of the Year were the Lord of the sign in which the eclipse was going to come, the ruin of the common people and their great impediment will be feared (instead of death); and this will be when the Sun arrives at the degree of the Ascendant of the middle of the eclipse; and this [will be] if the Ascendant of the eclipse were Gemini or Virgo or Libra, or the first half of Sagittarius, or Aquarius, according to the kind of persons who are signified by the sign of the Ascendant, and according to the other things signified by the signs, just as I have expounded to you above in the chapter on the impediments which the Lord of the ascending sign of the revolution introduces when he is impeded. And these significations will last according to the number which we said above–namely if it were an eclipse of the Moon, one month is signified for each hour; indeed if it were an eclipse of the Sun, one year is signified for each hour.

And Abū Ma'shar said,[474] after this, look to the portion [of the ecliptic][475] over which you measured from the place of the eclipse and the place of its

---

[474] Another of the strange paragraphs from a Latin translation of Abū Ma'shar.
[475] *Parti.* I take this to mean that we are to measure the distance between these.

Lord, according to the substance of both signs. And he said, look at the speedy [or flying] stars which are the stars of Jupiter, and always appear in the place of Mercury. If Mercury were in the east, they will be seen in the east; and if he were in the west, they will be seen in the west; and the combustion of Mercury will be their receding.

On the portions[476] of the planets in an eclipse

Abū Ma'shar said,[477] concerning the portions of the planets in an eclipse, if they were in the lower journey,[478] it will be bad for the role of Mars and Venus, which are southern and northern; and if they were in the upper journey, it will be bad for the role of Saturn and the Moon and the Sun. And he said, after this, look to see in which sign they appear, and of what sort is the condition of the Lord of the same sign in its place, and what kind of aspect the malefics and the benefics have to the Lord of the sign and the staying-place.[479] If it were in a sign of kings [a fire sign], and the Lord of the sign were to aspect from a strong place, it signifies that he will leave from the same side which contends in the kingdom [and will be of] the household members of the king, and he will be famous. And he said if it were in a sign of a kingdom in the way I said, and the Lord of the sign did not aspect, he will be of the sons of nobles, and he will be fit for a kingdom. And he said judge likewise with regard to all the signs. And he said, know that the signs of the Sun and Jupiter and Mars signify the sons of kings, and the signs of Saturn signify those famous in former times. And the domicile of the Moon is less than the domicile of the Sun; and the domicile of Mercury is less than the domicile of Jupiter, and the domicile of Jupiter is less

---

[476] *Partibus.* Again, we have the ambiguous word *pars.* Since Bonatti's Abū Ma'shar is speaking about aspects to the planets and their signs, I take this to mean the "portion" of the zodiac they occupy. *Pars* here could also simply be a synonym for "sign."

[477] Yet again, another garbled paragraph from the unknown source of Abū Ma'shar.

[478] I am not sure what Bonatti's Abū Ma'shar means by an upper or lower journey. It could pertain to (a) whether they are above or below the horizon, or (b) their place in their epicycles, or (c) their place in their deferent, or (d) their declination. But in the case of (a), I cannot see why he would group the planets like this; in the case of (b), the Moon and the Sun do not have epicycles (else they would go retrograde); option (c) makes more sense, in which case the "upper" journey might mean going to or from their apogee (and the "lower" journey to and from their perigee), but what would being northern or southern have to do with that (and the categorization still is opaque to me). Perhaps (d) is meant, but then again the categorization still does not make sense to me.

[479] *Mansionis,* usually "mansion." But in older astrological literature the planets are said to "stay" in signs, so I do not think Abū Ma'shar means the lunar mansions. This should probably be understood as "the sign and its place in the chart."

than the domicile of Saturn; and [know] that their circles are below the circles I stated. And he said, for Saturn in Aquarius is notable, and it is ascribed to the wise [that] in Capricorn he is bad. And he said, the staying-places in their rising place do not signify unless it is the condition of the vulgar, and generally [the condition] of kings and great men. Whence you ought to consider the ascending sign, or the staying-place, and judge about the aforesaid persons according to the Ascendant and according to its planet.

How the hour may be discerned

Again, Abū Ma'shar said,[480] indeed the understanding of the hour in which it will appear, that is, so you might number from the Ascendant of the eclipse, or from the place of the eclipse to the Ascendant of the middle of the eclipse for every sign and month. And he said, when you have gone to the sign itself in which it is (or [to] the Ascendant of the middle of the eclipse), without a doubt this will exist, whether it were good or evil; or perhaps this thing will appear if it were faster, at [or toward] the entrance of the Moon to the Ascendant (especially in an eclipse which is in days): [there will be] battles, corruption or mutation in weather and adversity.

Chapter 116: How one should proceed concerning the significators of the king and the rustics, according to Abū Ma'shar

Abū Ma'shar said if the signification of the Sun is over the condition of the rustics,[481] and you were to understand it, the significator of the king will be manifested to you, and it will reveal to you what should happen in his kingdom in that same year. And he said, know from the reception of the planets towards

---

[480] This paragraph describes (in confusing terms) how to predict the timing of the events heralded by an eclipse. Abū Ma'shar wants us to follow standard procedure and cast a chart for the moment of the middle of the eclipse, and measure the distance between the degree of the Ascendant and the degree of the middle of the eclipse (he seems to allow both the longer and shorter distances). But the timing is the problem, since he does not seem to follow Ptolemy's procedure. I take it that Abū Ma'shar thinks the event will occur when certain planets enter the sign of the Ascendant or of the eclipse by transit. So for instance, in cases where the events are supposed to happen soon ("in days," left undefined as to how to tell this), the events will happen at the entrance of the transiting Moon into the sign ascending at the time of the eclipse.

[481] I am not sure if this means that the Sun is the Lord of the 1st, or the Lord of the Year. Later in the sentence he makes it seem that the Sun (in his hypothetical example) is the significator of the king, as well.

one another through their lights, and the falling of their rays in the twelve houses of the circle, and what there is in the signs with regard to climes and cities, so that their destruction may be laid open to you; and the adaptation by the rays of the malefics being inimical, and by the rays of the contrary ones, and likewise by the rays of the malefics being amicable, and likewise by the rays of the benefics being friendly and inimical, and speak according to their friendship and enmity toward the domiciles. For the benefics, if they were made peaceful toward the domiciles (that is, if they were to aspect the places by a trine or sextile aspect), signify a multitude of goods; and if they were inimical (that is, if they were to aspect from the square or the opposition), they signify a scarcity of good. And likewise if the malefics are inimical to the domiciles (that is, when they aspect from a square aspect or from the opposition), they signify a multitude of evil. If however, they were made peaceful toward the domiciles (that is, [if] they were to aspect them from a trine or sextile aspect), they signify a scarcity of evil.

And he said, then look to see what is in each sign (in terms of lands) in the east and the west. And if a sign were impeded in the west, it signifies impediments from the lands which are in the direction of the east and west. And if there were an impediment in the Midheaven, it signifies impediment in the lands which are in the east and the west, and especially toward the north and south (namely in the areas of Mars and Venus, and in the land of the Ethiopians).

And he said this is an admirable example through which you may contemplate a revolution of the year, namely the twelve days remaining of the month of Ramadan, which is the ninth lunar month of the 35th year of the Arabs. And the year arrived to Scorpio, and Libra was ascending, fifteen degrees, the bound of Jupiter; and the planets and their rays [were] according to what they are in this figure.[482]

---

[482] I can state with certainty that this entire delination by Abū Ma'shar is taken from BN *lat.* 16204 (see Introduction), although I have not verified every word in it against the manuscript.

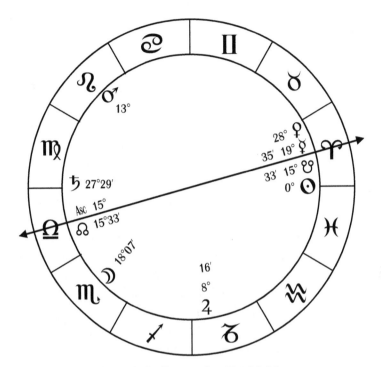

Figure 1: An Ingress by Abū Ma'shar

And he said that the[483] revolution was following Benesaphar[484] according to one equal hour and twelve minutes from the beginning of the Sabbath night, which begins to grow light on the 18th of the aforesaid month.[485]

And the[486] Ascendant (by the ascensions of Toledo) was Libra, fifteen degrees, the planets according to what I will tell you. For Saturn was in Virgo, 27° 29'. Jupiter in Capricorn, 8° 16'. Mars in Leo, 13°. The Sun in Aries, the first

---

[483] Omitting *si* ("if").

[484] Saphar is one of the months in the Islamic calendar, but I do not find a Benesaphar, unless perhaps it is someone's name–in which case it would read "the revolution was (according to Benesaphar) according to one equal hour..." But this seems rather awkward. The word could be *bāna Saphar* or "[the month of] Saphar becomes manifest," i.e., it was right after the beginning of the month, on the Sabbath night. This seems most likely. The construction of the sentence is also unusual because it begins with an antecedent "if" (omitted here) but no consequent.

[485] By my calculation this must have been the Aries ingress of March 656, AD, JC. Many of the planetary positions are roughly correct, but as I see it the Moon should be in Libra, not Scorpio. Perhaps a difference in calendrics is responsible for the difference.

[486] Again, omitting *si*.

degree. Venus in Aries, 28° approximately. Mercury in Aries, 19° 35'. The Moon in Scorpio, 18° and 7'. The Head in Libra, 15° 33'. And the Tail in Aries, 15° 33'.[487]

And the year arrived at Scorpio. And the erected angles, that is, the same signs, were by division and by number in the revolution of the year of the 35th year of the Arabs, with twelve days of the month of Ramadan remaining. And the Sun was in the opposition of the Ascendant, receding.[488] And the revolution was in the night, and the Moon was in her own descension in the second sign; and the benefics missing from her,[489] and she was joined to the malefics; and she was the Lady of the Midheaven. And Venus and Mercury were in the opposition of the Ascendant. And Mars [was] in the 11th (namely in Leo), received.[490] And Jupiter was in the 4th in his own descension, cutting off the light of the Sun from Mars.[491] And Saturn [was] cadent in Virgo, not received, in the 12th house [domicile?]. And Mars was the Lord of the domicile of the Lord of the Ascendant (namely of Aries, in which Venus was, and she was the Lady of the Ascendant), and the Lord of the domicile of the Sun and the Moon.[492]

And the Lady of the Year, the significatrix of the plebes, [was] Venus, who had more in terms of testimony;[493] and she was in an angle, in the opposition of her own domicile, going from the east toward the angle of the west, not received.[494]

And the significator of the king was the Moon, because the revolution was in the night, and it was her authority; and she was the Lady of the Midheaven and was joined to Saturn, who was cadent in the 12th house [domicile?], then was joined to Mars (and he was retrograde). [This signified] that the king of that same clime will be killed by his own rustics, because the retrograde Mars

---

[487] Note that no degree of the Midheaven is given.

[488] I.e., in opposition by whole sign, and "receding" by being cadent from the angle by degree.

[489] By whole sign the Moon is still configured with Jupiter; but Abū Ma'shar must mean that by degree she is separating from Mars and will soon be joined to Saturn.

[490] This means either that Abū Ma'shar allows reception by sign only (since Mars is in the Sun's domicile), or that he allows it so long as there is an applying aspect (even if it is outside of the orbs). See the comments on Jupiter's cutting off the light, and Venus, below.

[491] That is, because the Sun must perfect a square with Jupiter before he can be joined to Mars.

[492] This means that Mars will be key to the revolution, since he disposes both luminaries and the Lady of the Ascendant.

[493] *Plus testimonio.* Usually *plus* takes the genitive, but can mean "greater in number" without the genitive. I have translated it so here.

[494] But is she not received by Mars by whole sign, just as Mars is received by the Sun by whole sign? Or is he saying that Venus is not in an applying aspect to her dispositor Mars (whereas the Sun is, even though Jupiter cuts off the light)?

signified his killing (and he was the Lord of the domiciles of the luminaries, and the Lord of the domicile of the Lord of the Ascendant).[495] And on account of the falling of the Moon from the angle, it signified that he would be killed without contention, and he would not subdue the aforesaid citizens of his.

And he said, on account of the place of Venus and her being put down from her own rank,[496] and the opposition, with her being the Lady of the Year and the significatrix of the rustics, signified that the rustics, after this, will be given over to battles and the complication of war and contention in the kingdom.

And he said, on account of the place of the Moon from Saturn, and the rays of his sextile aspect, it signifies that these things will happen in the first quarter of the year. And from the place of the Sun (who is the Lord of the 11th, in the square aspect of Jupiter, committing disposition to him),[497] it signifies that he who will succeed [the king] will be just, and the rustics will be improved in his own time.[498]

And he said, on account of the light of the retrograde Mars in the 11th from the Ascendant, it signifies that he will scatter the houses of the king's treasures after killing him by a powerful killing and the shedding of blood. And he said, on account of the Mars's presence in the domicile of the Sun, it signifies the contention of noble men and their kings.

And he said, therefore the light of the opposition of the Sun and Mercury and Venus was in the Ascendant, and the rays of the second[499] square aspect of Jupiter, and the rays of the first sextile aspect of Mars.[500] This signifies there is going to be a contention in the clime of those signs, and shedding of blood. And there will be a battle in the area of Marmon[501] and Sigistan[502] and Aason,[503]

---

[495] But why would Mars signify the king's rustics, who would be better signified by the Ascendant (the common people)?

[496] *Propter...eius depositionem a suo ordine.* In other words, she is in detriment. This phrase must reflect an early and more literal translation of Abū Ma'shar.

[497] The wording (both here and in BN *lat.* 16204) makes it seem as though the Sun is receiving Jupiter (and thereby committing disposition to Jupiter); but the chart shows that Jupiter is receiving the Sun from his own triplicity and term in Aries, so that *Jupiter* is committing the disposition to the *Sun.*

[498] *In tempore suo.* It is unclear what this refers to; it could mean "in their own time," or simply, "during his reign."

[499] Again, the "first" aspect of a planet is the sinister aspect cast forward in the order of signs. The "second" aspect is the dexter aspect cast backwards against the order of signs.

[500] Note that Abū Ma'shar tends to use whole-sign aspects.

[501] Unknown.

[502] *Lat.* Sagesten.

[503] Unknown.

and their cattle will be profitable, and the land will be fertile; infirmities in boys, and the condition of their businessmen will be improved.

The second [sign] from the Ascendant was Scorpio, and the Moon was in it impeded, and the rays of the second trine aspect of the Sun, and the rays of the second sextile aspect of Jupiter, and the rays of the first square aspect of Mars, and the first sextile aspect of Saturn. And this signifies the shedding of blood and battles. And the beginning of these will be in the clime of the Arabs. After this it will change, because the Moon is impeded outside of the sign in which she is,[504] and after this it will be magnified, and there will be the shedding of much blood in it, and the condition of the clime of the Arabs will be made severe, and the death of their cattle, and the cold of their winter will be severe, and this will be because of the place of Venus from the Ascendant. And on account of her presence in an angle, it signifies that a foreign enemy will not enter upon them, and he will be in the east, and death by means of his role, and the greatest proportion will be in women.

The third [sign] was Sagittarius, and in it were the rays of the second trine aspect of Mercury, and the rays of the second trine aspect of Mars, and the rays of the first square aspect of Saturn; and its Lord Jupiter was in his own descension. This signifies infirmities and severities which will find the citizens of the first clime and the citizens of Spain; and a multitude of robbers, and the death of beasts, and it will be multiplied in the land, like in Upper Armenia, and more boys will die in this year.

The fourth [sign] was Capricorn, and Jupiter was in it, and the rays of the second square aspect of the Sun, and the rays of the second square aspect of Venus, and the light of the first trine aspect of Saturn, and the light of the first sextile aspect of the Moon. These signify the health of the clime in the day, and the goodness or fineness of their condition; also the fitness of the condition of their king, and the felicity of their land, and that they will beat those who contend with them; and the multitude of their wealth; and the fertility of the land of the citizens of Asamilier[505] and Almedehai,[506] and the security of their citizens together with their largesse and abundance; victory and the fitness of their king.

The fifth [sign] was Aquarius, and none of the planets was in it, but the light of the second sextile aspect of the Sun was there, and the light of the second

---

[504] I am not sure what Abū Ma'shar means by this—perhaps that she will be in Sagittarius, which Saturn aspects by a whole-sign square?
[505] Unknown.
[506] Unknown.

sextile aspect of Mercury, and the light of the first square aspect of the Moon, and the light of the opposition of Mars, and the light of the second sextile aspect of Venus–which signifies contention and war in the area of Kufa,[507] and in its rustics, and battle and rebellions and consuming [of food]. And he said, perhaps this will be in Egypt and Gurgan,[508] and on account of this occasion there will be the shedding of much blood. And he said many pilgrims will be congregated to those regions.

The sixth [sign][509] was Pisces, and none of the planets was in it, but the light of the opposition of Saturn was there, and the light of the first sextile aspect of Jupiter, and the light of the first trine aspect of the Moon. And he said the place of the opposition of Saturn signifies the severity of the cold in Tabaristan,[510] and in its direction, and a burden which will occur to its king in it, and this on account of the place of Jupiter and the weakness[511] in which he is. And the bad condition of its rustics, and they will have power over their king, and they will resolve among themselves, and there will be dissensions, and their rains and their profits will be multiplied, and their cattle will be fit, and likewise this will occur to the areas of India and the land of Armenia (of those who come up toward Romania).

The seventh [sign] was Aries, and the Sun in it, removed from the angle. Also Mercury and Venus were in it, and the light of the first square aspect of Jupiter, and the light of the second trine aspect of Mars (who is the Lord of the second [sign]). And on account of the place of Venus, which is in an angle, and the trine aspect of Mars, who is the Lord of the 2nd domicile (and he is in Leo retrograde), the Sun signified concerning the ruin of the king of Babylon, and that there will be contention and war in the clime of Babylon, and the shedding of much blood, and the destruction of their kingdom. And the beginning of these things will be in another clime, and this according to the place of Mars, and on account of the place of Mercury (who is the Lord of the ninth).[512] And the light of Jupiter (who is the Lord of the 3rd domicile), signifies that there will be in addition a loss of many men on the occasion of these wars. And he said there

---

[507] Lat. *Alcuphus.*

[508] Lat. *Urgen.*

[509] Reading *sextum* with the rest, instead of *sexta.*

[510] Lat. *Tabaribem.*

[511] Lit., "his weakness," but in this context it sounds unusual in English.

[512] Reading *noni* for *nonae.* The punctuation in the original is unclear, but I have ended this sentence here because Mercury is mentioned in connection with the other planets in the seventh sign, whereas the mention of Jupiter seems to indicate a new point. Bonatti's text is one long run-on sentence.

will be religion, and boys and camels and every hairy thing will be successful, and heat will be oppressive to them. And what I said will even be in the mountains and in Azerbaijan.[513]

And the eighth [sign] was Taurus, and none of the planets was in it, and its Lady Venus was cadent from it. However, the light of the first sextile aspect of the Sun, and the light of the first trine aspect of Jupiter, and the light of the second square aspect of Mars (who is the enemy of this domicile), and the light of the opposition of the Moon (who is the Lady of the exaltation of this domicile), signifies that the king of Antiha[514] and the city of Ortona[515] (which are said to be continuous with Nueria,[516] and particularly Sigistan[517] and Tabaristan,[518] because it is in the areas of the west) will go out upon all the enemies who are near them, and they will find severity from them; and robbers and arrogant men and contradictions will be multiplied everywhere; and their harvests will be destroyed, and the rustics will put down their king, and their cattle will perish, and their security will be from the king,[519] and they will find good from pilgrimage.

And the ninth [sign] was Gemini, and none of the planets was in it, but the light of the first sextile aspect of Mercury was there, and the light of the second square aspect of Saturn, and the light of the second sextile aspect of Mars.[520] The commixture of the light of Mercury (who is the Lord of the ninth)[521] signifies that those from Adaliam[522] and Exanos,[523] and their parts, [and] Thebut[524] will be strengthened over those who are inimical to them, and who are of their opposition and are enemies; and this will be on account of the strength of the place of Mercury and his reception. And on account of the commixture of Mars with Saturn, it signifies many infirmities and pains in these regions, and many men will die; and this will be particularly in youths.[525] And

---

513 Lat. *Arabigem.*

514 Unknown.

515 Unknown.

516 Unknown.

517 Lat. *Segestan.*

518 Lat. *Cabrus*, reading as a variant on *Cubrasten*, also attributed with Sigistan to Libra.

519 This should probably be read as meaning "they will be safe from the king"

520 Again, the punctuation is somewhat ambiguous.

521 Reading *noni* for *nonae.*

522 Unknown, but perhaps Daylaman, a region on the southern shore of the Caspian Sea.

523 Unknown.

524 Unknown.

525 Is this because Gemini is ruled by Mercury, or because Mercury's light is also commingled with that of Mars and Saturn? The punctuation makes this ambiguous.

because the second square aspect of Saturn has more degrees, it signifies that they will be satisfied with their king and will obey him. And he said, and what we said will be in Gurgan[526] and Lower Acebirutaba,[527] and Upper Alem,[528] and Amacil.[529]

And the tenth [sign] was Cancer, and none of the planets was in it, but the light of the [second] trine aspect of the Moon (who is the Lady of the 10th domicile) was there, and she is impeded in her own descension; and the light of the second sextile aspect of Saturn, and the light of the first square aspect of the Sun, and the light of the first square aspect of Mercury, and the light of the first sextile aspect of Venus. And he said, what I said is signified by the malignity of the Lord of the domicile and the Lord of the exaltation in addition to what the square of the Sun signifies, that the king of the clime of Iraq[530] will perish and their kingdom will be destroyed, and it will be mixed together,[531] and there will be contention between them in their princes, and there will be infirmity in men generally from cold and moisture, and their produce will be destroyed, and the condition of men will be oppressed, and acquisition will be decreased; and likewise the land of Balab[532] and Allaharara[533] (that is, of the two seas), and of Egypt, Emarius[534] and Addul.[535]

And the eleventh [sign] was Leo, and Mars is in it retrograde, and the light of the first trine aspect of the Sun, and the light of the first trine aspect of Mercury, and the light of the second sextile aspect of Saturn,[536] and the light of the second square aspect of the Moon, and the light of the first square aspect of Venus. And he said the place of Mars and the light of the second square aspect of the Moon (who is the luminary of the night, and the significatrix of the king), signify that in the clime of Altoio[537] and in Aeratus[538] there will be war and the shedding of blood, and detriment from robbers, and this[539] will be in Alba-

---

[526] Lat. *Iurgen.*
[527] Unknown.
[528] Unknown.
[529] Unknown.
[530] Lat. *Alirat.*
[531] *Commiscebitur.* I am not sure what Bonatti's Abū Ma'shar is getting at.
[532] Unknown.
[533] Unknown.
[534] Unknown, but perhaps Oman?
[535] Unknown.
[536] This does not seem right, since Saturn is in Virgo and cannot cast any sort of aspect into an adjacent sign.
[537] Unknown.
[538] Unknown, but perhaps Herat?
[539] Reading *hoc* for *hunc.*

frah,[540] and many men will perish in that same year, and there will be contention in the kingdom. And it will be on account of the light of the second square aspect of the Moon—understand this.

And the twelfth [sign] was Virgo, and Saturn was [there], retrograde, and the light of the first trine aspect of Venus, and the light of the second trine aspect of Jupiter, and the second sextile aspect of the Moon—which signifies infirmities from cold and dryness, according to the nature of this sign. And he said, on account of the place of Mercury they will be freed [from the infirmities] with the help of God, and they will not be destroyed. And their strength will not belong to the heat of summer[541]—understand this.

How the condition of the king might be seen in this year

The 10th of this figure was Cancer. And the Moon (who is its Lady), was the significatrix of the king, and she was cadent in the second place. And he said, therefore we looked to see whether her light was in the Midheaven (which is her place) or in the Ascendant. And the light of her trine aspect was in the eighteenth degree and seventh minute of Cancer. Therefore we looked to see to whom she committed her own disposition in this place, and it was to [the light] closer to her apart from the other lights, the light of the first square aspect of Mercury, and it was in the nineteenth degree and a fraction.[542] We subtracted the light of the Moon from this, and one degree and a fraction remained. We divided this by fifty-nine minutes and eight[543] seconds, and one day and a fraction came out. [Therefore] the Moon disposed one day and a fraction through her own light out of the Midheaven.[544] And because the disposition was committed to Mercury (who was the Lord of the house of enemies, and the Lord of pilgrimage and faith), this signifies the sorrow of the king in this disposition by the accusation of the religious, and [people] of faith, and from their sayings, and from enemies. After this, Mercury will receive the disposition from the Moon by his first square aspect. And he is the Lord of the 9th house

---

540 Unknown.

541 *Et non erit calori aestatis eorum fortitudo.* I believe this simply means that they will not have much strength in the heat of summer.

542 Here the disposition seems to be committed from the Moon to a degree in which Mercury's light falls; so far we have only seen disposition go directly to the planet itself.

543 Reading *8.* for *18.*, since the relationship between the degree of longitude and the day is 59' 8".

544 As we will see, Abū Ma'shar is letting the planets cast their rays into the sign he is interested in (the tenth), and taking the longitudes of the aspects in order.

[domicile?] and the 12th. His rays are in the 9th domicile from her;[545] [and] this signifies every work which is hoped for, having a good measure of accusation because of penances and prayer and fasting, and they will find marriage celebrations in that disposition.

Then Saturn will receive the disposition by the light of his second sextile aspect, from the light of the first square aspect of Mercury, and he will dispose the remainder of the sign in which his light is, in the following sign from the same place. And he is the Lord of the fourth and fifth (which is the eighth from the place of disposition). Therefore, in this disposition it signified in this place (because he received the light from the square aspect of Mercury), that little notes and rumors will come to him[546] in these days from the direction of the west, which will make him sad; and he will be confused about them, and he will be of bad mind over it, and he will envy the citizens their work, and his own children,[547] which will make him sad.

After this the Sun will receive the disposition from Saturn by the light of his first trine aspect (and he is the Lord of the 2nd domicile from the Midheaven,[548] and it is also the second [sign] from the house of the king), which signifies expenses because of women, and this is on account of the place of the Sun [in Aries], and because he commits disposition to Venus,[549] and Venus receives the light of her [his?] own first square aspect, and the light of the first trine aspect of the Sun, and Venus is the Lady of the Ascendant, and [Libra] is in his opposition.

Therefore [Venus] receives the disposition from the Sun and renders it to the Moon, and this signified the entrance or involvement in this disposition, and contention with the rustics because of the kingdom, and the marriage celebrations of his own son from the direction of women,[550] and their consolation by the light of the second square aspect from the square aspect of Venus (and [the

---

[545] Reading *ea* (indicating the Moon) for *eo*. Below we will see Bonatti point out that Saturn rules the 8th domicile from the 10th ("from the place of disposition"). Both the Moon and the 10th signify the king, the subject of this section.

[546] Perhaps because Saturn is in the third sign from the tenth?

[547] Perhaps because the Moon is in the fifth sign from the tenth?

[548] Reading *medii coeli* for *ascendentis*. The link between money and women seems to be because he rules the second sign from the tenth (wealth), and is located in the seventh sign (women, marriages).

[549] I do not understand the logic of the rest of this paragraph; there must be errors involved in the transmission.

[550] *Ex parte mulierum.* Obviously the marriage would be with women. Bonatti's Abū Ma'shar might be emphasizing that proposals come from women or from their families, since we are talking about the influences coming from the seventh house.

Moon] is the Lady of the Midheaven, and is in the 2nd from the Ascendant), which signifies the entering of the king [into these situations] in that same year, and in the same disposition, and generally in the disposition of the planets from the Midheaven up to the place of the cutting [of the light] by his [her?] rays, up to seventy-three and one-half days, and one-sixth of a day.[551]

Therefore consider by this, and what it is necessary for you to employ in it, in a revolution of years of the world, if you worked it out in the disposition of days by the projection of rays according to what I told you concerning the domiciles and their Lords, and the reception of light and its sending toward a reception from a trine or square aspect, or from the opposition. After this, know the light of the reception and its impulse,[552] and work in the lights of the contrary and inimical malefics, and in the lights of the harmonious or peace-making malefics. And he said, likewise [regarding] the inimical benefics, if they were inimical to the houses, say [there will be] a scarcity of good; and in the lights of the malefics (if they were inimical to the houses), and multitude of evil; and if they were pacified, a scarcity of good.[553]

Likewise concerning the two Parts[554] in a revolution of the years of the world

Abū Ma'shar said if you were to find two Parts in one place or sign, those people will prevail whose significator was better disposed. And that one will be called better disposed (how much it is) in this, who better aspects his own Part, or were joined corporally with it. And Abū Ma'shar said this is like if a Part is joined to its own Lord in the watery triplicity, and their presence or conjunction coincides in one of the signs of the triplicity from which the conjunction has

---

[551] *Ad sextam diei.* Meaning unclear. One would expect it to read: *ad sextam partem diei.* This 73-day period, multiplied by 59' 8", yields an arc of 71° 56' 44". I am not sure what arc is being referred to.

[552] This must refer to one of Abū Ma'shar's senses of "pushing," either "pushing power" or "pushing nature." See Tr. 3.

[553] Despite the odd wording (which I think might be based on Arabic), I believe these last sentences are simply standardized instructions for judging malefics and benefics making good and bad aspects.

[554] Just as in Ch. 34, there is some ambiguity about the word *pars*–whether it means a Part or "side," or what. I have translated *pars* as "Part," because the description of the method sounds much like the relationship between a Part and its dispositor. It seems we are to see whether the Lord of the 1st or the 7th (I am assuming a war context here) aspects the Part relevant to its side, but what Parts are meant? Abū Ma'shar speaks about a book he as written, called the *Book of the Two Lots* (see *OGC* II.V, 15-18), and there seems to have been a number of versions of "two lots" or "two Parts" in medieval mundane astrology. But this book of Abū Ma'shar's has not been identified, and accounts differ on what the Parts are. See Ch. 34. Of course, this passage could also be based on BN *lat.* 16204.

been changed. So Gemini: the conjunction is changed from it, and it will summon[555] its presence or conjunction in the circle of the conjunction, or in the two others outside that triplicity in Aquarius. Therefore in addition the citizens of this triplicity are strengthened. And he said if it were Saturn and the conjunction were in Scorpio, they will be strengthened. If however he were to receive the disposition of Mars in Scorpio, and he were in the Midheaven, and ruled the year, and Mars were in the Ascendant and ruled, with the commission of his own disposition to Saturn in the Midheaven in Scorpio, it signifies that the king will perish in the direction of the east, and he will leave his kingdom. And if it were to happen in addition that Venus were strong in her own exaltation, and the conjunction were in Scorpio, it signifies the strength of the Arabs, and their seeking in the kingdom.

Another chapter on the revolution of the years of the world according to Abū Ma'shar

If you were to erect the figure of the revolution of one of the years of the world, look at the significator or Lord of the Year, which is called the significator of the rustics. And look at the Sun and the significator of the king. Even see if one of them were to fall[556] in the opposition of Mars, unless perhaps Mars is made very fortunate (so that nothing bad can be said of him, which tends to happen most rarely): because it signifies wars and terrors and bloodshed. And if two of the aforesaid significators were to fall in the opposition of Mars, they will signify greater evil.

And Abū Ma'shar said the removal of the malefics from the angle into the third or ninth[557] signifies war and a scarcity of religion (both of the king and the rustics). You ought to consider the Sun and his condition, which if he were well disposed (namely made fortunate and strong), it signifies the good disposition and fitness of the land of Babylon and its citizens. If however he were impeded, it signifies their bad condition and the detriment of them and of their king. If the Sun were alone, impeded in the 2nd or in the 6th or in the 12th, or he were impeded somewhere by the conjunction or [square] aspect or opposition of one of the malefics, it even signifies the bad condition of the aforesaid king (namely of Babylon).

---

[555] *Conveniet.* This notion of "summoning" (or even "summoning before a tribunal") recalls the Hellenistic language in aspect doctrine, whereby one planet is "called to witness" for another.

[556] This may refer to the planet's falling on an individual degree, or it might mean that the planet is both "cadent, [and] in the opposition of Mars."

[557] Here "removal" implies cadence.

You will even see the disposition of the Moon: that if she were free (namely made fortunate and strong), it signifies the strength of the Romans and their king, and the weakness of their enemies. If however she were alone, impeded in whatever place she is (but more in the aforesaid houses), it signifies the impediment and evil of them and of their king, and the strength of their enemies.

But someone might say, "Why does the Sun signify the king of Babylon, and the Moon the king of the Romans—because the kingdom of the Romans is bigger than any other, and the Sun is the greater luminary?" To which it must be said that the Sun is the higher luminary, but he is not a universal participant in things like the Moon is; and the kingdom of Babylon existed before the kingdom of the Romans, nor is it a universal kingdom, wherefore the Sun was attributed to it as its significator. Indeed the Moon, because she is the universal luminary participating in every matter, was attributed as the significator of the kingdom and king of the Romans, because that kingdom is universal beyond all other kingdoms, to which all kings and all kingdoms were then subjected and put under.

You will even look at the disposition of Saturn: which if he were well disposed, and in the conjunction of the benefics, and especially from the Ascendant, and he were the Lord of the Year, free from impediments, he will not impede, nor will he be an evildoer then; and the impediment which he will bring into inferior subjects by nature will be removed if he were [not][558] impeded (and more powerfully if he were in Scorpio, and Scorpio were the Midheaven, because then the Ascendant will be Aquarius, and he will be the Lord of the Year). For it signifies the shedding of blood and other pestilences are going to come in that revolution; and it seems that the evil is supposed to begin when Saturn reaches his own bound. If however Mars were to aspect him from the opposition or square aspect, it will increase the evil; but if the aspect were a trine or sextile with reception, it will not bring in so much, and the evil will be decreased.

You will even look on at Mars, and you will see if he were to fall in Cancer (which is his detriment and descension). Because if it were so, Abū Ma'shar said it signifies that the citizens of the clime of Iraq[559] will fall into oppression because of the leader.[560] And likewise in Sagittarius. And he said, because these

---

[558] Adding *non*.

[559] Lat. *Alirat*.

[560] Reading *ex auctore* for *ex actore*. The text might also be read *ex actore* ("because of a disputant") or *exactore* ("by means of an extorter/accuser/tax collector"), but none of these readings seems to fit well with the syntax given.

signs belong to their clime, and that Mars is the significator from the leader;[561] and he said that Mars in the Ascendant signifies the diminishment of the eastern direction in that same year. And he said that the fitness of Venus in Pisces or in one of her own domiciles, signifies the fertility of the regions of the Arabs, and their security. And he said if she were to commit disposition from a place similar to a planet who receives her in the Midheaven, and she were in an angle, not removed, and receiving, and the luminaries were in the sign of the profection from Scorpio,[562] the Arabs will contend in the kingdom and will seek it from their own citizens because she is joined to a planet in the Midheaven, and had fallen in a good place (and even better if the sign of the Midheaven were to be congruent with her nature).

And he said, the fitness of Venus signifies the fitness of the Arabs in their own bodies, and the fitness of their sustenance [or way of life]. He said, if however she were to fall into the enmity of the Ascendant, it signifies wars and mutations in the middle of the year, and in ignoble people and robbers. And he said the impediment of the Lord of the Ascendant in a malign place[563] in the Midheaven signifies the oppression which will present itself to the rustics from their rulers. And he said the occurrence of a planet in the 7th from the Ascendant (which is the place of its enmity), signifies that the king will contend–if the signification of the planet in its[564] place were concerning the kingdom or concerning the year. And he said if the first party[565] were in the Midheaven[566] in its own dignity, and the second party were in the fourth, it signifies that war will generally abound in the earth.

In like manner you will see if one of the malefic planets were to fall in the second from the Ascendant of the revolution: because if it were so, and he were to impede the Lord of the second from the opposition or a square aspect, it signifies the destruction of substances, and their dispersion or expenditures, and often on useless things.

You will even consider the malefic planets, and you will see if one of them were opposed to the other: because if it were so, it signifies the coming of a great matter in the world, and in a time that is not far off. Likewise you will see

---

[561] See above.
[562] Again, is this a statement about Venus (who rules Arabs), or Abū Ma'shar's application of a general rule to his chart above?
[563] "Place" (*loco*) here must mean "sign."
[564] I.e., the planet's place at the time of the revolution.
[565] Here *pars* definitely means "side"–in this case, the Lords of the 1st and the 7th would be in their own 10th, and opposed to one another.
[566] In this instance, the Midheaven is being equated with the tenth whole sign.

whether Mars is found to be combust (unless perhaps he were in the *kasmīmī* of the Sun), and he were the Lord of the sign of the 10ᵗʰ house and removed from the angle: because if it were so, it signifies that one [man] will go out from the kingdom, who will punish [the kingdom], and the end of this matter will be by the sword. And if the Sun were then to commit disposition to Saturn, and Saturn were the significator of the rustics, and the Ascendant were Capricorn or Aquarius, and he were to aspect the Ascendant with an aspect of friendship, and were in a good place from it, and the authority were the Moon's,[567] and she were to commit disposition to him from the Ascendant, it signifies that the rustics will conspire together toward the ruin of their king, and death by them will be feared for him in that revolution.

And if Saturn were the Lord of the year, and the *al-mubtazz* of the Midheaven were impeded by him, not receiving him, but there were no testimony on the condition of the rustics from Venus and the Moon to the Lord of the tenth (and Saturn were in the eleventh),[568] and the Moon (whose authority it is) in the Ascendant, Saturn is given more testimony in the condition of the rustics.

And Abū Ma'shar said if Mars does not aspect his own place [or domicile], nor is he received, nor likewise the Moon, Saturn signifies from the place of the Moon (who is the luminary of the night) what the matter of the Sun signified.[569] And by the committing of disposition and strength to Saturn, the king will perish in that year, and the rustics will kill him. And he said there will be poverty and tribulation in the rustics, and likewise oppression and a battle, and the burden of the *annona*, and it will be in the sixth month, on account of the fact that there are 6° between them.[570] And he said the cattle will be profitable in that same year; and the cold of their winter will be middling.

You will even see at the hour of the revolution if Saturn were the significator of the vulgar or the Lord of the Year or the *al-mubtazz* over the Ascendant of

---

[567] I.e., in a nocturnal chart.

[568] *Sed non fuerit testimonium in esse rusticorum Veneris atque Lunae & fuerit Saturnus in undecimo domino decimi.* An awkward sentence and I am not completely sure of its meaning.

[569] This might mean, "Saturn will signify what the Sun signifies *instead of* signifying what the Moon does." That is, since the Moon in the nocturnal chart is weakened, her authority reverts to the Sun—and therefore Saturn, who often signifies kings along with the luminary in charge, will participate with the Sun. Latin would normally have used slightly different wording to say "instead of," but saying "from the place" might have been an early, standard astrological way to phrase this idea. The phrasing might also be a slight play on words, since "instead of" in Latin is literally "in the place of" (*in loco* + genitive), and *locus* ("place") is a standard astrological term for a sign or house.

[570] This statement seems to refer to a particular chart—but it cannot be the chart above, since none of the planets besides Mars and Mercury have six degrees between them by aspect.

the year, nor did Mars impede him, and the benefics were in the Ascendant, and Mars cadent from them and from the Ascendant: because it signifies the fitness of the affairs of the vulgar (and more strongly so if he were in an angle or in another good place from the Ascendant, and [Saturn] were to receive the benefics).

And Abū Ma'shar said moist and watery planets in the Ascendant signify the cold of the year in that same city or region, and locusts and the fitness of cattle; and likewise if the benefics were to descend in the Ascendant with the Sun.[571] And he said the presence of the Lord of the Midheaven falling into the third with Jupiter, signifies the ease of the king and his being dispatched throughout his rulership.[572]

---

[571] "Descend" here could simply mean "*be in* the Ascendant."
[572] I.e., the third signifies short journeys. So the king will make many trips through the lands he rules.

TREATISE 10:
HEAVY RAINS

On heavy rains and on mutations of the air, and what is associated with every part of them

Preface

Since[1] it would seem to me that I have satisfactorily observed the things promised (of those which I promulgated in the beginning of this work) in what has preceded, lest perhaps you would say you are deceived in something I think it would be appropriate, in this Treatise, to make mention of the mutation of the air–and of those things (of those mutations) that coincide with them, and what will result from that coinciding, and of those things which we can perceive from thence, and to which the human mind can attain–as compendiously as I can.

And even though the action of heavy rains (and of other things which coincide with the mutations of the air) is very particular, and more particular than the rest of the other particular things, still those things which can be said of it, and known, do not seem to me they should be omitted; and according to the sayings of our wise predecessors and [according to] those things which, besides, will be able to be seen, which would seem will be useful; [and according to] the truth of it, just as one will be able to discuss [it] more certainly; nor to deviate from their opinions;[2] according to to how it seemed to our most reverend predecessors Jafar [the Indian][3] and Lencuo, Ptolemy, and others who strove to light the way for us in this. To put it briefly, therefore, so we can more quickly arrive at the main topics devised, and not to [make] a great introduction to the

---

[1] This Treatise is drawn from Jafar (often almost verbatim), whose Latin text is choppy and almost in a faux-classical style, often leaving words out and using a minority terminology for "conjunction," "aspect," *etc.* The style does not reflect Bonatti's own.

[2] The long portion "[according to] those things…from their opinions" reads, *et ea quae insuper videri poterunt quae videantur utilia fore veritatem eius prout certius poterit discurrere nec ab eorum sententiis deviare.* The translation is somewhat uncertain, and it seems that in the interest of appearing more classical the original author or Bonatti has either let certain words simply be understood (and perhaps he has omitted some verbs). This sort of monstrously long sentence is not typical for Bonatti, nor is the construction of the individual clauses.

[3] Jafar Indus. See my Introduction.

beginning of this, I do not intend to make you burdened by means of a lengthy talk, but to [arrive] at those things which will conduct you more quickly to the desired matter, and to focus my mind and intention faithfully on them.[4]

What things are set out in this work

Among[5] those things which pertain to this work are all the planets and the mansions of the Moon (even though certain other things are considered at first, as is necessary). And as has already been said, it is necessary to consider the Moon before the others, and that her conjunction with the Sun be considered, and their opposition, not to mention their square; and then to their aspects of others[6] and their corporal conjunction, and even the increase of the light of that luminary [the Moon] and the speed and slowness of her course, and her rising, ascent, descent, and likewise setting, not to mention those things which seem to make for generation and corruption from her motions:[7] because in the aforesaid times the effects of the mutations of the air, and their coincidings are apprehended more, just as will be shown extensively in the following, God willing.

And Jafar said,[8] nevertheless also, [her] quite similar [departure and] return into the south[9] and the north, and the application of the same, and whatever things happen to the figure, this same thing is brought in, the actions of all of which (and her efficacy, and the power[10] of the Moon, by means of begetting animals and of the earth, the which things sense perceives and vision discerns), are easily distinguised.[11]

On the knowledge to be had of the benefics and malefics,
and of all temperate or convertible things

If[12] it is intended that a greater knowledge of the mutation of the air be had, it must be known first which of the planets are benefic, which malefic. Likewise

---

[4] *Sub breviloquio igitur cum quo citius potest ad excogitatorum proposita perveniri* [sic?] *nec magnum accessum ad principium huius, nec te multiloquio gravem facere intendo, sed ad ea quae ad rem optatam citius te perducunt, et circa illa mentem atque intentionem fideliter adhibere.*

[5] Based on Jafar, §§2-3.

[6] *Tunc ad eorum aliorum aspectus.* Usually Bonatti does not say "aspect *of* another," but so the text reads. Moreover, this clause is missing a verb.

[7] Omitting *considera* dangling at the end, as it is not needed.

[8] See Jafar, §3.

[9] *Austrum.*

[10] Reading *potentia* (with Jafar) for *patientia.*

[11] Reading *discernuntur* (with Jafar) for *differrentur.*

[12] See Jafar, §4.

it is necessary for you to know first which are now for fortune, which now for misfortune. For as the ancient sages unanimously decreed, it is true that Jupiter and Venus are naturally benefics and workers of fortune. Indeed Saturn and Mars are naturally malefics, and of their own nature bring in misfortune, just as the same sages affirm, and [as] will appear by the most open test of truth. Indeed they said the Sun and Mercury and the Moon are common and temperate: namely [they say] the Sun sometimes [works] fortune and sometimes misfortune, but Mercury and the Moon are convertible, so that they are converted to the nature of those to whom they are applied (whether they are benefics or malefics).[13]

To know when coming rains would be signified, and when not

Indeed[14] in the knowledge to be had of future rains, it is necessary for you to consider the conjunction of the Sun and the Moon (as was touched on above), and [to consider] if any of the planets is then joined with them, or aspects them by any aspect. Because if Jupiter or even Venus is joined corporally to them, or Jupiter aspects them from a trine or sextile aspect, nor did one of the malefics appear[15] with them, nor does it project its rays to them, or [Jupiter] were to aspect [the Moon] after her separation from the Sun, it will indubitably deny future rains. If however the aspect of Jupiter to the luminaries were a square or opposition, without the admixture of the malefics, as I said, it will signify there are going to be light rains or practically none. But if one of the malefics were to aspect, without the aspect of a benefic, or after the conjunction the Moon were first joined corporally or by opposition [to it], without a doubt you could announce future rains.

For[16] the peculiar nature of the benefics is naturally to make the air fine, and to clear it of thick vapors, and likewise to resist the malice of the malefics; and on the other hand the malefics strive to resist the goodness of the benefics. And because the nature of their heaviness and impurity agrees with the thick vapors collected together in the air, they generate heavinesses which bring in a disturbance of the air into the lower parts, on account of that heaviness and impurity

---

13 I.e., they are "common" (having two different effects), but for different reasons. The Sun's action depends on whether he is burning or not (which is usually said to pertain to his squares, the conjunction, and opposition).

14 See Jafar, §5.

15 *Extiterit.* In this context, it means "is joined with."

16 See Jafar, §5.

of the air, and likewise [they bring in] powerful rains descending into the thickness.

Nevertheless, even though Venus is of the fortunate stars, still, because her nature comes down[17] in a certain manner on the side of moisture, if she is mixed with one of the malefics (nor were another benefic to aid [her]), it allows rains to move–not, however very harmful ones, unless perhaps she were exceedingly weak, and strong malefics were found, so that she could not mitigate their badness (however she always alleviates something).

On the prognostication of rains in general

However, in the prognostication of rains it is necessary that you bring discernment to bear, and that you consider the places, sites,[18] seasons, climes, regions, and the like which occur to you to be considered. For the mutations of the air tend to be diversified in different ways: for it most often and most forcefully tends to rain and likewise snow in the Alps than in flat places, on account of the thickness of the air and the rushing of vapors; more in the seventh clime (on account of the aforesaid reasons) than in the sixth; more in the sixth than in the fifth; more in the fifth than in the fourth; more in the fourth than in the third; more in the third than in the second; more in the second than in the first–and you may understand thusly for every clime, and every region according to its nature, and according to their sites.

Which mansions of the Moon are wet, which dry, and which common[19]

You[20] will even consider in which, and from which mansions of the Moon, the aforesaid conjunctions and aforesaid aspects come to be. Because certain of the mansions are wet, certain ones dry, certain ones common, certain ones lucky or fortunate, certain ones unlucky or unfortunate, just as I will expound to you in what follows.

---

[17] The author frequently uses *declino* ("decline, come down") to describe on which side of a choice (between colors, benefic and malefic affects, *etc.*). It does not seem to be used for astronomical purposes (like declination, or setting).

[18] *Situs*. This word appears a number of times in this Treatise. It carries connotations both of local position or a site, as well as how something is "situated." Its technical meaning is unclear to me (as well as how it relates to "places" (*loca*), which in a planetary context would seem to be the signs (in this sentence it seems to refer to geographical place).

[19] In this section, "common" and "temperate" should be understood in their traditional senses of being "mixed"–just as the common signs are said to partake of both movable and fixed characteristics.

[20] See Jafar, §6.

For indeed the aforesaid mansions are 28,[21] of which:[22]

The first is called:	Albarain,
the second:	Altamazer,
the third:	Aldebaran,
the fourth:	Albachia,
the fifth:	Alvata,
the sixth:	Alziraa,
the seventh:	Albiathia,
the eighth:	Altarfin,
the ninth:	Algetua,
the tenth:	Alaracen,
the eleventh:	Alzarfa,
the twelfth:	Alafraze,
the thirteenth:	Alzamee,
the fourteenth:	Achafre,
the fifteenth:	Alzebene,
the sixteenth:	Aliachil,
the seventeenth:	Alchabin,
the eighteenth:	Astiala,
the nineteenth:	Abuaarca,
the twentieth:	Albelaca,
the twenty-first:	Azea,
the twenty-second:	Bolah,
the twenty-third:	Zacazad,
the twenty-fourth:	Alasboa,
the twenty-fifth:	Alhumadez,
the twenty-sixth:	Almaiehe,
the twenty-seventh:	Alahut,
the twenty-eighth:	Anathe.[23]

And each one of the stated mansions contains 13 degrees and 20 minutes, to which another 28 secondary [mansions] are subordinated (that is, they are enclosed by them). Namely:

---

[21] I note that there can only be 27 mansions if each is really supposed to be 13° 20'. But the traditional number of mansions is 28.

[22] Below Bonatti attributes this to a "Johannes," who is probably John of Seville. The names differ slightly from Jafar's in §§15-18, but for the most part only with trivial spelling differences. The reader should consult the Appendix with mansion names found in Burnett (2000). Until more is known about the use of these mansions and whence Bonatti is getting his names, it is difficult to say more.

[23] Or *Anate* (1491).

The first is:	Alazelazenet,
the second:	Agasie,
the third:	Azulierie,
the fourth:	Alchil,
the fifth:	Alchali,
the sixth:	Alzula,
the seventh:	Almara,
the eighth:	Albeldie,
the ninth:	Alzabel,
the tenth:	Alialciz,
the eleventh:	Zaudazaa,
the twelfth:	Zaudolabia,
the thirteenth:	Alsuganfaboel,[24]
the fourteenth:	Alsurgalabet,
the fifteenth:	Racamavide,
the sixteenth:	Alnatha,
the seventeenth:	Albucan,
the eighteenth:	Alciraze,
the nineteenth:	Aldabaran,
the twentieth:	Alchada,
the twenty-first:	Aluzana,
the twenty-second:	Alamoha,
the twenty-third:	Alirazma,
the twenty-fourth:	Alcaubua,
the twenty-fifth:	Alcebira,
the twenty-sixth:	Alararen,[25]
the twenty-seventh:	Alzaut,
the twenty-eighth:	Alaacen

—just as these names were found in the translation of John.

And the secondary ones are subordinated to the aforesaid primary ones, in this way.[26] For:

---

[24] Or *Alsugamfaboel.*

[25] Or *Alararem.*

[26] I.e., in order: the first secondary mansion is subordinate to the first primary mansion, and so on.

Alazelazenet	is subordinated to:	Albaraya,[27]
Agasie	is subordinated to:	Altamazer,
Azulierie	is subordinated to:	Aldebaran,
Alchil	is subordinated to:	Albachie,[28]
Alchali	is subordinated to:	Alvata,
Alzula	is subordinated to:	Alziraa
Almara	is subordinated to:	Albiathia,
Albeldie	is subordinated to:	Altharfin,
Alzabel	is subordinated to:	Algetua,
Alialcim[29]	is subordinated to:	Alaracen,
Zaudazaa	is subordinated to:	Alzarfa,
Zaudolabia	is subordinated to:	Alafraze,
Alsuganfaboel	is subordinated to:	Alzamee,
Alsurgalabet	is subordinated to:	Achafre,
Racamavide[30]	is subordinated to:	Alzubene,[31]
Alnatha	is subordinated to:	Aliachil,
Albucan	is subordinated to:	Alchabin,
Alciraze	is subordinated to:	Astrala,
Aldabatan[32]	is subordinated to:	Abuaarca,
Alchada	is subordinated to:	Albelaca,
Aluzana	is subordinated to:	Bolah,[33]
Alamoha	is subordinated to:	Azea,
Alirazma	is subordinated to:	Zacazad,
Alcabua	is subordinated to:	Alasboa,
Alcebira	is subordinated to:	Alhumadez,
Alararen	is subordinated to:	Almaiehe,
Alzaut	is subordinated to:	Alahut,
Alacen	is subordinated to:	Anathe.

Twenty-seven of which twenty-eight mansions, with their subordinates, are reckoned in their effects. The twenty-eighth, namely that in which the conjunction of the Sun and the Moon is, is not reckoned (even if, nevertheless, it does

---

[27] Was: Albarain.

[28] Was: Albachia.

[29] Was: Alialciz. 1491 has Alialciz for both, but this may be a misunderstanding for the abbreviation for *m*.

[30] 1491 spells this: Racaviavide (but the *vi* are shaped similarly to *m* in the gothic print).

[31] Was: Alzebene.

[32] Was: Altabaran. The above is probably a misprint, since this mansion is undoubtedly named after the star Aldebaran.

[33] This pairing appears in the wrong order in 1491 and 1550.

something practically imperceptibly).[34] But the virtue which the Moon has in that mansion is bequeathed to the Sun (likewise the strength of that mansion). Nevertheless however, the Moon gives to [the Sun] the virtue which she acquires for herself (which belongs to a planet when she is joined to him).[35]

Of which mansions, six are dry: Alzarfa, Alafraze, Alzamee, Alchabin, Alasboa, Albelaca. Of which six mansions, four are lucky and fortunate, namely: Alzarfa, Alzamee, Alchabin, Alasboa. Indeed the other two, namely Alafraze and Albelaca, are unlucky and unfortunate.

Indeed nine are wet, namely: Altamazer, Aldebaran, Albachia, Alziraa, Albiathia, Abuaarca, Bolah, Alhumadez, and Alahut. Of which seven are lucky and fortunate, namely: Albachia, Alziraa, Albiathia, Bolah, Abuaarca, Alhumadez, Alahut. However, two are unlucky and unfortunate, namely Altamazer, Aldebaran.

The thirteen left over are temperate or common, which are: Albarain, Alvata, Altarfin,[36] Algetua, Alaracen, Achafre,[37] Aliachil, Astiala, Azea, Alzebene,[38] Zacazad,[39] Almaiehe,[40] Anathe. Of which thirteen, six come down more on the side of fortune than misfortune, namely: Altarfin,[41] Algetua, Alaracen,[42] Astiala, Azea, Zacazad. Indeed five come down more on the side of misfortune than fortune, namely: Alvata,[43] Achafre,[44] Aliachil, Almaiehe,[45] Anathe. The other two, namely Albarain, Alzubene, remain in their own quality, not coming down more on the side of fortune than misfortune.

All[46] of these having been individually considered, you will look to see in which of the aforesaid mansions both of the luminaries come together, and in

---

[34] This indicates a problem that plagues the doctrine of mansions–are there 27 or 28? Jafar (and this text) says the mansion occupied by the luminaries at the conjunction counts as the 28th, and is ignored (§12). But the problem is not whether or not to pay attention to the mansion, but how we can even speak of one to begin with, since each of the 28 is supposed to be 13° 20' in longitude, which is impossible.

[35] See Jafar, §12. Jafar puts it more starkly: "after the Moon recedes from the Sun, applying or conjoined to another star, the whole of the signification, even the efficacy and power, is relinquished right over to the Sun, the Moon and mansion being cast away."

[36] Reading *Altarfin* for *Alcarfin*.

[37] Reading *Achafre* for *Azafre*.

[38] Reading *Alzebene* for *Alzubene*.

[39] Reading *Zacazad* for *Zazacad*.

[40] Reading *Almaiehe* for *Almaie*.

[41] Reading *Altarfin* for *Altharfin*.

[42] Reading *Alaracen* for *Alacaren*.

[43] Reading *Alvata* for *Alnatha*, else the list would not make sense.

[44] Reading *Achafre* for *Azafre*, as above.

[45] Reading *Almaiehe* for *Almaie*, as above.

[46] See Jafar, §21.

what sign and in what place of the circle, and which of the planets regards her, and to whom the Moon is first joined by body or by aspect after the separation from the Sun, and in which of the mansions he is (to whom she is then joined). For if the conjunction of the luminaries were in a wet mansion, and in a wet sign, without the aspect or corporal conjunction of some benefic, and the said planet were in a wet sign or in a wet mansion, without a doubt you could announce an abundance of future rains. Nor could you resist that in any judgment (and more so if the aspect were from the square or from the opposition, and the planet to which she is joined were a malefic).[47] But if it were a benefic, it will mitigate the badness in a certain sense. If however the conjunction of the luminaries were as I said, and the planet to which the planet is joined were in a dry mansion, even if it were in a wet sign, [and] even if it were a malefic, still the rains will be somewhat more decreased (indeed if [it were] a benefic, they will be decreased more). Which if it were a dry mansion and a dry sign, the rains will lighten more. But if the aforesaid conjunctions and aforesaid aspects were in dry signs and dry mansions, the rains might cease altogether, whether the one to whom the Moon is then joined (or whom she aspects) were a benefic or a malefic, unless the planet whose dignity the mansion was, worked to the contrary. For if it were the dignity of Venus (because her nature comes down more on the side of moisture), it will help the rains somewhat, and will temper the dryness somewhat (even if not much). And our ancient sages wanted to note all of these things carefully.

And Jafar said[48] they were drawn out by means of a center of lines in the circles, namely whose arcs are referred to the tetragon, trigon and hexagon, by means of a certain condition[49] of knowledge. Nevertheless also the places (out of which the application of each of the stars comes to be), strongly configured to the place of each star, obviously whence they apply from (he said) a masculine or feminine one, obviously of the nature of the places related to the four elements; even thence if they might apply themselves from a certain longitude and latitude.[50]

---

[47] See, e.g., Jafar, §24.

[48] Jafar, §6.

[49] Reading *habitudine* (with Jafar) for Bonatti's *beatitudine*.

[50] Both Bonatti's rendering and my Jafar are confusingly (and I think ungrammatically) constructed, though Bonatti's is smoother. Bonatti reads: *Nihilominus quoque loca ex quibus stellarum fit applicatio fortius utrunque loca stellae configurate, undeque videlicet applicent de loco, inquam, masculino vel foeminino, ex natura videlicet locorum ad elementa quatuor relatorum, inde etiam si de certa longitudine et latitudine se applicent.* Jafar reads: *Et nihilominus quoque loca ex quibus stellarum fit applicatio fortis utriusque loco stellae configurata; unde terminorum videlicet applicetur; de loco inquam*

Therefore, the application of the stars from places of this kind having been understood, the matching [or agreeing] and firm reception that is had [shows][51] the effects and means. Learned antiquity[52] wanted to sketch out and distinguish[53] these mansions (which it called "knots" or rather "bindings"), to note them, and to attend to their effects; for they wanted us to consider all the aforesaid, so that definite judgments could be handed down on rains and the mutations of the air.

On the air's mutation and its variation, and the knowledge of future heavy rains

For[54] the knowledge of the mutation of the air and its variation (and likewise of heavy rains), it is necessary to know the degree of the conjunction of the luminaries, and the degree of their opposition, and the last [degree], I say, of the first quarter, and likewise of the second one, and the middle [degree] of the quadrature of any lunar month (even though these four aforesaid places are secondary), and principally [those] of the dichotomies. Indeed[55] it is necessary to consider more principally the conjunction and prevention, and even certain other things which will be said in their own place and time (namely that other places are subject to these aforesaid places).

And[56] these twelve are called the *centra*[57] of the Moon, which are when the Moon stands up from [or leaves] the degree in which her conjunction with the

---

masculino sive feminino ex natura videlicet qui ad elementa quattuor referuntur. I cannot be sure what exactly it means.

[51] Adding *monstrat* with Jafar. Note that he does not say anything about what "reception" means here—it could simply mean residing in one of the mansions.

[52] See Jafar, §7.

[53] Reading *discernere* for *discernente*.

[54] See Jafar, §8.

[55] See Jafar, §10-11.

[56] See Jafar, §11.

[57] Reading *centra* (with Jafar) for *cera*. The word literally means "centers," but I do not believe this is what is meant. In Hellenistic astrology, *kentra* (sing. *kentron*) were the angular degrees, meaning "goads"—i.e., degrees which "goad" planets to more vigorous action when they are near them (just as planets are said to be quantitatively stronger in their action when they are angular). In Indian astrology, this term was transliterated and assimilated directly as *kendra* (I note that in Jafar's text, the translator also speaks of Jafar and "the Indians" in the third person, which Bonatti omits here). Now, since Jafar has been speaking about the key points at which we determine the Moon's applications, this leads me to believe that these key points themselves are the *kentra/kendra* which stimulate weather. The problem with Jafar's text (and Bonatti's appropriation of it) is that he mentions only eight key points—but then immediately seems to identify the *centra* with the standard 12° on either side of the Sun's conjunction or opposition, saying there are "twelve" *centra*. But it is not normal in medieval astrology to individually isolate these degrees. Therefore I believe there must be some distortion or error

Sun is supposed to come to be, by exactly twelve degrees in front or behind; but in the prevention it does not happen so necessarily, indeed in the angles of the dichotomies more repeatedly, than it is used to happening in the prevention.

And Mecra said,[58] for this reason they wanted principally and especially to note that which is called Biabene,[59] because the two stars fill up the sign of Libra and its figure in every way. And he said, for, the Moon is snatched in the hands of Virgo,[60] and nowhere else. Even in the same way, because that degree, where these two stars are placed, sits in the beginning of Scorpio;[61] and there the Moon tarries while she walks that path, the peculiar nature [of which stars] they henceforth took up [in] an introductory speech.

Indeed Mecra[62] preserved all of these hidden things from the ancients so far as reason goes, not so far as the effects of [their] operating. And he said, for how it is with the rest of the mansions of the Moon and the things connected to that, let the business of this follow [later]. I will bring it up in what follows, even though above it was spoken about this when I was going to speak about the natures of the mansions; and I will adjoin the opinions of individuals which pertain to this chapter in the required places. For the greater clarity of the reader I will preserve [it] by means of a fitting order, and I will disclose [it] in the following, in the way I ought to proceed in these [matters].

Indeed Jafar[63] listed the names of certain aforesaid mansions, just as is found in another translation.

For he calls the first of them (which signify moisture, and which have the virtue of making rain fall) Aldebaran,[64] which above was called Altamazer.

---

in Jafar's text. He must be making a general point about eight *centra/kentra/kendra* (i.e., stimulating degrees), and making the additional point that with the conjunction and opposition there is a broader span of degrees to be taken into account.

[58] Unknown, but in the sentence corresponding to Mecra below, Jafar reads "Mercurius." Could this be a reference to Hermes?

[59] This must refer to the mansion which includes the claws of Scorpio. See Jafar, §13, who reads "axa bene." But note that *Biabene* is very similar to the Latinized *Belbeny*, derived ultimately from the Persian (Pahlavi) *wiyābān*, "desert stars." See Pingree, 1989, p. 233.

[60] This may not be right–perhaps the author is referring to the claws of Scorpio in *Libra*, which seems to be the focus of his interest.

[61] Again, I believe the author is speaking of the claws of the constellation Scorpio, which became the pans of Libra.

[62] The sentence ends with the unknown word *cilcivius* (Jafar reads *tillemus*). The medieval *tilo* comes from Gr. *tillō* ("to pluck"), but I am unsure of its role here or what Bonatt thought it meant (if he did not simply copy it from his source text). Note the similarity between *cilcivius* and Tilcinius (below).

[63] See Jafar, §15. Here and below Jafar spells the mansions differently.

[64] Reading *Aldebaran* for *Aldebaram*.

The second one he called Alzama, which was called Aldebaran.[65]

The third he called Alialbetha, which was called Albachia.[66]

The fourth he called Alzarfa, which was called Alziraa.

The fifth he called Alzafra, which was called Albiachia.

The sixth he called Alichil, which was called Abuaerca.[67]

Indeed the seventh [he called] Autiaim, which was called Bolah.

Indeed the eighth Alelelach, which was called Alhumadem.[68]

The next, the ninth, he called Alfaraz,[69] which was called Alahut.

Of which aforesaid mansions, six signify rains more so than the other three, namely: Aldebaran, Alziraa, Alialbetha, Alzarfan, Alzafra, and Alithil. Indeed the remaining three are less wet, and signify rains less so than the aforesaid six.

Whence[70] if the Moon were in one of the now-stated mansions, and especially [in one of] those six which I said earlier (and more strongly [if] she were to appear joined or applied with one of the stars signifying dew), without a doubt you could announce future heavy rains. But in the other three, it will be less than this, and all of these according to the nature of him to whom she were joined or applied. If however you were to find her in dry mansions, you could announce dryness according to the aforesaid reasons. Which if she were in one of the ones which were called temperate or common, you could judge the coming disposition of the air according to the disposition and nature of him to whom the Moon were joined or applied; likewise in the three of the temperate

---

[65] Reading *Aldebaran* for *Aldebaram*.
[66] Reading *Albachia* as in the first list, but note the confusion of *ch* and *th*.
[67] Reading *Abuaarca* as in the first list.
[68] Reading *Almuhadez* as in the first list.
[69] In 1491: *Alfarz*.
[70] Jafar, §16.

ones, obviously in those [of] which Jafar[71] called one Alanatha, and the other Atumech, indeed the third Adalaz, which come down more to dryness than to moisture.[72]

From whatever kind of mansion the conjunction or aspect was, the effecting of the matter will be according to its nature, whether from a wet one, or a dry one, or from a temperate or common one (and more strongly for rains, if the aspect were from the square or from the opposition; however in the prohibition or rains, if it were a trine or sextile, always by considering that the benefics add in the good and subtract in the bad). And Jafar said,[73] for Anathe and Altarfin[74] and Alibee,[75] Avaula,[76] Alnayn,[77] and the belly of Pisces,[78] take up that effect,[79] and with the rest that follow them, as it was had in the figure of rains, and it will be something to pursue. And this is a table:

Signs	Complexion	Complexion	Complexion
♈	12° 15' Temp.	14° 23' Dry	4° 0' Temp.
♉	8° 30' Temp.	13° 36' Wet	9° 0' Dry
♊	10° 17' Dry	7° 9' Temp.	13° 0' Wet
♋	12° 25' Temp.	13° 13' Dry	5° 0' Wet
♌	8° 14' Wet	13° 26' Temp.	9° 0' Wet
♍	10° 17' Wet	7° 9' Temp.	13° 0' Temp.
♎	12° 51 Wet	13° 13' Wet	5° 0' Wet
♏	8° 9' Wet	13° 26 Dry	9° 0' Wet
♐	10° 17' Wet	7° 7' Wet	13° 0' Temp.
♑	12° 51' Wet	13° 13 Temp.	5° 0' Temp.
♒	8° 34' Temp	12° 26 Dry	10° 0' Dry
♓	10° 17' Dry	7° 9' Dry	13° 0' Temp.

Figure 2: "One way of [presenting] the mansions of the Moon in a table"

---

[71] Referring perhaps to Jafar §17.

[72] It is impossible to say (based on the text) which mansions (whether primary or secondary) these names apply to–except perhaps "Alanatha" (which was called Anathe in the primary list and Alnatha in the secondary list).

[73] See Jafar, §§18-19.

[74] Reading *Altarfin* for Atarfin.

[75] Unknown mansion.

[76] Perhaps Alvata?

[77] Unknown mansion.

[78] Does this refer to a mansion?

[79] What effect?

A chapter on rains and the mutations of the air

If[80] however if suits you to prognosticate on rains and the mutations of the air, and on clouds signifying rains or dew, or on clouds signifying neither of them, and on future winds, and likewise at what time and in whatever part of the year, and at what hour [would be] the coming of the aforesaid (or any of them), and on their increase or diminishment—it will be necessary for you to know (as Jafar testifies[81] he heard it from the most experienced[82] of the Indians) according to the site[83] of the circle of signs at the hour of the conjunction and prevention of the Sun and Moon which immediately preceded the entrance of the Sun into the first minute of Libra; and [to know] the local disposition[84] of all the other planets in the circle—however, principally that of the luminaries.

And[85] it is even necessary for us to consider (after the Sun enters the first minute of Libra), his progress up until he has walked through the whole scorched path,[86] and another five degrees of Scorpio besides; and this happens in the middle of the seven climes, because Libra and the first 20° of Scorpio have a signification over rains and winds and mutations of the air in the whole fourth clime, and likewise in the last half of the third, and in the first half of the fifth.

And the Indians said,[87] the Sun and the Moon having finally been rectified to those two hours of the coming-together,[88] (he said) and of the opposition, or to the aforesaid two signs,[89] therefore it will be necessary to direct the mind with the greatest[90] exertion regarding the mansions to be discerned. Therefore from here onwards the task will be to discern the mansions so, because wherever the

---

[80] See Jafar, §§19-20.

[81] Jafar, §19.

[82] Reading *a peritissimis* for *apertissimis*.

[83] *Situs.* Perhaps this means how the zodiac is "situated" relative to the horizon, i.e., in terms of whole sign houses?

[84] *Situalem…dispositionem.* Again, this probably means in what whole sign (or perhaps quadrant) houses the planets are in.

[85] See Jafar, §20.

[86] *Viam perustam,* a variant on the more familiar *via combusta.*

[87] Reading *Indi rectificatis* for *in directificatis.* The following is a paraphrase of Jafar Indus, §§20-21.

[88] *Conventus,* the original author's standard term for a corporal conjunction. Clearly he is only concerned with the conjunction of their bodies (as in an eclipse), and not with their conjunction by orbs.

[89] Aries and Libra. Jafar is interested in the Sun's entrance into Aries, as well (Bonatti only mentions Libra above).

[90] Reading *summo* (with Jafar) for Bonatti's *uno.*

conjunction or opposition of the luminaries were, from the beginning of Aries to the end of the signs themselves, you will grant 13° 20' according to equal degrees. And if you were to seize on the place of the conjunction or prevention, you will see whether the mansion is dry or wet or temperate (or common). You will even see in which mansions the other planets are found, just as you considered[91] for the Moon. Which if you were to do this, you will see to whom the Moon would apply after the coming-together or the prevention, or [to whom] she would be corporally joined. Because according to how her conjunction or application with some planet in the circle were to appear,[92] so will be her signification over rains or no rains, or winds, or dew, or mutations of the air.

For[93] if the Moon were joined to or were applied to Saturn, with her being of good condition and well disposed, and in a wet mansion, likewise without any other application, without a doubt you could announce temperate and suitable heavy rains (likewise dark clouds filling up the whole air). And if Saturn were impeded or badly disposed, it will increase rains and winds and the darkness of the clouds, and all the aforesaid, to the contrary of the good; and all the significations according to the places, the sites,[94] the significations of houses, mansions, conditions, conjunctions, aspects or applications, as was said above when we spoke of the complexions of the mansions of the Moon and what belongs to them.[95]

And[96] if Venus and Mercury were to apply their own testimonies and the virtues which were said, they[97] will be very much increased (and more so, and more strongly so, if their conjunction or application were in the angles or from angles,[98] for then clashings of winds will be feared, and their fury; even the ruin of certain houses, and the breaking of trees, and even the eradication of certain ones of them.

---

91 Reading *consideravisti* for *considerasti*.
92 *Extiterit.*
93 See Jafar, §21.
94 *Situs.* Again, it is unclear how "sites" differ from "places."
95 *Ipsarumque.*
96 See Jafar, §22.
97 I.e., the heavy rains.
98 Bonatti has rarely spoken of houses–perhaps the references to "places" and "sites" are relevant here?

On the hour of showers, heavy rains, and winds

However,[99] in order to know the hour of the aforesaid events, it is necessary for you to know the hour of the conjunction (if your consideration were [of] a conjunctional one) or the hour of the prevention (if your consideration were [of] a preventional one), and see by how many degrees the fullness[100] of the conjunction or application or prevention or tetragon were distant from the aforesaid places. Because the effecting of rains or the mutation of the air will arrive up to so many days or hours, just as the aspects or applications or conjunctions were from such signs. For if they were from fixed signs, they will signify days; if from common ones, hours. But if from movable ones, hours–but the aforesaid movable ones will portend more quickly than the common ones. The coming of the aforesaid will even hasten by one-sixth if the course of the Moon were quick, or even [if] the increase of her light were not missing. But if just one of them were present, the coming will hasten somewhat less than this.[101]

If however you were to find the Moon in a place of the degree opposite to the conjunction (or the prevention), or her course were slower, the coming of the aforesaid will slow down according to the sign or place in which she was, like it was said regarding [its] hastening. Indeed if the Moon were to apply to one of the benefics after the coming-together of the Sun, and the benefic were to aspect Saturn from some aspect, and were to receive him from some dignity of its own (or he it)–and the more so if each receives the other and is received by [the other]–the aforesaid [effects] will be altered. However, they will not exceed [their proper] measure, and they will signify slowness, and their coming will be prolonged by one-sixth of the total. If[102] however the Moon would apply to [Saturn] from a square aspect or the opposition (nor would [it] impede any of the others[103] in the effecting of rains), a delay will not interfere with her parts,[104]

---

[99] See Jafar, §23.

[100] *Complementum.* In this context, this word probably means "the degree of the exact conjunction/aspect."

[101] I do not know what is meant by her increase of light being "missing," and what is supposed to be "present" (*defuerit, affuerit*).

[102] See Jafar, §24. But most of this sentence is Bonatti's own elaboration (or based on his edition of Jafar or another source). The meaning simply seems to be that if the Moon is in the square or opposition of Saturn, it will definitely bring rains without delay, and especially if the inferiors are involved.

[103] *Aliquas aliorum.* This phrase does not make grammatical sense, as *aliquas* is feminine (referring perhaps to rains), and *aliorum* is masculine. It probably should be read as *aliquos aliorum* (same English translation).

and especially if the two aforesaid inferior [planets] attest to them; and they would grant their own support, as was said, just as they meet each other,[105] nor will they waver, nor even will they be decreased.

When Saturn prohibits rains

Indeed[106] if Saturn were to reside in a dry mansion, and the Moon were to apply to him in a dry mansion, nor are the supports of others exhibited to them, rains will not be present, even if perpetual clouds disturb the air much.

On the application of the Moon with Jupiter

And[107] if the Moon were to apply to Jupiter from the aforesaid or similar places, or she were with him in the same place or mansion (one which is wet), and Venus and Mercury were to exhibit their own testimonies, clouds with dew and soft (or practically no) rains will be signified. If however Venus and Mercury did not exhibit their testimonies to them, the rains will cease completely. But if one of them were to help them, indeed the other not, something of the making of rain will come, even if however middling. And then if Jupiter would apply to Saturn, it will signify part of the aforesaid (but not, however, exceeding measure) is going to come.

But[108] if the Moon would apply to Mars from the aforesaid places or mansions after [her] separation from the Sun, and [if] Venus or Mercury were to aspect them by the testimony of some masculine planet,[109] and such an application were in an angle or from an angle, and in a wet mansion, or from a wet mansion, it will signify a gathering and commixture of clouds, but it would portend little dew (or practically none). However, it could signify thunders, and flashings of light likewise; and in the seasons and in the regions fit for this, there are going to be lightning bolts without a multitude of rains, provided that Mars would then apply to Saturn or Jupiter: because if he were then applied to them, it will indicate future rains.

---

104 *Partes.* Perhaps, "roles"?
105 *Se convenient.*
106 See Jafar, §26.
107 See Jafar, §27.
108 See Jafar, §28.
109 *Alicuius planetae masculini testimonio.* Jafar says *feminarum* [sic] ("of feminine ones").

And Jafar said,[110] even this presents itself to be noted, because Mars would increase exceedingly the signification of heavy rains from any aspect;[111] and the Moon (and stars) to which he were to apply here in the generating rains helps utterly;[112] for there is already a delay especially and principally by that.[113] And he said,[114] indeed if it were to happen otherwise, he will not signify this, and the same corrupts; however, the clouds which the Martial nature brings forth, having saffron radiance from above [are] not without radiance.[115]

On the application of the Moon with Mars

Again,[116] if the Moon were to withdraw after the conjunction with the Sun [and] were to apply at the same time to Mars and Saturn, and she were to remain in a wet mansion, and they likewise, it would portend future, immoderate rains. Which if she were to approach only one[117] of them (or to both), and the matter would behave that way,[118] and they were even in temperate mansions, it will signify rains. Indeed if she were to remain in a wet one, and those two in dry ones (or *vice versa*), it will often mitigate future heavy rains. Likewise[119] if the Moon were joined to the Sun and then she would be joined to Jupiter at the same time (or she were to apply to him by aspect), and they both (or one of them) were to receive her, they will prohibit heavy rains from remaining so they do not overflow.

And Jafar said,[120] for indeed [if] the Moon [is] precisely then in an optimal place (that is, under one of the *centra*),[121] that is, [in] places dedicated to this signification, wherefore she is made fortunate, it would cancel her peculiar nature and pervert her command, until she has agreed with fortunate [planets] in

---

[110] Jafar, §29.

[111] *Respectu.*

[112] But Mars cannot apply to the Moon; Jafar must mean that the Moon applying to Mars will help in generating rain.

[113] *Illa enim eadem & proprie & principaliter iam est dilatio.*

[114] See Jafar, §§29-30.

[115] Punctuation and clauses unclear, as well as the translation: *idem corrumpit, nubes autem quas martialis producit natura, croceum candorem desuper non sine candore habentes.*

[116] See Jafar, §30-32.

[117] Reading *uno* for *uni.*

[118] *Res ita se habeat.* Meaning unclear.

[119] See Jafar §34.

[120] Jafar, §34.

[121] Here we see yet another meaning of "optimal place." In this case we are probably dealing with her position in one of the four dichotomies.

some configuration.[122] And he said, therefore these[123] general occasions must always be noted. And he said, even the white clouds which are generated will portend much and inconstant dew.

On the application of the Moon with the Sun

And[124] if you were to find the Moon in the corporal connection of the Sun, nor is one of the other [planets] looking at them nor joined corporally with them, it will prohibit heavy rains so they do not come. Which if one of the others were to apply to them then, and [the other planet] were in a wet mansion (and the more so if this were in an angle), and the Sun were outside his own dignities and his strengths; and he[125] would apply to Saturn and Mars at the same time (or would separate from one of them and apply to the other), it will announce strong rains are going to come about. If however he were to apply to only one of them, nor would he be separating from the other one, the heavy rains which it would signify will be half, or at least one-third, or at least one-fourth, below the aforesaid; and in the aforesaid cases he will bring in between grey or saffron and semi-red and dense clouds; nor quickly dissolving ones; but after they were unleashed,[126] they will announce the air to be slight and fair. Indeed if the Moon, after her separation (whether they are joined by body or aspect),[127] were to apply to the Sun from a triangle, [effects] will come into action according to the nature of the houses [domiciles?] or mansions in which their significations were. And Jafar said,[128] concerning the coming-together and opposition, in no way is it called an application.[129]

On the application of the Moon with Venus

If[130] however the Moon would apply to Venus after her separation from the Sun, and she [were] in watery or airy signs (but less so airy ones) and in wet mansions, without a doubt it will announce coming rains; and the more so, and

---

[122] Uncertain of this last clause: *dum iam fortunatis aliqua configuratione respondit*, translating *respondit* as "agreed" (with a dative object).

[123] Reading *hae* for *haec*.

[124] This seems to be based on Jafar, §43*ff.*

[125] I do not know if this means the Sun or the third planet involved.

[126] Or "dissolved away"?

[127] I think the aspect the author means is the opposition.

[128] Jafar §31.

[129] This simply means that the conjoining of the luminaries at the New and Full Moon is not an "application."

[130] See Jafar, §§33-34.

more certainly and ineffably so, if Mars and Saturn would aspect them. But if only one of them aspects them, their signification will be something below this, nor will it be necessary that Mercury extend some help to them in one of the aforesaid cases; but if he were to extend it, it will increase the future rains. But if the aforesaid malefics did not aspect them, but Jupiter were to aspect them (or she[131] were otherwise made fortunate), the rains will cease without a doubt, nor will they come. If however Venus were to apply to one of the three superiors in the same knot,[132] nor did it[133] impede any other signification of Venus, it will portend there are going to be perpetual (nor moderate) rains. And the aforesaid will happen more strongly so, if their application were to appear[134] from out of a wet mansion or a watery sign. But if Venus were free, made fortunate and strong, nor is the Moon found joined to her in the same knot (nor in a watery sign [or] wet mansion, or she even remains fortunate),[135] this will signify that the aforesaid heavy rains will not happen. Nevertheless, if Venus (as was said) behaved in this way, and the Moon would be joined to her, there will not be rains, but clouds and some dew will appear in the air.

On the application of the Moon with Mercury

Again,[136] you must look to see if the Moon, when she is joined to the Sun (or when she is separating from the Sun after her conjunction), would first apply to Mercury in the same place, and in a wet mansion, without the aspect and conjunction of another: because it will indicate continuing heavy rains without a delay in time. Which if she were joined, you could announce for sure [that] they will come, [but] not exceeding their proper measure. Indeed if Mars and Saturn attested at the same time to their conjunction, announcing horrendous and threatening and submerging rains (and constant ones) is not be doubted. But if Venus were thus far a participant of the aforesaid conjunction from some dignity of hers, from the aforesaid places, it will be doubted that the rains will exceed proper measure. If however, at the hour of the conjunction of the Moon with the Sun, Mercury [were] applied to Venus in the same place, knot, and a

---

[131] *Ipsa.* This probably refers to the Moon.

[132] Recall that "knot" is a synonym for "mansion."

[133] I do not know if this refers to a particular planet, or to "it" in the impersonal sense of the situation as a whole.

[134] *Exstiterit.*

[135] It is unclear to me whether all of the conditions between the parentheses should be read with a "nor," so that none of them is supposed to apply.

[136] See Jafar, §35-42.

watery sign, and likewise in a wet mansion, it will indicate rains exceeding proper measure. Indeed if you were to find the aforesaid from other signs and mansions, you could certainly announce a middling amount of rains. And Tilcinius said, likewise with Mercury looking to [aspecting] Venus from a watery sign and wet mansion, or located in the same knot or joining, the rains will exceed their limits. If however Jupiter (or another of the benevolent [planets], however he is the strong one) were then to aspect the aforesaid malefics, you will judge mediocre rains. And if only Mercury were applied to the Moon, and he were to signify dew and rains, [if] Jupiter's aspect to him were with reception from his own domicile or exaltation, or from two other dignities, Mercury would assume the nature and significations of [Jupiter] for himself, nor would he permit the Moon to exercise her significations; and he will bring in serene air, however with a multitude of winds; and the quality of the winds will be according to the nature of Jupiter or another star to whose nature he were applied, if you were to find him turned around[137] and applied to some other one.

However,[138] if the Moon, after the separation from the Sun, applies to Mercury and Venus at the same time, before the other aforesaid places, or even to Mars and Saturn, as was said, they will pervert the things signified by the Moon, and [the things signified] will be made manifest, unless, he said, Jupiter and the Sun worked to the contrary, from whatever aspect or aforesaid conjunction this were to come about; and more strongly and ineffably so, if the conjunction were with the aforesaid malefics—the rains and dew will be increased, and likewise the air will become misty. And if the aforesaid benefics worked to the contrary, they cancel the dew and rains (still they could not prohibit clouds from being present). And may you remember in no way to hand over the aforesaid [points] to forgetfulness, but keep them always in the secret [recesses] of your mind, so that you will be able to reply eagerly, and likewise to know and see them ahead of time for your own usefulness.

On the application of the Moon with the benefics or malefics

And[139] if the Moon were to apply to one of the benefics after her separation from the Sun, it prohibits coming rains. Which if she is joined to one of the

---

137 *Conversum.* This could mean "retrograde," or simply that Mercury is aspecting another planet in addition.
138 Based on Jafar, §35-42.
139 This seems to be based at least on Jafar, §§32.

malevolent [planets], or were to aspect from any aspect, and her application were to depart from that benefic up to 5° or less without the aspect of a benefic, it will announce future rains in that same week. Which if the Moon (he said) is joined to one of the planets after her separation from the Sun, and this were to happen in a wet mansion, or even in some other one of the places of the circle, nor is she impeded nor received[140] by any, it will humidify the air, and will signify clouds and dew and diverse rains, and the filling up of the clouds of the air; indeed the incitements [of these things] will come to be due to diverse winds, and sometimes flashings of light and lightning bolts.[141] Indeed, if after this the Moon were to apply to one of the planets who makes her fortunate, or he himself were made fortunate, it will improve [or amend] all the aforesaid, and convert them into their contrary. If however he were a malefic, or he himself were made unfortunate, the aforesaid things will be increased and grow so much that they will seem to be doubled. But if she were malefic and of bad condition, and badly disposed, in the observance of malefics, she will be found [to be] strong of promise and stronger, nor from the observation of the aforesaid, will it weary [or vex] another.[142]

And even though (of those things which are now and were said in the past) it should be held more openly that the Moon is converted into the nature of him to whom she is applied (and that is true), still, thus far it does not seem that I should omit to tell you again that if she were applied with the benefics or other stars who are applied to benefics (as was said), or she were to appear[143] without any impediment of the benefics in their own dignities (as was said), it will not make heavy rains remain (even though it does not resist them). But if she were applied to malefics, just as was said with the benefics, it will announce future heavy rains.

And Jafar,[144] explaining the general influence[145] of the Moon with individual stars (like in Aligistivia[146]), that is, [explaining] the coming-together,[147] said: for

---

[140] Reading *recipitur* for *recipiens*.

[141] Somewhat uncertain about this sentence. *Incitationes siquidem ventorum diversorum & aliquando coruscationum & fulgorum causa fiet.*

[142] Very uncertain of this sentence. *Observatione* ("observation") sounds like it might be an alternative word for "aspect"; but then the second half of the sentence seems to contradict the first and then turns to the notion of wearying or vexing. *At si fuerit ipsa infortuna & mali esse, & mala disposita, in observatione malorum fortis promissionis atque fortior invenietur, nec a praedictorum observatione alium fatigabit.*

[143] *Extiterit.*

[144] See Jafar §45.

[145] *Ducatus.*

[146] Jafar reads *Alestima*. I do not know if this is a book, or mansion, or what.

indeed in those things which it will seem necessary that they must be had for the knowledge of this, the which [points] written above, I have devised in a fitting order; therefore, next will be expounded how it ought to be done in the opposition and the tetragons.

On the four tetragons, or on the four dichotomies or the four figures

In[148] this matter it is necessary to look principally at seven places in the circle: namely the degree of the conjunction of the luminaries, its tetragons (which are distant from it, one in front, the other behind, by 90°),[149] and its opposite degree, and the degrees of its dichotomies. The first of which is in the beginning of the month up to seven days, and is the first dichotomy. The second is from the said seven days up to another seven, and it is the second dichotomy, and it is even the degree of the prevention. The third is from those fourteen days up to another seven (namely twenty-one), and it is the third dichotomy. The fourth is after those aforesaid ones up to the following conjunction, which is the fourth dichotomy.[150]

Secondarily, you ought to look at another ten places without the aforesaid, of which the first is three days[151] before the hour of the conjunction of the Moon with the Sun. The second is three days after. The third is three days before the first dichotomy. The fourth is three days after it. The fifth is three days before the prevention. The sixth is three days after it. The seventh is three days before the second dichotomy. The eighth is three days after it. The ninth[152] is twelve degrees before the opposition, and the tenth is the same amount after it.

---

[147] *Conventum.* This is Jafar's standard word for the corporal conjunction–now he will turn to oppositions and squares.

[148] Jafar, §46-47.

[149] I believe that by "in front," Bonatti means the leading or "first aspect" ahead in the order of signs. By "behind," he means the following or "second aspect" backwards against the order of signs.

[150] Bonatti uses "dichotomy" principally to indicate the degrees marking the ends of the lunar quarters, which are not 90° from each other (since the Sun's motion affects the lunar phases). The best I can make out is that we are looking at a configuration composed on two zodiacal shapes: one tetragon marking points based on the degree of the New Moon (all spaced out by 90° intervals), and a skewed rhomboid marking the points where the beginnings of each lunar quarter *actually* takes place. The two shapes coincide on only one point–the degree of the New Moon–so there are seven points to look at.

[151] This refers to a precise (or roughly precise) time, i.e., exactly three days before, *etc.* See also Ptolemy, *Tet.* II.13).

[152] Here we see that these positions could count as the *centra* mentioned above.

Whence, if in the space of three days after the coming-together [of the lumi-
naries] you were to see her slender and clear around evening, likewise glittering,
without a cover of clouds, nor is she otherwise impeded by the malefics while
she stood in that sign, it will signify the air to be serene. Which if she were
slender, and her color declining to redness [or blush], and the parts of her which
were not illuminated likewise glittering, and they seem to be moved almost like
shaking, it will show that winds are going to come from that direction against
which she is seen to decline.[153]

Which if the Sun were to remain then in Capricorn or in Aquarius, and the
Moon were found in Taurus or in Virgo,[154] and she were to have some meet-
ing[155] with Saturn, then coming cold winds will take place, and the more so if
Saturn were then found in Capricorn. If however she were to come down on
the side of blackness or practically greenishness, with some density, or un-
doubted thickness, it will indicate threatening rains and even [regular?] rains.
However in the other aforesaid places, you will announce the future disposition
of the air according to the signs and according to the mansions and according to
the conjunctions or aspects of the planets with her.

In order to know the qualities which will be prolonged more than one day

Which if you wished to know ahead of time the qualities of the air whose
space [of time] are prolonged more than one day, as Ptolemy said,[156] you will
consider the hours of the partnerings[157] of the luminaries in the figure: because
for every quality of the figures which there is from the hour of that figure up to
the hour which follows it in the figure, it will signify to the majority. Moreover,
it appears to have seemed to Ptolemy that we should consider the hour of the
conjunction of the luminaries and its minute, and erect the figure to the
Ascendant of that minute, and construct the four angles, and to see which of
the planets is then stronger over that Ascendant: because he will rule over the
disposition of the air until the Moon then arrives to the next angle of the said

---

[153] In this case, *declino* seems to refer to the Moon's movement, and not something qualitative.
But I am unsure what exactly the author means. Perhaps *declino* is a synonym for "be," so if
she is in the south, winds will come from the south, *etc.*

[154] This could only happen in different situations, i.e. before or after the Full Moon, not after
the New Moon (which is what was just discussed). Moreover, this could only happen in
winter (in the northern hemisphere).

[155] *Convenientiam.* Not a corporal conjunction like when the author uses *conventus,* so it must
refer to other types of aspects.

[156] See *Tet.* II.12.

[157] *Societatum.*

figure (namely the second one); and the air will be disposed according to how that *al-mubtazz* is disposed, unless something else were to work to the contrary, which it will be necessary that you consider by your own industry, by considering the things which were said above, and still will be said.

You will even consider when the Moon will enter the first minute of the said angle,[158] and you will see which of the planets is *al-mubtazz* over that Ascendant which it then was, because he will rule over the disposition of the air until the Moon were then to arrive at the third angle of the said figure of the conjunction, which will be disposed according to the disposition of the *al-mubtazz* of that Ascendant.[159] Again, you will look to see when the Moon will enter the first minute of the degree which will be opposite the degree of the designated conjunction,[160] because according to how the *al-mubtazz* of [that] Ascendant were disposed, so will the air be well or badly disposed until the Moon then arrives to the first minute of the fourth angle of the said figure ([provided that] nothing else works to the contrary).

Afterwards, you will consider when the Moon arrives at the minute in which the aforesaid conjunction is: because then the air will be disposed according to how the planet who was the *al-mubtazz* over the Ascendant (which then was) were disposed, until the Moon then arrives at the minute of the following conjunction, unless something else works against it–namely that one of the malefics impedes the said *al-mubtazz,* or [the *al-mubtazz*] himself is in a mansion or sign contrary to the nature of any of the aforesaid Ascendants, and the like; or even the season works against it, namely by adding or detracting according to what Ptolemy testifies, just like it is if that lunar month were in the summer, and [also] the significators (namely those signifying moisture or rains), wherefore rains and moisture will abound less. If however it were winter, and they were significators signifying little moisture, more rains than would seem to be signified will follow from thence, and *vice versa.*

---

[158]By "angle," Ptolemy must have in mind the degrees that are square and in opposition to the degree of the conjunction of the luminaries (see below), as they are viewed in the chart erected at the New Moon.

[159] But by "ascendant" does he mean we ought to cast a new chart? Or does he simply mean that that the *al-mubtazz* of that sign will be treated as though he were like the Lord of the Ascendant for that quarter?

[160] But, again, the beginning of the third lunar quarter (which is the degree of the prevention) does not coincide with the degree opposite the degree of the Full Moon or conjunction. For, since the Sun also moves, the Full Moon will be approximately 210° away from the degree of the conjunction.

Indeed 'Ali[161] seems to have said that Ptolemy divides the lunar month into only four divisions, namely according to the four dichotomies. But if I remember rightly, what was expounded above is enough.

And always make the Moon a participator with the *al-mubtazz* of the Ascendant of every one of the aforesaid angles, according to how you were to find her in the places or signs or mansions (whether dry or wet or common).

Moreover,[162] it is necessary for you to attend to the condition of the Sun and the Moon when he enters the first minute of Libra (from that minute until he were then to traverse the twentieth degree of Scorpio)–[namely] what kind of condition he has either with the benefics or with the malefics, and in what mansion the Moon is then running through, and likewise in what kind of sign, and the site[163] of the other planets, and with which of them one of the luminaries is applied: because the air will be disposed according to the significations which there were then, until the entrance of the Sun into Aries–however, with the admixture of the significations which will happen in the comings-together[164] of the luminaries up until then.

And Jafar said,[165] for, these things (which I put down) having been more fully carried out, no variation or ambiguity will come, concerning the renewal of the air. In a like way the Moon is to be looked at, to see whether she is traversing in a dry or equal[166] mansion, and applies Venus or Mercury. Or [whether], as Jafar testifies,[167] she is staying in watery signs, and were applied to Saturn or Mars: she will indicate future rains. And he said that the Moon and Mercury are stars signifying dew. Likewise he said that if, therefore, they are looking at the Moon from, and staying in, signs of this kind, [and] even the Moon is applying to them from places of this kind, it means heavy rains. And he said, verily the Moon applying or looking [from] dry or equal places, on the whole brings in mediocre rains. And he said, likewise the Moon, by her unique and peculiar nature, conveys white and thin fog and clouds.

---

[161] Bonatti probably means 'Ali ibn Ridwān's commentary on *Tet.* II.

[162] See Jafar, §52.

[163] *Situs.*

[164] *Conventibus.* Here, *conventus* seems to refer to any aspect between the luminaries–or at least, the tetragons. So it seems that the testimony of the Sun when he enters Libra will be dominant, and the lunar phases for the semester will be subordinate?

[165] Jafar, §46.

[166] I.e., "temperate" or "common," i.e., a balance of both moisture and dryness.

[167] See Jafar, §§53-54.

On the circles which are made around the Moon and the Sun,
likewise around the other stars (both the wandering and not-wandering [stars])

However,[168] it is necessary to attend to the circle which is made around the Moon, and to see whether it is only one or more. However, if it were only one, and it were thin and clear and of little durability, and it is gradually moved back step-by-step and conceals itself, it will signify fair weather and clear and pure air. Indeed if they were more, they will signify winter wind. But if they were coming down more to a clear redness, and they seem practically to be cut off piecemeal, they will indicate the confusion of the air from wherever it comes to be, on the occasion of the winds. Indeed if they were disorderly with thickness, and obscure, it portends the disturbance of the air by cold and winds and snows.

And Ptolemy said[169] if they were to come down on the side of a black greenness, they will signify winter air which happens through the occasion of each, namely through winds and cold and snows. And he said if the circles were many, the things they signify will be many, according to what we have said before.

And Ptolemy said[170] [if] a circle will appear around the wandering and the lucid not-wandering stars, it will signify by way of similarity those things by means of the colors of their circles and of their stars which are enclosed.[171]

And he said[172] it is fitting for us to observe even the non-wandering stars, like the Pleiades and Alfecta, and those similar to these, and of their stars in which many more stars approach each other; we should look at the collections of the erratic ones, [their] colors, and apprehend their quantities or number. For if they were to appear of greater light and of greater quantity than they were made out to be, they will signify blowing winds that are going to come from that direction in which they are stationed. You would say the same about certain other stars which are called Praesepe, and those similar to these which seem practically misty [or nebulous]: which if they were to appear while the air is serene, almost spreading or decreased in light and thick (just as Ptolemy testifies), they will indicate the disturbance of the air and a multitude of rains.

---

[168] *Tet.* II.13.
[169] *Tet.* II.13.
[170] *Tet.* II.13.
[171] Ptolemy is refreshingly clear: "And the halos that gather about the stars, both the planets and the brilliant fixed stars, signify what is appropriated to their colours and to the natures of the luminaries which they surround."
[172] *Tet.* II.13.

But if you were to see them come down on the side of gleaming and clarity, you could announce powerful future winds.

And Ptolemy said[173] the method even of those (of the appearances or the other signs) which happen to take place in some season, is likewise.[174]

On comets and tailed stars

Indeed[175] comets, which are called "tailed," when they appear, will signify winds and the dryness of the air, especially if they appear almost cloudy [or nebulous]; and the strength of their significations will be according to the multitude and scarcity of them, and their length and shortness.[176]

On the hurling of the stars

Indeed[177] in the hurling of the stars, you will look in calm weather, to see when they are seen, and if the stars fell, [when] they are moved–the which motion, and the hurlings, from whatever direction they were, will announce the blowing the winds is going to come from that direction; and by how much more and thicker the hurlings were, by that much more will the thing they signify be increased and hasten. If however they were from different directions, they will portend disorderly [or irregular] winds are going to come from here and there. But if you were to see such significations appear everywhere, [they will portend] the disturbance of the air everywhere, and likewise thunders and flashings will be looked for from thence, and they will happen. You would say approximately the same thing if you were to see clouds likened to light flecks of wool.[178]

On the significations of diurnal and nocturnal qualities

In[179] investigating diurnal and nocturnal qualities, it is necessary for us to consider the body of the Sun in that very hour, and in that minute, when he begins to appear above the horizon, and to understand well and to see whether

---

[173] Perhaps an allusion to *Tet.* II.11?

[174] The gist of this sentence seems to be that we should apply similar rules to anything else he hasn't already mentioned.

[175] *Tet.* II.13.

[176] I am not sure if the author means how long they remain visible, or how long their tails are.

[177] This section derives from *Tet.* II.13, on "rushing and shooting stars."

[178] *Leveflochis.* Compare with *Tet.* II.13, "flocks of wool." *Flochus* definitely is related to *floccus,* "wool," and the *leve-* prefix must be a variant on *levis,* whose paronyms all signify things that are light or trivial.

[179] *Tet.* II.13.

his body rises clear and gleaming. Because if it were so, on that day it will indicate fair weather. But if you were to see the contrary, you could judge the contrary. If however he were to set, it seems the same should be prognosticated concerning the qualities of weather of the night. Which if his body were of diverse colors, as Ptolemy said, or were to come down more to a fiery red, or the rays of the Sun which proceed from him or around him were red, or if the clouds which enclose him on account of excessive clarity were to come down to reddish, and his rays were extended very far, and were separated from each other outside the circle, they will signify very strong winds whose blowing will proceed from the angles in which these signs (which we talked about) were to appear:[180] which if they were to ascend black, or decline[181] to greenishness in mists, or one or two circles were around him, or were to have around themselves clouds which are called "suns,"[182] and their rays were coming down to greenness or they were black, they will indicate stormy air[183] and rains.

On the rainbow, if it were to appear, and in what times, and what it would signify

You[184] will even look at the rainbow, and see in what weather it were to appear, and in what weather its appearance will be. For if it were to appear in fair weather (nor were the fair [weather] of a long time and great dryness, because then its signification will not be necessary), still one will hardly or never be deceived, because it will signify either winter air or rains. And this will happen because the vapors which had been thin, begin to thicken: because often, or rather almost always, a rainbow will not appear unless vapors are rarefied or thickened. If however the winter [or stormy] season were fair, it will demonstrate it is going to be a serene season, because then the vapors begin to be rarefied and dried out and annulled, as Ptolemy says.[185]

---

[180] Ptolemy says "to which the aforesaid signs point," indicating that "signs" here refers to "atmospheric signs," not zodiacal signs. The chapter in which this and previous sections appear in Ptolemy, is about atmospheric signs.

[181] This means "setting," per Ptolemy (*Tet.* II.13).

[182] I.e., "parheliac clouds." These are vertical bars of colored light (formed by sunlight shining through water crystals in the atmosphere) which appear on either side of the Sun. They are also called "sun dogs," and my own guess is that this phenomenon was behind the "apparition of three Suns" in 1644 to which Lilly devoted his *The Starry Messenger* (1645).

[183] Reading *hyemalem* as "stormy," with Ptolemy.

[184] *Tet.* II.13.

[185] Ptolemy simply says that a rainbow in clear weather signifies coming storms, and after storms it signifies clear weather (*Tet.* II. 13).

Generally,[186] we add that for the most part the peculiar colors which appear in the air will signify qualities similar to the accidents signified by the aforesaid colors.

On the investigation of the year, if there should be rains

If[187] however you cared to know whether the year would be rainy, as was touched on above, you will consider the entrance of the Sun into the first minute of Libra, and [consider] what kind of condition he has, until he had traversed through the twentieth degree of Scorpio. You will even see what kind of condition the Moon has with other stars in those times [seasons?], because the signification of that year will be taken from them. Therefore you will even look, in that entrance, to see to which of the planets the Moon is first joined, corporally or by aspect. Because if the planet were oriental, as Jafar testifies, it will show the end of the year or month or week to be rainy. If however it were occidental, it adorns the beginning of the aforesaid heavy rains with benefit.[188] However this application will signify (particularly when made with Venus or Mercury) the things which are aforesaid. But if she were applied to them (with one oriental, the other occidental), from the middle,[189] it will demonstrate common[190] and great rains are going to come throughout the whole year.

And he said,[191] the said multitude of rains while Venus and Mercury hasten to enter Scorpio, Capricorn, Aquarius and Pisces, particularly threaten. And I say more strongly so, if their application appears[192] from wet places or mansions, with the Moon in them. Which if they were to behave this way, they show general rains but useless ones. And if the Moon were applied to another one who regards her by means of a noted aspect, however long such an application were to last, and to the full amount of the application or aspect or conjunction, a multitude of rains will cease.[193]

---

[186] This sentence comes right from the penultimate paragraph of *Tet.* II.13.

[187] See Jafar, §52.

[188] Reading *beneficio decorat* (with Jafar) for *beneficio declarat*.

[189] I am not sure what "middle" refers to–this does not appear in Jafar.

[190] This may be a synonym for "temperate."

[191] Jafar, §52.

[192] *Exstiterit.*

[193] I believe this simply means that there will be no rain at least until the aspect is perfected.

On the application of the Moon with Saturn and with the rest of the planets

Ptolemy said[194] if the Moon were applied to Saturn, it will signify that soft and sweet or temperate rains are going to come, unless Mars or Mercury worked to the contrary.

For[195] indeed Jupiter has a serene air and uncommon[196] winds; also, not otherwise does he help the adjoinings of the rest of the stars. Should there be a community or admixture of bodies (as was said above), he will show efficacy, but [he will show] even the chief[197] and alternating colors of the clouds and variations of the air. It will be permitted to look through the whole year, these things having been weighed first.

Which[198] if the Moon were applied to Mars, it will signify clouds between saffron and reddish [in color], having radiance from above; and thunders, likewise flashings, and even lightning in seasons fit for this–unless Jupiter worked to the contrary. But if you were to see her applied to the Sun, it will indicate saffron clouds, and rains having great drops of water. If however the Moon would apply to Venus, it will generate soft and continuous rains, and much dew (practically like clouds). If however the Moon were applied with Mercury, it will show heavy rains and savage winds, and their severity, and likewise[199] dispersed and diverse clouds, likening to smoke [or steam].

On certain extraordinary things[200]

There are certain other extraordinary things which I do not remember having found in the sayings of any of the philosophers (but I have seen them to be often and most of the time veridical), and they especially have a place here in the whole sixth clime,[201] and on the edge of the fifth, and in the south of the seventh. Namely, if the Sun were to set (even though in other parts the air might seem clear and the weather fair), and where his body were to set there were clouds just like a cloth,[202] that it will signify, in that same night or in the

---

[194] This is also Jafar, §53.

[195] Jafar, §57.

[196] *Proprios.* Jafar reads *prospicios.*

[197] *Ducatus.*

[198] Jafar, §§54-57.

[199] Reading *necnon* for *nec.*

[200] *Partibus.* I am not sure why Bonatti (or his editor) chose this word.

[201] The author of this passage must live in the sixth clime.

[202] *Mappa.* This word can mean a napkin, or cloth, or a signal flag waved at the beginning of a race. I am not sure exactly what sort of shape the author means.

following day, winds or rains or both. For if the cloth were thick, and likewise dense, and along with it there was clear air and fair weather, it will usually indicate winds. Indeed if some little cloud almost like a little cushion[203] [were] next to the cloth, just like the *matizotius*[204] of paintings, it will indicate rains. But if he were to set in serene air, and after his setting up to the completion of dusk the air seems red, likewise it will signify there is going to be serene weather in that same night and in the following day.

And Christianus says you will consider what kind of weather there was on the second day of Subat,[205] because up to the entrance of the Sun into Aries, you will expect the contrary of the weather which there is at that time. And Gerardus[206] said, you will see when thick and obscure clouds from out of the direction of the north (directly under the arctic pole or coming down somewhat to the western direction), were contiguous with the horizon, because then it will rain practically immediately. But if mountainous clouds were to appear almost like the bed of a river, and were set apart from the horizon, they will signify the harmonizing of the air. Likewise, if you were to see flashings in the same direction in a late hour, they will show the disturbance of the air is near, so that the arrival of the disturbance will not be prolonged beyond eight days easily,[207] unless a great dryness worked to the contrary.

And Alanus said you will even see if clouds opposite the plain and especially opposite the north, were to seek higher mountains, because it will be a sign that rains are going to come that same day, or the next one at the latest. The same tends to happen when thick and dense clouds surround the peaks of mountains, announcing that winds are going to come at that time. And the aforesaid will happen more strongly, if the clouds are extended out from an eastern or northern wind. If however the clouds were to seek the plain from the mountains, you will announce it is a sign of the alleviation of the air and its improvement (unless much humidity worked against it), and by much more if it is moved by a western wind.

And there is another accident which often, or rather most of the time, I have seen to be veridical–that if a rainbow were to apply in the morning, then it will

---

[203] *Lictura.* Perhaps: "couch?"

[204] Unknown word.

[205] Here is another indicator of the oddness of this Treatise. *Subat* is the second month in Turkish, not Arabic (it seems to be equivalent to Safar). In Tr. 4, Bonatti clearly refers to Safar, but nowhere else draws on Turkish. Either "Christianus" or the author, or both, must have studied or lived in and around Turkey.

[206] Undoubtedly Gerard of Cremona.

[207] *De levi.*

indicate rain, unless a great dryness of the air worked to the contrary. If however it were to appear around the evening, then the weather will be made fair, unless a great moisture of the air worked to the contrary. Even when a great and dusky thickness of the stars, or the greatest thinness were to appear, then the alteration of the air will be signified, to put it briefly. These accidents, even though they are often true, still are not necessary.

On the accidents whose spaces of time are prolonged for a little while

You will see, in accidental things, those whose spaces of time are prolonged a small amount. I think the Sun, if you were to see him in the southern direction, and Venus were hidden under his rays, with the Moon applying to them or to one of them (especially to Venus) by conjunction or by aspect, you will announce heavy rains are going to come on that same day, likewise at that same hour, and its minute at which such a conjunction were in that land. You could say the same if you were to find Mercury in the southern direction with the application of the Moon; or if she did not apply to him by conjunction [but] she is joined to him diametrically opposite (and more strongly so, if then the Moon is found in Scorpio). You could say the same if Mars and Venus are found together in Scorpio.

And Jafar said,[208] moreover, with the Sun in Aquarius and the Moon applying to him, or placed in his opposition, and Venus is staying in the same place, there will be rains present in that hour. And he said in the same way also, the application of Mars or Venus to the Sun, and the Moon traversing in their opposition or square, while Venus were burned [combust], makes the judgment of rains certain. Indeed, as was said, if Venus applies to the Sun, and Mercury were conjoined to her, or at least they to Venus, it will announce rains are going to come on that same day. Moreover, if you were to find the Sun in Libra, but Venus in Sagittarius, and the Moon joined to them (and especially to Venus), minute by minute, it will show heavy rains that are going to be in the land in which you are, on that same day. But if the Sun were in Aquarius or in his own exaltation, and the Moon were to remain in Leo, it will show many heavy rains are going to come in the day and hour of their conjunction or application. You could judge the same about Sagittarius as I said about Leo, because according to the authors who testify [on this matters], the images are said to be of a river.[209]

---

[208] I am unsure of the source of this quote.
[209] I am not sure what is meant by this. Moreover, the constellation of the river Eridanus is near Taurus, not Sagittarius.

Nevertheless, Leo effects a greater multitude of heavy rains than Sagittarius does, and likewise he makes them denser; the same thing tends to happen in the first face of Taurus. However Sagittarius, even though it does not make as much rain, still it makes thicker drops of water. And the aforesaid will happen more strongly and certainly so, if the Sun were in Sagittarius or were to aspect it, and the Moon were to aspect Mercury or apply to him; and he pursued Venus, and on that same day their efficacy will be made known [or spread wide]. Things like the aforesaid will be generated in the domiciles of Mars and in the domiciles of Venus: great falling rains, flashings, thunders, and hail.

And Jafar said,[210] on the other hand, the Sun traversing in Pisces or in Aries, the Moon staying in Virgo or Libra or in Sagittarius (that is, in vaporous places),[211] it will bring in a profusion of heavy rains on that same day. Again, if Venus and Mercury are joined to the Sun in one of the aforesaid places outside Leo, and the Moon applies to them (and the more so if she were applied from Leo), it will show flashings and thunders, even though with little or practically no rain. And the more so, if the Sun is found to be joined with one of them (whether it is direct or retrograde) directly opposite.[212] If however the Sun were in Aquarius, or in Aries, or in Leo, or in Libra or Scorpio, and the Moon were directly opposite, namely minute by minute to him, or opposite to Venus after rains or falling showers, it will signify luminous flashings and likewise thunders. And more strongly than that if the Moon is exposed[213] before [or opposite to] her from Leo, because then with the flashings and thunders, if the air were disposed to this, it will demonstrate generative[214] lightning bolts.

And Abū Ma'shar Trax said,[215] the said things [will] also [take place] in a like manner in regions subject to the equinoctial line in the second clime, in the fourth and in the third; their moderateness [or mean] will be more relaxed[216] in the fifth and in the sixth. But if you were to find the Sun or Moon in Pisces, and Mars were to aspect them from the square or from the opposition without the support of some benefic, they will signify an abundance of rains, lightning,

---

[210] I am unsure of the source of this quote.

[211] Mansions?

[212] But neither Venus nor Mercury can ever be opposite the Sun.

[213] *Obiicitur.* This probably refers to the Moon moving out of the Sun's light after the New Moon, so it simply means that the Moon applies to Venus from a New Moon in Leo.

[214] *Generativa.*

[215] Unknown–I have never heard of anyone else with the name "Abū Ma'shar," and I do not know what "Trax" means.

[216] *Remissius,* i.e., "remitted" as opposed to "intensified."

thunder, and flashings. And Trax said even the Sun in Aries, Scorpio, the Moon in Leo in the coming-together of the Sun,[217] prefigures the same.

On the consideration of the places of rains

Even if you have apprehended the other, aforesaid considerations, still you should not forget to consider the places of rains (which are Cancer, Leo, Capricorn, and Aquarius).[218] Whence, if you were to find the Moon in one of those signs, and she were applied to Venus corporally or from some aspect, and especially from the square or from the opposition, you will announce there are going to be heavy rains. And the more so, if the conjunction were completed before, from one degree or less.[219] However, the first half of Capricorn is less malefic than the other preceding ones; indeed the last [half] signifies more cold than rain. However, you will consider all of these with discernment.

On the signs and places signifying less rain than the aforesaid signs

However, there are certain other places in certain signs signifying less rain than the aforesaid: and these are the last bound of Aries (and this because of certain moistures which are found in those bounds); Gemini, Virgo, and Libra are even of the places signifying fewer rains.

In the conjunction of what planets rains are signified

If however the Moon, after the coming-together [with the Sun], is joined immediately to Mercury and Venus and Mars, or to one of them corporally, or through some aspect, [then] unless Jupiter were to speak against it, it will announce rains are going to come. If however she were to apply to Mars or Venus, it signifies that rains will come to be that same day. If to Mercury, the footsteps of him to whom Mercury were to adhere.[220]

---

[217] It seems as though this means the Moon is joined to the Sun by trine or square (in which case, *conventus* here means "aspect" instead of the usual "conjunction").

[218] I.e., the domiciles of the luminaries and their opposites.

[219] Perhaps this means, "if it had been completed with one degree or less, just before the chart were cast."

[220] In other words, since Mercury's effects depend on his aspects, look to another planet he aspects in order to determine the effects.

If you wished to know, of some month, whether it would be rainy or not

If however in any month you wished to prognosticate[221] whether there are future rains, in the beginning of any one of them you will raise up [erect] the figure required for it, and you will adapt the twelve cusps to it, and you will regard the hour and minute of the coming-together of the Sun and the Moon, and you will see which of the planets then regards them, or to whom they apply, and from what places, and from what mansions the application was. Because if they were to apply to stars bringing in rains, and from wet mansions, they will indicate stormy rains. If however they were to aspect planets signifying rains from dry places, their significations will be less than the aforesaid by at least one-third or one-fourth.

You will even see if Venus is joined with Saturn, and more so if Venus were to transfer the light of Mars or Mercury or Jupiter: because then you could announce future rains indubitably. And if apart from this the aforesaid planets were to have an application with the Sun, they will indicate some kind of rains, because the nature of the Sun in this case comes down more to dew than to dryness. You will even consider if the Sun and Venus were to travel in the same knot, and are in a mansion of the nature of one of them, and in addition both or one of them are joined to some star [who is] the ruler of the place which they occupy, and [the star] were in a good place of the figure; and [the star] were to receive one joining to it: without a doubt heavy rain will be signified. Moreover, if the Moon were to transit the degree of her conjunction with the Sun, and were joined to Jupiter and Mercury at the same time (or to one of them) in a watery or airy sign (and the more so if she were in the southern direction,[222] and more strongly so if reception were to enter between the aforesaid planets), great rains will be shown, nor in any way will it be contradicted by them.

On the conjunction of the Moon with the planets,
and on the conjunction of the other planets individually to each other

You will look, in the forecasting of rains, to see if one of the inferior planets is joined with one of the superior planets in the southern direction, and some inferior will be applied to by the superiors, and one of the inferiors [to or by]

---

[221] Reading *pronosticare* for *pronosticari*.

[222] I am not sure if this means in the southern *direction* (say, in the 10th house), or in a southern ecliptical *latitude*, or even in a southern *declination*.

them,[223] because immediately when the aforenamed inferior one were separated from the superior one, rains will be expected necessarily.

And Abū Ma'shar (the most experienced of the ancient astrologers) said, on the other hand, looking at the places, still they took care to attend to the names, whose discernment is this: how many times the Moon is going back[224] from Venus, the signification of rains is certainly reduced.[225] And he said, [the Moon] going away from Mercury and applying to Jupiter or the Sun, or *vice versa*, no other judgment is available. And he said, these are individually the [types of] information, and [they are those] certain things which the openings of the planets (suitable enough) are formally named.[226] And he said, the opposition of these stars from the third clime to the fourth, it flows with its own rains toward the southern direction [or part],[227] and from that same direction, the significa-tion of rains happens all together.

And Jafar said,[228] on the other hand again, indeed those things which were said regarding the opposition in the signs which signify waters, the application having been made (namely in their degrees) and the coming-together,[229] or by chance the aspect[230] being unobserved, and the Moon in her own domicile, applying to Saturn, it brings in manifold heavy rains.

---

[223] This clause is ungrammatical, and is perhaps a combination of an error and a redundant repetition: *fueritque inferior aliquis a superioribus & aliquis ex inferioribus applicetur illis.* It is also possible that the author is speaking of planets in southern latitudes, and their mutual application by latitude there–but it still would not make the sentence grammatical.

[224] *Rediens.* This might mean "separating from," as the author uses *recedens* below. Or perhaps this should be read as *recedens*, too.

[225] Meaning unclear: *nomina autem attendere curaverunt, quarum haec est discretio, quotiens Luna a Venere rediens pluviarum significatio profecto reducitur.*

[226] Again, practically incomprehensible because it is out of context–I do not even know what the topic of the sentence is. *Et dixit, haec autem sunt singulariter et notoria, et quaedam quae planetarum apertiones satis congruae nuncupantur.*

[227] Omitting *deprehensa*; perhaps it pertains to an earlier clause in Bonatti's source text, but he has uncritically copied it here.

[228] I am not sure where Bonatti is getting this quote, nor do I understand it.

[229] *Conventum.* This seems to be in the wrong case, and at any rate I do not understand its role here.

[230] *Respectu.*

BIBLIOGRAPHY

Abu Bakr, *Liber Genethliacus* (Nuremberg: Johannes Petreius, 1540)

Abū Ma'shar al-Balhi, *The Abbreviation of the Introduction to Astrology*, ed. and trans. Charles Burnett, K. Yamamoto, and Michio Yano (Leiden: E.J. Brill, 1994)

Abū Ma'shar al-Balhi, *Liber Introductorii Maioris ad Scientiam Iudiciorum Astrorum*, vols. VI, V, VI, IX, ed. Richard Lemay (Naples: Istituto Universitario Orientale, 1995)

Abū Ma'shar al-Balhi, *The Abbreviation of the Introduction to Astrology*, ed. and trans. Charles Burnett, annotated by Charles Burnett, G. Tobyn, G. Cornelius and V. Wells (ARHAT Publications, 1997)

Abū Ma'shar al-Balhi, *On Historical Astrology: The Book of Religions and Dynasties (On the Great Conjunctions)*, vols. I-II, eds. and trans. Keiji Yamamoto and Charles Burnett (Leiden: Brill, 2000)

Abū Ma'shar al-Balhi, *The Flowers of Abū Ma'shar*, trans. Benjamin Dykes (2nd ed., 2007)

Al-Biruni, Muhammad ibn Ahmad, *The Chronology of Ancient Nations*, trans. and ed. C. Edward Sachau (London: William H. Allen and Co., 1879)

Al-Biruni, Muhammad ibn Ahmad, *The Book of Instruction in the Elements of the Art of Astrology*, trans. R. Ramsay Wright (London: Luzac & Co., 1934)

Al-Fārābī, *De Ortu Scientiarum* (appearing as *"Alfarabi Über den Ursprung der Wissenschaften (De Ortu Scientiarum),"* ed. Clemens Baeumker, *Beiträge zur Geschichte der Philosophie des Mittelalters*, v. 19/3, 1916.

Al-Khayyat, Abu 'Ali, *The Judgments of Nativities*, trans. James H. Holden (Tempe, AZ: American Federation of Astrologers, Inc., 1988)

Al-Kindī, *The Forty Chapters (Iudicia Astrorum): The Two Latin Versions*, ed. Charles Burnett (London: The Warburg Institute, 1993)

Al-Mansur (attributed), *Capitula Almansoris*, ed. Plato of Tivoli (1136) (Basel: Johannes Hervagius, 1533)

Al-Qabīsī, *Isagoge*, trans. John of Spain, with commentary by John of Saxony (Paris: Simon Colinaeus, 1521)

Al-Qabīsī, *The Introduction to Astrology*, eds. Charles Burnett, Keiji Yamamoto, Michio Yano (London and Turin: The Warburg Institute, 2004)

Al-Rijāl, 'Ali, *In Iudiciis Astrorum* (Venice: Erhard Ratdolt, 1485)

Al-Rijāl, 'Ali, *Libri de Iudiciis Astrorum* (Basel: Henrichus Petrus, 1551)

Al-Tabarī, 'Umar, *De Nativitatibus* (Basel: Johannes Hervagius, 1533)

Al-Tabarī, 'Umar [Omar of Tiberias], *Three Books of Nativities*, ed. Robert Schmidt, trans. Robert Hand (Berkeley Springs, WV: The Golden Hind Press, 1997)

Alighieri, Dante, *Inferno*, trans. John Ciardi (New York, NY: Mentor, 1982)

Allen, Richard Hinckley, *Star Names: Their Lore and Meaning* (New York: Dover Publications Inc., 1963)

Aristotle, *The Complete Works of Aristotle* vols. I-II, ed. Jonathan Barnes (Princeton, NJ: Princeton University Press, 1984)

Bloch, Marc, *Feudal Society*, vols. I-II, trans. L.A. Manyon (Chicago: University of Chicago Press, 1961)

Bonatti, Guido, *Decem Tractatus Astronomiae* (Erhard Ratdolt: Venice, 1491)

Bonatti, Guido, *De Astronomia Tractatus X* (Basel, 1550)

Bonatti, Guido, *Liber Astronomiae: Books One, Two, and Three with Index*, trans. Robert Zoller and Robert Hand (Salisbury, Australia: Spica Publications, 1988)

Bonatti, Guido, *Liber Astronomiae Part IV: On Horary, First Part*, ed. Robert Schmidt, trans. Robert Hand (Berkeley Springs, WV: The Golden Hind Press, 1996)

Boncompagni, Baldassarre, *Della Vita e Della Opere di Guido Bonatti, Astrologo et Astronomo del Seculo Decimoterzo* (Rome: 1851)

Brady, Bernadette, *Brady's Book of Fixed Stars* (Boston: Weiser Books, 1998)

Burnett, Charles, ed., *Magic and Divination in the Middle Ages* (Aldershot, Great Britain: Ashgate Publishing Ltd., 1996)

Burnett, Charles and Gerrit Bos, *Scientific Weather Forecasting in the Middle Ages* (London and New York: Kegan Paul International, 2000)

Carmody, Francis, *Arabic Astronomical and Astrological Sciences in Latin Translation: A Critical Bibliography* (Berkeley and Los Angeles: University of California Press, 1956)

Carmody, Francis, *The Astronomical works of Thābit b. Qurra* (Berkeley and Los Angeles: University of California Press, 1960)

Dorotheus of Sidon, *Carmen Astrologicum*, trans. David Pingree (Abingdon, MD: The Astrology Center of America, 2005)

Grant, Edward, *Planets, Stars, and Orbs: The Medieval Cosmos, 1200–1687* (New York, NY: Cambridge University Press, 1994)

Haskins, Charles H., "Michael Scot and Frederick II," *Isis*, v. 4/2 (1921), pp. 250-75.

Haskins, Charles H., "Science at the Court of the Emperor Frederick II," *The American Historical Review*, v. 27/4 (1922), pp. 669-94.

Hermes Trismegistus, *Liber Hermetis*, ed. Robert Hand, trans. Robert Zoller (Salisbury, Australia: Spica Publications, 1998)

Holden, James H., *A History of Horoscopic Astrology* (Tempe, AZ: American Federation of Astrologers, Inc., 1996)

Ibn Labban, Kusyar, *Introduction to Astrology*, ed. and trans. Michio Yano (Tokyo: Institute for the Study of Languages and Cultures of Asia and Africa, 1997)

Ibn Sina (Avicenna), *The Canon of Medicine (al-Qanun fi'l tibb)*, ed. Laleh Bakhtiar (Great Books of the Islamic World, Inc., 1999)

Kennedy, Edward S., "The Sasanian Astronomical Handbook Zīj-I Shāh and the Astrological Doctrine of 'Transit' (Mamarr)," *Journal of the American Oriental Society*, v. 78/4 (1958), pp. 246-62.

Kunitzsch, Paul, "Mittelalterliche astronomisch-astrologische Glossare mit arabischen Fachausdrücken," *Bayerische Akademie der Wissenschaften Philoso-phisch-Historische Klasse*, 1977, v. 5

Kunitsch, Paul, trans. and ed., "Liber de Stellis Beibeniis," in *Hermetis Tris-megisti: Astrologica et Divinatoria* (Turnhout: Brepols Publishers, 2001).

Kunitzsch, Paul and Tim Smart, *A Dictionary of Modern Star Names* (Cambridge, MA: New Track Media, 2006)

Latham, R.E., *Revised Medieval Latin Word-List from British and Irish Sources* (Oxford: Oxford University Press, 2004)

Lemay, Richard, *Abu Ma'shar and Latin Aristotelianism in the Twelfth Century* (Beirut: American University of Beirut, 1962)

Levy, Raphael, "A Note on the Latin Translators of Ibn Ezra," *Isis*, v. 37 nos. 3/4 (1947), pp. 153-55.

Lilly, William, *The Starry Messenger* (London: Company of Stationers and H. Blunden, 1652). Reprinted 2004 by Renaissance Astrology Facsimile Edi-tions.

Lilly, William, *Anima Astrologiae*, trans. Henry Coley (London: B. Harris, 1676)

Lilly, William, *Christian Astrology*, vols. I-II, ed. David R. Roell (Abingdon, MD: Astrology Center of America, 2004)

Long, A.A. and D.N. Sedley, *The Hellenistic Philosophers*, vol. I (Cambridge: Cambridge University Press, 1987)

Māshā'allāh *et al.*, *Liber Novem Iudicum in Iudiciis Astrorum* [Book of the Nine Judges], ed. Peter Liechtenstein (Venice: 1509)

Māshā'allāh, *De Receptione* [*On Reception*] and *De Revolutione Annorum Mundi* and *De Interpraetationibus*, in *Messahalae Antiquissimi ac Laudatissimi Inter Arabes Astrologi, Libri Tres*, ed. Joachim Heller (Nuremberg: Joannes Montanus and Ulrich Neuber, 1549)

Māshā'allāh, *On Reception*, ed. and trans. Robert Hand (ARHAT Publications, 1998)

Maternus, Firmicus Julius, *Matheseos Libri VIII*, eds. W. Kroll and F. Skutsch (Stuttgard: Teubner, 1968)

Michelsen, Neil F., *The Koch Book of Tables* (San Diego: ACS Publications, Inc., 1985)

Mantello, F.A.C. and A.G. Rigg, eds., *Medieval Latin: An Introduction and Bibliographical Guide* (Washington, DC: The Catholic University of America Press, 1996)

New Oxford Annotated Bible, ed. Bruce M. Metzger and Roland E. Murphy (New York: Oxford University Press, 1994)

Pingree, David, "Astronomy and Astrology in India and Iran," *Isis* v. 54/2 (1963), pp. 229-46.

Pingree, David, "Classical and Byzantine Astrology in Sassanian Persia," *Dumbarton Oaks Papers*, v. 43 (1989), pp. 227-239.

Pingree, David, *From Astral Omens to Astrology: From Babylon to Bīkāner* (Rome: Istituto italiano per L'Africa e L'Oriente, 1997)

Pseudo-Ptolemy, *Centiloquium*, ed. Georgius Trapezuntius, in Bonatti (1550)

Ptolemy, Claudius, *Tetrabiblos* vols. 1, 2, 4, trans. Robert Schmidt, ed. Robert Hand (Berkeley Springs, WV: The Golden Hind Press, 1994-98)

Ptolemy, Claudius, *Tetrabiblos*, trans. F.E. Robbins (Cambridge and London: Harvard University Press, 1940)

Ptolemy, Claudius, *Quadripartitum* [Tetrabiblos], trans. Plato of Tivoli (1138) (Basel: Johannes Hervagius, 1533)

Sahl ibn Bishr, *Introductorium* and *Praecipua Iudicia* [The Fifty Judgments] *De Interrogationibus* and *De Electionibus*, in *Tetrabiblos*, ed. Girolamo Salio (Venice: Bonetus Locatellus, 1493)

Sahl ibn Bishr, *De Electionibus* (Venice: Peter of Liechtenstein, 1509)

Selby, Talbot R., "Filippo Villani and his Vita of Guido Bonatti," *Renaissance News*, v. 11/4 (1958), pp. 243-48.

Seneca, *The Stoic Philosophy of Seneca*, ed. and trans. Moses Hadas (New York: The Norton Library, 1968)

Stegemann, Viktor, *Dorotheos von Sidon und das Sogenannte* Introductorium *des Sahl ibn Bišr* (Prague: Orientalisches Institut in Prag, 1942)

Thomson, S. Harrison, "The Text of Grosseteste's *De Cometis*," *Isis* v. 19/1 (1933), pp. 19-25.

Thorndike, Lynn, *A History of Magic and Experimental Science* (New York: The Macmillan Company, 1929)

Thorndike, Lynn, *The* Sphere *of Sacrobosco and Its Commentators* (Chicago: The University of Chicago Press, 1949)

Thorndike, Lynn, "A Third Translation by Salio," *Speculum*, v. 32/1 (1957), pp. 116-117.

Thorndike, Lynn, "John of Seville," *Speculum*, v. 34/1 (1959), pp. 20-38.

Utley, Francis Lee (review), "*The Legend of the Wandering Jew* by George K. Anderson," *Modern Philology*, v. 66/2 (1968), pp. 188-193.

Valens, Vettius, *The Anthology*, vols. I-VII, ed. Robert Hand, trans. Robert Schmidt (Berkeley Springs, WV: The Golden Hind Press, 1993-2001)

Van Cleve, Thomas Curtis, *The Emperor Frederick II of Hohenstaufen: Immutator Mundi* (London: Oxford University Press, 1972)

Weinstock, Stefan, "Lunar Mansions and Early Calendars," *The Journal of Hellenic Studies*, v. 69 (1949), pp. 48-69.

Zoller, Robert, *The Arabic Parts in Astrology: A Lost Key to Prediction* (Rochester, VT: Inner Traditions International, 1989)

Zoller, Robert, *Bonatti on War* (2nd ed., 2000)

INDEX